JACK LONDON
AND
HIS DAUGHTERS

Joan London
Introduction by Bart Abbott

Heyday Books • Berkeley
In Conjunction with Rick Heide

ISBN: 0-930588-44-4 (hardcover)
ISBN: 0-930588-43-6 (paperback)
Library of Congress Card Catalog Number: 90-80392

Printed in the United States of America
10 9 8 7 6 5 4 3 2 1

Produced by Bookmakers:
    Production coordination by The Compleat Works,
        Berkeley, CA, and Rick Heide
    Cover and interior design by DuFlon Design Associates,
        Berkeley, CA
    Typeset in Aldus by Archetype, Berkeley, CA

Grateful acknowledgment is made to Waring Jones for permission to reproduce the photographs from *Joan, Her Book* and for his extraordinary cooperation. We also wish to express sincere gratitude to Milo Shepard of the Irving Shepard Trust for permission to quote from letters written by Jack London. Thanks as well to Stanford University Press for permitting us to print the full text of the letter that appears in the Appendix from *The Letters of Jack London*, edited by Earle Labor, Robert Leitz, and Milo Shepard (Stanford, 1988). This letter, from the collection of Waring Jones, has also appeared in *Letters from Jack London*, edited by King Hendricks and Irving Shepard (New York, 1965).

Cover and dustjacket photos courtesy of Bart Abbott.

Published by Heyday Books
              P.O. Box 9145
              Berkeley, CA 94709

PREFACE

This book gestated for a long time. Forty some years that I know of, and perhaps it was on my mother's, Joan London's, mind as a writing project since adolescence. It was a search for personal answers far more than a daughter's public recollections of a famous father.

Her relationship with Jack London, who died when she was sixteen, was strange, mystifying, and troubled. With maturity came flashes of understanding and insight, but a hurt bewilderment nevertheless predominated at least until the biography of her father, *Jack London and His Times*, was completed. The careful research, interviews, and countless discussions with friends, acquaintances, and scholars allowed her to fill out a childhood picture. The man who visited only for short periods, and who all too frequently allowed years to pass between them—this man became a person. He was no longer only a famous author, a teller of tales of the sea, the Klondike, the South Sea Islands, a daddy of happy occasional afternoons. With the biography she now saw someone who had been a schoolboy, had friends, worked inhuman hours on barbarous jobs, struggled through high school, adventured on San Francisco bay, became a deep-water sailor, read voraciously, aspired to be a writer, fell in love, got drunk, became a socialist, longed for marriage and later for children. Jack London became a human being with color and depth, breathing, complete—almost.

An enigma nevertheless remained for Joan. In many ways the most important questions, never fully answered for her, revolved around the nature of the relationship between Jack London and his daughters. Why, during these long-ago visits, was there such an air of poignant hope, unfulfilled yearning, frustrated seeking? Because my mother often spoke of these things during my adolescence and young manhood, I know that they were always in the fore of her mind.

Jack London and His Times was written and published in the late 1930s, while I was still in high school. In 1951 I moved with my family to a ranch in Northern California for a year, and there Joan visited us a couple of times a month. During one of those weekend visits she observed grandchildren and neighbor kids swirling through a score of restless plans and activities.

"Let's go to Glenbrook and ride the horses," someone suggested. A three-year-old granddaughter's eyes glowed. She was ecstatic with the joy of having a plan, of being part of it. "I want to go. I'm going!" Eight-, ten-, twelve-year-old eyes rolled up to the sky. "You can't go to Glenbrook with no clothes on, no shoes. Go put them on and catch up with us down the road. We'll start off slowly."

Of course, the little nudist couldn't find shoes or clothes, and the big kids were swiftly out of sight, as they had undoubtedly intended. For that disappointed, betrayed, sad granddaughter, Joan was ready with a piece of candy, a story to read, and comfort to give.

I tell this family anecdote because within an hour Joan announced that it was time for her to begin *Jack London and His Daughters.* From the start the book went slowly. Always made aware of her writer-father, much was expected of Joan from grammar school composition onward, and no one expected more than she did of herself. Her writing was always work, rework, change, cut, add, polish, repolish, cut again. *Jack London and His Daughters* was the most difficult project Joan ever worked on. It dealt with questions that had baffled her all her life. "How did my father feel toward me, us? Surely he loved us. How could he have abandoned us, rejected us when we were so young, so vulnerable?" And the terrible conflicting loyalties. She loved her mother so very much. She adored, was dazzled by, her father.

What happened to her was what has occurred countless times before and since. Children of broken homes are often made pawns in a game that is over. When a marriage is dead it must be buried with dignity, and while the parents go their separate ways the children must be allowed to thrive in the love of each parent and be free to return that love without conflict.

This didn't happen at all in the divorce and subsequent lives of Jack and Bessie London. Surely the fault lay with both parents. Who was most at fault matters little. For Joan the seeds of conflicting loyalties were planted very early, and those seeds bore bitter fruit that she tasted for the rest of her life.

My parents separated and divorced before I was two years old, and they deliberately tried to avoid competing for my love. The attempt wasn't perfect, but for the most part they were successful. Thus I know that Joan, at least by age twenty-two, had accepted the fact that people cannot be expected to stay together when a marriage is over, abrading each other and their children. Perhaps by understanding this, she laid to rest the question "Why did they do this to me? I loved them both with all my heart, so why?" However, while the concept can be understood, it can almost never be felt or accepted fully. So Joan continued to struggle with her childhood's prime question: "Did Daddy really love me?"

Under these circumstances writing was slow. Many other things also interfered. Joan was working for the California Labor Federation as research librarian, and would continue to do so for another twelve years. She also carried on an extensive correspondence with friends and strangers across the country and around the world.

I must explain that the strangers were an astonishing number of people who somehow found her address and hoped for answers to questions about Jack London or his daughters, or who just wished to add another word of praise to Jack's worldwide reputation; as so many wrote, "My whole life has been affected by reading your father's books."

Also during the 1950s and '60s there was much correspondence with organizations: Camus' committee to help Republican refugees from Franco's Spain, the American Civil Liberties Union, Amnesty International, Women's Strike for Peace, and many others opposing United States participation in the Vietnam War.

The cause to which she was most committed during the last ten years of her life was the organizing of California's migrant farm workers. From the beginning efforts by Cesar Chavez and the United Farm Workers Union to improve the life of California's most exploited workers, Joan offered help in whatever way she could. Most of her time eventually went into a book on the history of California's farm workers and their many attempts to form unions and improve the dreadful conditions under which they worked and lived. This book, *So Shall Ye Reap*, written with Henry Anderson, appeared in early 1971. It was reviewed in the *San Francisco Chronicle* on January 21, 1971, the day before her death.

All in all, it is not surprising that *Jack London and His Daughters* stops somewhat short of being finished. The last section of the book appears as a synopsis, written by Joan but with the intention of later expanding it. Even if the book had been completed, however, the unanswered questions might still never have been resolved.

This book was, as I have said, a search for personal answers. But behind that search lay another purpose, really more important to Joan.

When Joan, the grandmother, empathized so keenly with the poignant yearnings of her granddaughter, when Joan saw her own three-year-old yearnings mirrored so vividly in another child—that is when she resolved to begin work on this book. It was to be a book that might encourage readers to bend every effort to fulfill childhood's grand hopes and wondrous dreams—dreams that stay whole even after a family has been broken.

I wish to acknowledge the help and encouragement I have received from Tony Bubka and Jim Sisson, and of course from my wife Helen.

—*Bart Abbott*
Arnold, California
January 15, 1990

Oh, that we had some deeper love and knowledge,
that no child will ever again be hurt!
—*Alan Paton*

ONE

There was a field in which golden poppies grew in deep, sun-warm grass, wild barley and sweet to smell. There was a row of pines, dark against grey-green eucalyptus up the hill. Unseen meadowlarks flung their arabesques of song into the luminous sky. And when the breeze quickened, the lovely silver-gilt surface of the barley swayed as if a gentle hand had passed over it.

Nested snugly in the grass, drowsy and content, an enchanted little girl watched a man who was flying kites. That man was Daddy, and the little girl was Joan, myself.

This I remember.

And this I know: the poppy field was in the Piedmont hills. Up the slope was the Bungalow, where *The Call of the Wild* had just been written. It was the springtime of 1903, and I was nearly two and a half years old.

These are facts, but they have no place in my earliest, most cherished of memories. This was the golden beginning of my awareness of being alive. Magically compounded of sunshine, deep-hearted poppies and swaying barley, of lark-song and fabulous kites straining into the sky, and of Daddy and being with him—this memory has existed apart from everything else, timeless, intact, perfect. All my life I have summoned it at will, and it comes back, unbidden, whenever I see grass rippling silver and gold under an unseen hand or hear meadowlarks call across the fields.

Of the time before the poppy field and the kites, and for almost a year after they had vanished, I remember little, but I know a good deal. There were the stories told and retold by Mother and Grandma

London and Aunt Jennie. Much later, George Sterling, Carlton and Laura Bierce, Frank and Madge Atherton, Ted Applegarth, Docky and others, including even Charmian, gave me glimpses of my small self. And there was the photograph album.

To a little girl, and then to a girl growing into and out of her teens, this album offered tangible evidence of unremembered years when, as often happened, she sought assurance that such years had really existed at all. Most prized of possessions, here was a gift of love from Daddy, conceived and executed by him with joy and pride. Here was the proof that Daddy and Mother and Bess and I had once been a family. And here, too, was the inspiration of many childish fantasies that somehow it might turn out as the fairy tales did, and we would again be a family and live happily ever afterward.

Joan, Her Book was stamped boldly in gold on the black leather cover. Inside was page after page of pictures, taken, developed and printed by Daddy, of myself and of everyone I had always known—Daddy and Mother and, later, Bess, Aunt Jennie and both my grandmothers—and of a few others whom, by the time I was four or five, I could no longer recognize. Underneath most of the pictures were captions, written and typed by Daddy.

A magic book! One of the pictures could only have been made by a sorcerer, while the captions, composed in a curious, archaic style and full of incomprehensible allusions, pleasantly baffled me for years.

"Here Beginneth the Story of Joan," he wrote on the first page, and the pictures which followed were taken at short intervals for two and a half years, from the time I was twelve hours old until the fatal summer of 1903 when our life together came to a sudden end.

With the very first picture, the story of Joan begins. Here, on carefully propped pillows, lies a baby in a long white dress, the tiny features dim but discernible. Underneath is written:

> *Joan, at twelve hours, who weigheth nine pounds and who looketh as though she hath been out all night.*
>
> *N.B. It happeneth to be only half the night. This we know.*
>
> *N.B. The night of January 14th, 1901, which, for her, commenceth in the morning of January 15th.*

Long afterward Ted Applegarth found among his papers and sent to me a one-cent postal card, postmarked on the front "Oakland, Jan 15, 01" and on the back "San Jose, Jan 15, 01," which tells a little more of that night. Scrawled in pencil is a brief message:

Jan 15/00
2:25 AM

A Girl.

> *Jack London*

The caption under the second picture in the album reads:

And this the Room. Behold the Books, wherefrom her
Progenitor extracteth knowledge.

It was not a very large room. The camera must have been placed in
the most advantageous corner, but it captured only the opposite corner
and a portion of one wall. Across an expanse of snowy counterpane
towers the ornate headboard of a large double bed; beside it a marble-
topped table holds a shaded reading lamp (the hose connecting it to the
unseen gas fixture in the center of the ceiling is a vertical black line on
the white wall) and seven or eight books, open and placed face-down,
one upon the other, as their reader completed his nightly stint in each
of them; next, almost in the corner, is a small round stove, half-hidden
by a table, its top tilted to display a single—magazine? containing one
of Daddy's stories?—it is impossible to guess, but it must have been
important to him, for the table has obviously been placed in front of
the stove solely to be within range of the camera.

I have heard the story of my birth many times: my reluctance to be
born, my mother's long hours of labor, the doctor's desperate decision
to use instruments "to save the mother, if not the child," and finally
the forced entry into the world of a mangled baby who did not breathe.

"Oh, let it die, let it die!" they said Daddy cried in anguish, sure that
a child with so misshapen a head, forceps-torn ear and crushed temple
would be a monster if it survived at all.

The doctor had made his choice. Wordlessly, he placed the baby in
Grandma Maddern's waiting hands, while he and the nurse turned their
full attention to Mother.

Melissa Maddern, who had borne six children of her own, and under
whose beneficent hands babies thrived, flowers bloomed and fruit ripened,
broken-winged birds flew again and ailing kittens and puppies returned
to health, harbored no fears. Life was her métier, not death, and she
knew many ways, ancient and modern, to establish and maintain life.
She tried them all—spanking, chafing and rubbing the tiny wounded
body, immersing it alternately in hot and cold water, placing drops of
brandy in the unresponsive mouth and, finally, for long minutes, forcing
air from her own lungs into mine in the old-fashioned, time-tested way,
now new-fashioned again. Then reluctantly conceding defeat, she laid

me against her shoulder for the last time, patting me gently and murmuring words of pity and love.

My thin wail transfixed everyone. In a moment the doctor and nurse had assumed charge, and Melissa turned to her next task.

Daddy was beside himself. "What have you done?" he accused. "You should have let it die!"

"Your baby is going to be all right, Jack," she comforted him.

"But that head! How can the poor thing live? How can you want it to live?"

She drew the distraught young man to her and kissed him gently. "Dear Jack, you have a fine, healthy daughter. How else could she have survived what she has been through? And don't be concerned about her head. In a day or two, you'll see, it'll be round and sweet like the head of every girl-baby."

And so, with patience and affection, she wrought her second miracle on that morning of January 15th.

Reassured by Melissa that his daughter would be neither a monster nor an idiot, and by the doctor and Mother herself that all would be well with her, Daddy's immense relief changed swiftly into the slightly lunatic exuberance of all young fathers. It is not difficult to picture him, hair tousled and eyes shining, beginning to be glad, and, quitting the crowded, disordered little room, running lightly down the stairs to tell someone, everyone, his news.

He scribbled his postal cards, forgetting in his elation that for two weeks he had striven to date his correspondence with the new year, 1901, and then he must have ridden his bicycle along the deserted streets to the main post office in downtown Oakland, for the card addressed to Ted Applegarth could not possibly have been postmarked in San Jose on the same day it left Oakland if it had not been with the mail that went south on the early morning train.

I wonder if it was rainy or foggy or frosty-clear on that January morning as he rode through the sleeping town. Whatever the weather, I think he rode joyously, accepting without reservation the happiness and fulfillment that had come to him after the bitter, lonely years of struggle. He was just twenty-five, but already fame was beginning to touch him and the future was bright. He had a wife, a home, friends, and now a child of his own. On that morning I do not believe he asked for more.

All that day he was busy, although he did no story-writing. A passionate amateur photographer at that time, he conceived the idea of taking a picture of his baby at the earliest possible moment. A dozen times he went upstairs to share his plans with Mother; by midday they had been expanded to include the entire album project, which he proposed to continue through all the years of my growing up. Even Mrs. Havens, Mother's nurse, finally yielded to his coaxing, and against her better judgment, consented to put me in the long white dress with the deep, lace-trimmed ruffle and pose me on the pillows. Camera, tripod and flashpan were arranged and rearranged, and when I was barely twelve hours old, the picture was made. *Joan, Her Book* was underway.

In the light of much that happened later, it often seemed to me that my birth, so eagerly desired by Daddy, had been a great disappointment to him. I had failed him in three important ways: I was a girl, I arrived in bad shape, and I was not born on his birthday as scheduled, but three days later—on Melissa's birthday as it happened, to everyone's belated surprise and pleasure.

It is true he had wanted a son. In a note to Anna Strunsky nine days before the event, he had written: ". . . Possibly ere that time, the boy—I do pray for a boy—shall have arrived . . . it will be in itself a dear consummation."

But his desire was for a child, son or daughter, and his disappointment was brief. Three weeks later, writing to another friend, he spoke only of the almost incredible happiness of realizing his ardent wish to be a father, and boasted of his baby, "a damn fine healthy youngster," who ate well and slept well, and could lie awake between times for an hour without a whimper.

Only one name had been chosen by Mother and Daddy for their first child: Jack. The possibility that I might be a girl had, of course, occurred to Mother, but each time the thought had been sternly repressed, so deeply did she want Daddy to have his longed-for son. Now I was two days old, and still nameless.

As I remember Mother across the many years I knew her, she possessed a miraculous gift of finding a way out of painful dilemmas, producing solutions which not only comforted, but usually substituted enchanting new vistas for the frustration and pain. How often when Bess and I were children did Mother magically transform sorrow to delight!

Lying in bed in unaccustomed idleness, she turned over in her mind the problem of a name for me. She knew that Daddy, although rejoicing in fatherhood, had not yet taken me wholly to his heart. Studiously avoiding calling me even "Baby," he was still referring to me as "it," and while he often peered at me as I slept in my converted clothes basket and watched, pleased and content, while I was being nursed, he had shown no inclination to pick me up or hold me.

Jacqueline? she wondered, but it smacked of compromise and then, as always, she wanted the best for me. Melissa? This was tempting, but it belonged so uniquely to her imperious, auburn-haired mother that it seemed absurd to bestow it on a baby. Elizabeth, her own name? This was instantly rejected; she had only recently emerged victorious from her years-long, determined refusal to be called Lizzie.

She awoke on the third day after my birth, aware of the slow, sure return of her strength and vigor, and simultaneously remembered that she had a choice of two names for me.

Daddy was an inveterate note-taker, jotting down ideas on scraps of paper as they occurred to him, and since their marriage Mother had undertaken to file these for quick reference. A few months earlier she had come upon the memo that she now recalled. It bore only six scribbled words: "Heroines—favorite names: Eve and Joan."

All morning she thought about them: Eve, the first woman, made from Adam's rib; Eve who was tempted by the serpent, ate of the fruit of the tree of the knowledge of good and evil and, with Adam, was banished from the Garden of Eden . . . Joan, Joan of Arc, who listened to her Voices, crowned a king and saved France from the English; Joan, who was brave and fine and true, and was burned at the stake. Eve London? Joan London? She could not decide.

Afternoon came and Mrs. Havens went off duty for a few hours. After a bit Daddy tiptoed up the stairs to see if Mother wanted anything.

"Yes," she told him, suddenly sure. "Will you bring Joan to me?"

He stood quite still for a moment. "Joan!" he repeated softly. "That beautiful name! Oh Bess, how did you know? It's perfect!" He went to the basket and picked me up for the first time. "You bet I'll bring Joan to you!"

I was forgiven, I was accepted, I was Joan.

When, as a little girl of five or six, I first began to search the album for confirmation that once my life had been lived with Daddy—days and days and nights and nights, one after the other, under one roof that sheltered us as a family—the house in which I had been born impressed me as being very old. But it was not old, merely old-fashioned, as nearly all two-storied, bay-windowed houses soon became during the heyday of the bungalow. It was good-sized and comfortable, and certainly the finest house that Daddy had ever lived in. It still stands, on East Fifteenth Street just off Twenty-third Avenue, looking not a day older than when Daddy photographed it in 1901 and pasted the picture proudly in the album.

This unpretentious house was my home for only two months, then, for half a year, we lived (rent-free in exchange for boarding the owner, a sculptor friend of Daddy's) in La Capricciosa, an ornate, rococco Italian villa close to Lake Merritt. It had a large, beautiful terrace high above the street, with pots of flowers and trailing vines, a pepper tree and a handsome pergola supported by neo-Corinthian columns, but Mother remembered it chiefly as chilly, badly planned, with small, dark rooms in which keeping house and caring for a baby were difficult.

The beginning of my life coincided with the last of Daddy's struggle to become a successful writer. Unaware that he was so close to his goal, he was driving himself relentlessly, writing, reading, studying, strictly rationing his sleeping hours and those he spent with his growing circle of friends and admirers. Yet, as the album attests, he somehow found time to take, develop and print pictures of his baby daughter, and to compose and type the captions that went with them—those whimsical, mysterious, baffling captions, full of his love for her and pride in his fatherhood:

> Joan meditateth on the Mystery of Things, Vieweth life Pessimistically, And striveth hard to be Reconciled—all at Three Weeks Old.
>
> Joan, at Two Months. Behold! she sporteth High Chairs, and reclineth at ease in the Clothes Basket.
>
> She twisteth her Eyes—And straighteneth out, with difficulty . . . at Two Months.
>
> She Smileth at Three Months . . . And cryeth immediately after . . . at Three Months and Five Minutes.
>
> N.B.—And Weigheth Fifteen Pounds.
>
> What maketh the Funny Noise? No, it is not the Camera that maketh the Funny Noise. It is the Squeaky Pig, which the Purple Cow Man giveth her at Five Months.

At six months, Joan "sitteth on the Beach at Sunny Cove and looketh Sphinx-like"; at seven months, she "repeateth the Performance—at the Cliff House." And the very next picture is the one that must have been taken by a sorcerer: sitting beside Mother on the open front end of an old-time cable car, Joan stretches her hand toward Mother's lap, across which two three-masted square-riggers are majestically sailing. Underneath is written:

> She reacheth out for the Earth and its fullness, and the Sea and its Ships.

Here, on page after page, are pictures of a happy family, a smiling mother and father, and a baby whose tiny face, laughing or sober, is relaxed and content. And here are pictures that reveal, from month to month, how the family's fortunes are improving. Gone are the hard times of the preceding year when publication plans for a novel had fallen through, stories either did not sell at all, or when they did brought in only a few dollars and, until she grew too large with me, Mother had continued the private teaching by which she had earned her living before she married.

There is a vacation at Camp Reverie that first summer, including a forty-mile trip in a horse-drawn stage. And a month or so later, after what Daddy called the beginning of the "migration to the hills," appears my third home, a large, imposing, even elegant dwelling on Bayo Vista Avenue in the Oakland hills, situated in a neighborhood of similar fine homes. It furnishes the background of a picture in which, warmly dressed, capped and mittened, for it is an October day, and looking very pleased, I am riding with Daddy on his bicycle, snugly fitted into a baby-carrying contraption fastened to the handlebars:

> *At Nine Months she Biketh with the Pater, Who is the Pater*
> *no longer, but Daddy. Behold Joan's House in the Distance.*

Sometimes when wind blows lightly across my face and past my ears, ruffling my hair in an oddly familiar way, I know an instant of sharp recognition which eludes me briefly and vanishes as I try to name it. Seeking to understand what I almost but never quite remember, I have thought that the touch of wind on face and hair is surely one of man's most ancient memories, and that it is familiar to me because it was a common experience of all my forebears back to the dim beginning of the time of man. But sometimes I have wondered if it might not be that my face and my hair are remembering what I cannot—the rides with Daddy on his bicycle.

Mother and Daddy were busy and happy in the spacious Bayo Vista house, with its large garden and view of the bay. Mother always recalled it affectionately, and sometimes, reminded of an incident or someone who visited them there, she would muse, "Perhaps it would have been better if we had stayed there and not moved to Piedmont at all."

Although never as inspired a housekeeper as she was a teacher, she found it relatively easy to run this big, well-planned house which at last met all their needs, including the solution to a problem that had begun to take on alarming proportions—guests. Old friends and new—Mother and Daddy delightedly welcomed them all. For Mother, it was a continuation, in her own home, of the hospitality which characterized the Maddern's family life, but for Daddy, with lonely years not far behind him, it was a new and exhilarating experience to be a host. Nevertheless, friends were coming in ever-increasing numbers, and, arriving unexpectedly and usually staying on for dinner, they willy-nilly made a shambles not only of Daddy's carefully planned work schedule, but of Mother's slim household budget as well.

They talked it over: if they were to set aside one evening every week for informal entertaining, the strain on Mother and the budget would be eased, and Daddy, with interruption of his work reduced to a minimum, could wholeheartedly enjoy himself. The plan was tried and met with instant success. Their first two homes had been too small to accommodate more than a few friends at a time, but in the Bayo Vista house there was room for dozens. And dozens there were who gathered there on the memorable "Wednesday nights," sharing the good talk and lively discussion, and the buffet suppers Mother prepared.

And at monthly intervals, the pictures for *Joan, Her Book* were taken, developed and printed, pasted in the album and captioned. Daddy was becoming a successful writer, Mother and Daddy together were building what promised to be a successful marriage and I was growing and learning to walk:

> *Joan standeth upright on her two Legs, at Nine Months, and preventeth the Chair from Tumbling Over. Also she Holdeth it Down.*
>
> *At Ten Months she Walketh, in the Walker, likewise by holding on to Things and preventing them from Tumbling Over.*
>
> *At Eleven Months she stoppeth the Rocker.*
>
> *And at Twelve Months, which is her Second Birthday, she holdeth her First Birthday Party.*
>
> *And at Fourteen Months, having completed the Migration to the Hills, she Diggeth in the Dirt and Walketh Upright under the Sun.*

Shortly after my first birthday, we moved to the last house we were to share, the Bungalow, always capitalized thus when written, and pronounced by Mother and Daddy so that the large B was almost visible.

The Bungalow was large, rambling, many-leveled and many-roomed, with redwood-panelled walls and ceilings, and redwood shingles outside, bronzed by summer suns and winter rains. The living room in the Bayo Vista house had been large, but the Bungalow's living room was huge.

Daddy used to say that the floor space of four cottages such as he had lived in as a boy would have fitted into that one room alone. The fireplace was big and welcoming, and every window framed a view of hill or bay. From spring to autumn, a broad, long, vine-covered porch was a second living room, for the Bungalow and its five acres of orchards, gardens and fields was sheltered by the eucalyptus-forested hills that rose steeply behind it and by a grove of tall, old pines on its northern side.

Over and over again when we were children we heard about the Bungalow from Mother and Daddy. There was a small, steep-roofed cottage where Grandma London lived, a barn large enough to hold a dozen horses, chicken houses and yards, a big pigeon loft, a separate laundry, even a creamery—and all for the even then unbelievably low rent of thirty-five dollars a month. They spoke of it always with love and regret, recalling the pink and white mist of blossoms in the springtime orchards and the fruit-laden trees in the summer and early fall, the riotous blooms in the garden, the little reservoir—"What a fine swimming pool it would have made," Daddy always said. And they spoke, too, of the famous view from the Bungalow: Oakland was spread out in a great half-circle, with marsh-edged Lake Merritt in the foreground, and a little further west, the silver line of the estuary fringed with the masts of sailing ships; across the bay, San Francisco climbed its many hills; straight ahead was the Golden Gate with ships almost always moving in or out; beyond lay the Pacific where, low on the horizon on clear days, loomed the Farallones; and to the north was the long, lovely slope of Tamalpais, purple against the sky.

But surpassing even these marvels was the unguessed and improbable, the never-to-be-forgotten poppy field. When they first came to live in the Bungalow the field had been like almost any California wintry hillside, with the new growth evoked by the autumn rains barely visible under the bleached, bent ghosts of last summer's grasses. But as the spring advanced and the wild barley grew lush and tall, the lacy, silver-green sprays of California poppies appeared, and seeking their multitude, Mother and Daddy realized that this would be no ordinary grassy slope, but a field of poppies.

"Every day," Mother used to tell us, "we would walk down the path to see how much taller the poppies had grown since the day before and to look for the first buds. How impatient we were for the coming of the poppies!"

At last the slender bud-cones began to shed their silver caps and the first blossoms gleamed like little heaps of gold amid the swaying barley. "It's a good omen!" Mother and Daddy told each other joyfully. And when the blooms reached their peak and the golden flood lapped at the

Bungalow porch and spread across the field and down the hill, their happiness and confidence were boundless.

How well it began, the year and a half we were to live in the Bungalow; how rich in fulfillment, creativeness and promise it continued to be for all of us almost to the very end.

Suddenly, magically, Daddy was famous. Critics and reviewers were saying, "A new star has risen in the West." Book sales leaped (there were three); editor and author exchanged roles: now they were begging Daddy for stories. The first summer in Piedmont a press association asked him, a struggling unknown only a few years before, to go to South Africa and do a series of articles on the Boer War. Hostilities being practically at an end by the time he reached England, he stayed in London to gather the material for and write *The People of the Abyss,* then traveled for several weeks on the continent. Six of his books were published during the Piedmont period, and many magazine stories and articles. *The Call of the Wild* was written in the Bungalow and *The Sea Wolf* begun.

At certain especially grim moments when he was still striving to be an author, Daddy used to announce defiantly, "If cash comes with fame, come fame; if cash comes without fame, come cash!" Now both were his, and although he began at once to live beyond his income, so secure was his fame that his credit was always good. From this time on he earned a great deal of money from writing; I was still a little girl when I read in a newspaper that he had become the highest paid author in America. Surely, though, no other literary man, with the possible exception of Balzac, was to mismanage his financial affairs more completely.

But now the hard times were over at last. Mother's faith in Daddy and Daddy's faith in himself had been brilliantly justified. They were very proud and happy, and a little incredulous, I think, that success had come so quickly, for both were prepared for a longer pull. Daddy continued to work steadily and well—the quantity and quality of his output attests to that—but he began to spend more time than formerly enjoying himself and relaxing. He fashioned great, brightly colored box kites and flew them in the poppy field, fenced and boxed, went on picnics in the hills beyond Piedmont, pursued his early love, photography, with even greater zeal, bought a small sloop for bay sailing.

Meantime, the family had grown. On October 20, 1902, while Daddy was still in Europe, my sister, Bess, was born—a second girl, but Daddy was undaunted. "The next one will certainly be a boy," he assured Mother, and boasted to everyone of his new daughter. "And after the boy comes," he would plan with Mother, "we'll buy a boat and sail around the world with the youngsters! . . . Would you like that?" he would suddenly ask Mammy Jennie, who had been his wet-nurse and who had come to live in the Bungalow and help Mother with the new baby. "We'll never be able to manage without you, you know," he would add, laughing at her astonishment.

A relationship that was fine and good was coming to maturity in the Bungalow. In the few photographs that include Mother at this time, she is smiling, and those of Daddy reflect his own contentment. Especially beloved by me are two pictures, taken by Mother and pasted in the album, showing Daddy and me on the front steps of the Bungalow: in one of them Daddy, tousled head on one side, is carefully extracting a splinter from the finger of an equally tousle-headed and very interested little girl; in the other, the album itself is open on Daddy's knees and I am pointing delightedly to one of the pictures.

Then there were the love-names Mother and Daddy used for each other. Girl and Boy they had been in the beginning, and after I was born they became Mother-Girl and Daddy-Boy—genuine, unaffected, frankly sentimental in that long-ago uncomplicated day before "sentimental" became an epithet. For several years after their separation Daddy continued to call Mother thus in letters and in the inscriptions he placed in her copies of his books, just as in October 1902 he had written in her copy of *The Cruise of the Dazzler*:

> Dear Mother Girl:—
>> Some day you can read this
>> aloud to the two youngsters.
>> With love from
>> Daddy-Boy

Something of this warmth and affection was to survive the crash of all their hopes and plans and somehow to be always associated with the Bungalow. During Daddy's visits to us later, especially when Bess and I were small, they would often reminisce, exchanging news of old friends and acquaintances and recalling incidents of the past. Almost invariably, their conversation would turn to the Bungalow. Intent, vicarious, I would listen eagerly, my eyes moving from one loved face to the other, undisturbed that they frequently spoke of people whose names I did not recognize. But when they talked about the Bungalow, their voices were different, they smiled and laughed as if only the happy times they had known there remained to be remembered, and suddenly I was shut out, unable to follow them into a past somehow barred to me.

The last spring in Piedmont was almost hectically gay. Servants, generally two, were there to assist Mother in her greatly increased duties as hostess, for guests not only thronged the Wednesday nights but often came on Sundays as well. In addition, there were nursemaids, one of whom, fourteen-year-old Docky, I would always remember, whose sole but fulltime task was to keep an eye on me.

And it was in the midst of this glad time of triumph and fulfillment and confidence in the future that the spinning of the gossamer-grail threads of memory began for me.

Daddy and Mother, Grandma London and Mammy Jennie, Docky and others who used to visit the Bungalow told me when I was a little older of how I used to elude the vigilance of everyone and vanish utterly on solitary explorations. Once I fell asleep in a woodcutter's shed far up among the eucalyptus, awaking happily when Daddy found me at last after a frantic two-hour search. As punishment and to prevent further disappearances, they staked me out in the garden with a rope around my waist. This restrained me for two days. On the third morning, before even the first routine check had been made, a telephone call from the entrance to Piedmont Park, some eight blocks away, brought Daddy hurrying down the hill to retrieve his daughter, who sanctimoniously explained that she had gone to the park merely "to get Daddy's mail."

For a long time my favorite goal after escaping my guardians was any of the numerous faucets in the garden and orchard. No one had been able to understand how and where I was getting myself thoroughly drenched. Trailing me on one occasion, the last, Daddy watched me turn on the faucet and settle myself in the deep grass directly under the flowing water. This time, as he carried me back to Mother for dry clothes, I explained that I was a water fairy. "I'll water-fairy you," Daddy threatened, "if you do it again!" But from then on the faucets could not be turned on without a wrench. And from then on, Docky was in charge.

I remember none of this.

I was outraged when Bess was born and could not be reconciled. I took her bottle away from her whenever I could, and until I was caught in the act they could not understand why she cried so much. When Daddy proposed to give her back to the doctor, I agreed so enthusiastically that they were forced, the doctor cooperating, into playing a tragi-comedy. They dressed her, wrapped her in blankets, packed her clothes and diapers, and actually started out the door to the doctor's surrey before I relented. I had sternly superintended the entire operation, but, standing on the porch, small, determined, I was apparently struck by the realization that this was something of mine that was being given away. To everyone's immense relief, I cried out imperiously;, "Give me back my baby sister! You can't have her!" Pictures in the album show my mulish unwillingness even to have my picture taken with the usurping baby, and it was some time before I truly accepted her.

I have no memory of this, either.

Long, long afterward, Charmian unexpectedly gave me a glimpse of myself in the Bungalow. "I wish," she wrote me a few years before her death, "I could wind something round and round in space and time, so that you could see yourself when I came to the Piedmont house of old, light right out for the Charmian you tried to pronounce, as your tiny hand searched my palm and pulled me straight for your piano." I like to think of myself as part of the Wednesday nights, even for the little while before I was carried off and put to bed. Almost I can see myself then, beguiling as any two-year-old, unabashed by the crowds, darting confidently among them, flattered by their attention, blissfully happy near Daddy, the center of it all.

But I don't remember those evening, or Charmian, or any of the others who came so often; I don't even remember Daddy or Mother or myself in the Bungalow.

My nascent memories were not of people, but of the physical world about me. A beloved child, secure in the matrix of my family, I accepted Mother and Daddy without question, while my awakening senses were thrall to the enchantment of field and garden, trees and flowers, wind and sun. Sounds, colors and smells, the shapes and textures of the things I saw with my eyes and touched with my hands and the intangible things without shape that I could neither see nor touch but could sense most distinctly—these became the almost-memories which later were to merge with the real.

Heliotrope bloomed in the sun against ruddy-brown shingles, its fragrance warm and prickly, the tiny flowerets pyramiding delicately from purple to lavender to pink to make the royal blossom, and the leaves furry, so different from rose leaves. . . . Wind, sweeping through my hair and along my outstretched arms, flattened the grass, set the pines to talking and roared among the eucalyptus up the hill, but when I turned on the faucet in the garden, the water swept through my hair and along my outstretched arms and was lost in the grass; and neither wind nor water could I hold in my hands to know its shape. . . . My fingers caressed the silken velvet of poppy petals and learned to trace the golden chalice from sturdy base to flaring lip. . . . In the summertime, the evenings were so filled with fragrances that I tasted them, saw their colors, heard their music, touched them with my hands: honey-suckle, jasmine, stocks and roses, new-mown grass, the pungencies of pine and eucalyptus.

The change-over from impression to memory and its linkage to place were to occur at different times and over a period of years. I remember that once, when I was twelve, I stopped short, shaken at the sight of blossoms as tenderly blue as an April sky. The barely uttered word of recognition—"bago"—was overheard. "Oh yes," the neighbor said, "the plumbago is especially lovely this year." Plumbago had grown in the Bungalow garden; I had not seen it since.

The process was always the same: a flower, a scent, a sound of wind or water, would bring an instant of bewildering recognition, and then, as I struggled to understand, it would come back—a time of joy, a garden and a poppy field where the sun always shone, a sense of marvel and of loss. It would pass quickly, but a memory had come to birth.

Our last summer together began. Toward the end of May, while the poppies still blazed in the field below the Bungalow, Mother and Mammy Jennie and Bess and I left for a camp resort in Sonoma County; Daddy, who had injured his leg in a buggy accident, remained in Piedmont until he could walk again and joined us a month later. Pictures that were taken that summer, showing me paddling in the creek, playing under the trees with other children, are pasted in the final pages of *Joan, Her Book*, but they have no captions.

Everything seemed all right. Urging a friend to join us at the camp, Daddy wrote in July that he was working well, turning out fifteen hundred words a day on *The Sea Wolf*, and that he expected we would stay there for at least another month. And yet, scarcely two weeks later, we were back in Piedmont, and Mother and Daddy were packing to leave, not only the Bungalow, but each other.

When next the heart-lifting call of the meadowlarks across the fields and the sight of wind gently stroking the silvery heads of wild grasses awoke in me memories of a vanished poppy field and a man who was flying kites and who was Daddy, a long time had passed.

TWO

I was ill for a long time, who had never been ill before. A heavy cold contracted on the sudden journey back to the Bungalow from Sonoma County and persisting through the disorder and confusion of packing and moving was succeeded by pneumonia, the first of the many attacks that were to plague my childhood.

My memory of the next year or so is a darkness out of which emerge dim and unrelated impressions of people and places, and three distinct incidents.

We moved several times: to Melissa Maddern's big house and garden on Broadway near Twenty-fourth Street, to a flat nearby, to another flat on the fringes of West Oakland. I am not certain of the chronology of these moves, but I know that it was the West Oakland flat we left for the newly built bungalow at 519 Thirty-first Street, near Telegraph Avenue, which was to be our home from the autumn of 1904 to the early summer of 1913.

When I look back to this shadowy time to find Melissa Maddern, it is her hands that I see first, small, swift, capable hands, always in motion, and almost always one of them is using a tool. I remember them, as I remember Mother's, as pretty, and perhaps they were, but then I have always found beauty in skillful hands.

I see them mostly in her garden, lightly working the soil with a trowel before giving bulbs or seeds or little plants into its keeping; or prying up dandelions with a blunt, short-bladed knife, a little reluctantly because she liked their sunny faces, but determinedly nonetheless because she liked her daisy-starred lawn more; or parting green heart-shaped leaves

17

to surprise me with the first of the white and purple violets; and some-times just touching with the tips of her fingers the bright leaves and blossoms and the delicate ferns that filled her small conservatory. But I can also see her hands busy in her big, fragrant kitchen. Fluting pie crust, pitting cherries or peeling potatoes in long, paper-thin spirals. Most clearly of all I remember them one sunny afternoon when she taught me how to shell lima beans—and much else.

Perhaps Mother had left me in Melissa's care that afternoon and she talked as she did to divert me, or perhaps it was she who needed diversion. Blessed with children and grandchildren and many friends, she was never alone in those last years of her life, but I think she was often lonely. My grandfather had died not long after I was born, and burdening no one with her grief, she remained inconsolable.

How to shell lima beans I have remembered unaided, but over many succeeding years my fragmentary memory of what Melissa taught me on that long-ago afternoon was made whole by Mother and her sisters, whose conversations so often began with "as our mother used to say. . . ."

Sitting on the sun-dappled front steps, the conservatory behind us and the garden spread around, Melissa showed me how to hold the cool, fleshy pod, slit it open with a carefully inserted thumb nail, and then scoop the fat green limas into the waiting colander. Because I valued her praise, I tried earnestly to follow her instructions, but soon her words snared me and I sat enthralled, pod in hand, listening.

Under her spell, I saw the limas as ovals of pale jade, heard the music they made as they fell rhythmically into the colander, which had magically become a burnished silver bowl, and watched the swift, precise move-ments of her hands and fingers weave the patterns of a dance. With the skill and art of an alchemist, she was transmuting a humble domestic task into the color and shape, the sound and motion, of beauty.

Almost, almost, I think I can hear her low, pleasant voice telling me, as she had so often told her daughters who were later to help me re-member, that beauty was everywhere, in everything you saw and did—in the lima beans, for example, and the shelling of them, in shining dishes and pots and pans and everything-in-its-place in the kitchen, in taking tiny, evenly spaced stitches in cloth, or fashioning warm and lovely garments from yarn with knitting needles or crochet hook, and always and most richly in anything you did in a garden. "And when you grow up and have a home of your own to care for," she told me—and this I am nearly sure I remember, "never clean it just to make it clean; clean it to make it beautiful; and wash your windows the same way, so that all the beauty outside can come in without blemish."

The last of the beans fell into the silvery colander. I can see her very clearly then, gathering the discarded pods into her apron, and, clasping her hands over them, gazing dreamily across the lawn to where a bed of asters glowed against dark shrubs. "How bright and beautiful they are," she murmured, so softly that I could just hear her. I like to remember her that way, smiling into her garden.

On another sunny afternoon I sat with my friend Annie at the top of the long flight of steps in the exact center of her high-basement, one-story house across the street from our West Oakland flat. I greatly admired Annie's house because it was painted snowy-white, while ours was a dull and melancholy grey, and I loved Annie.

She was a big girl, almost twelve, just the age for lavishing an almost maternal affection on a small one. Mother was always glad to let me play with Annie for she knew I would be safe from harm, and I was flattered and proud to be with her. She cut out paper dolls with me, tried to teach me how to play Jacks, sang the loveliest songs, and sometimes read me stories out of her book of fairy tales.

There were other children on the block, boys and girls older than I and a few even older than Annie. But I was a newcomer, an outsider; I did not know their rhymes or games and was confused and bewildered by their slang. I played with them seldom and then not very happily, even with those my own age.

From the high top step Annie and I watched the boys drifting aimlessly down the street that afternoon, quarreling half-heartedly, looking for something to do. At the foot of Annie's steps they paused, looking up at us with no especial interest. Then one of the boys said something we could not hear, and the others began to titter and guffaw, and when they looked at us, their eyes slid past us in a curious way.

Annie sat quite still. I moved a little closer to her, but she did not seem to notice. They were still laughing and whispering together, and now they were a group, their separateness and their quarreling gone.

The boy whose remark had started the laughter shouted suddenly, "Hey you, Joan, why do you always want to play with that nigger?"

A burst of laughter swept the group. I stared down at them blankly. Here was another word I had never heard before.

"I don't know what you mean," I said uncertainly.

They found this excruciatingly funny.

"That black girl up there with you is what I mean!" the boy yelled back.

I was speechless, understanding nothing.

"You must like those dirty niggers a lot!" the boy went on with relish. "Why, there's one at your house right now—that dirty old black woman!"

This time I at least knew whom they were talking about. There was only one old person in our house that day, and that was Mammy Jennie. But she wasn't dirty! And she certainly wasn't black!

"She's *not* black!" I shouted.

"She's black and dirty and a nigger!" he retorted.

"She's *not!* She's just like everybody else!"

I started down the steps. I would show them that Mammy Jennie wasn't black! They fell back to let me through the gate, then turned as one, still jeering, to watch me race across the street and down the side of the flat to the back porch.

"Mammy Jennie! Mammy Jennie!" I cried, climbing the steps as fast as I could. Flinging open the screen door, I stormed into the kitchen, and stopped short.

It was true, it was true, Mammy Jennie *was* black. I had not known.

She must have started toward the door when she heard me calling. Now she, too, stopped short. For an eternity we stood there, the length of the kitchen between us, looking at each other. Then, as if at a signal, we rushed together, she kneeling so that when I reached her arms it was against her loved and comforting shoulder that I buried my face and wept.

Gently rocking and patting me as she always did whenever I was cross or ill or unhappy, she kept murmuring, "Child, child, it's all right. Don't cry, baby. It doesn't matter. It doesn't matter at all." And I realized that somehow she knew what had happened and why I was crying.

After a bit my tears ceased, though my body still shuddered from the excess of my grief and rage. Out of the pocket of her big, white apron came a freshly laundered handkerchief for my wet eyes and nose, and then her panacea for all my bad moments—a peppermint lozenge.

"Someone said something?" she asked quietly. "The children on the street?"

I nodded, my hatred of them still too great for speech. If only I were not so little so I could punish them, hurt them, annihilate them!

"Don't pay any attention to them," she said firmly. "They just don't know any better."

She took my small, clenched fists in her hands, stroking them until they slowly relaxed and opened. Suddenly I remembered and sprang up. "Annie!" I had left her on the steps. I must go back right away.

"Wait." From a cloth-covered plate on the table, Mammy Jennie took two cookies, still warm from the oven, and put one in each of my hands, then led the way to the front door.

Annie was no longer on her steps. Our tormenters, tired of waiting for me to reappear, had wandered on and were standing irresolutely at the corner half a block away.

At the opposite curb I turned and waved confidently to Mammy Jennie, still watching from the doorway, then, holding the cookies carefully, I started up the long flight of steps to find Annie—Annie, who was also black, beloved Annie who was my friend.

When we lived in the West Oakland flat I was three going on four, and in October, Bess would be two. Slowly recovering from pneumonia, I had not been aware that Daddy had gone on a journey—to a faraway place called Korea, Mother said when I asked her. He had been away a long time, it seemed to me, but I never doubted that he would be back some day.

What worried me was that Bess did not know who Daddy was. On the wall in the dark front hall was a large framed picture of him. Daily, I would stand under it with Bess, anxiously making sure that her eyes followed my pointing finger, and then I would say as clearly as I could, "My Daddy!" She gave no sign of understanding what I was trying to tell her other than the pleased smile she bestowed impartially on everything that was brought to her attention, from toys to mashed potatoes.

She was a round, sturdy, sweet-tempered baby who rarely cried, but she had never made the slightest attempt to talk. Hiding her growing fear that perhaps the little one was mute, Mother used every loving device to evoke the beginnings of speech, but without success. Bess communicated her wishes only to me, in a rich variety of grunts emphasized by gestures, which I unaccountably understood and translated to Mother.

It was a formless, uneventful time. The summer days were long and quiet, I remember, with lingering twilights filled with the twittering of sprarrows. Mother put us to bed early, but even after she had read me a story I was rarely able to fall asleep right away. Lying wide-eyed in the dim room, I would listen to the cries of the children still playing in the street and the low rumble of their fathers' voices talking across the hedges while they watered their tiny lawns or smoked their pipes in the gathering darkness. Sometimes I heard the mutter of a lawn mower, and after a while the fragrance of fresh-cut grass would drift through the open window, awakening for a moment remembrance of other places, other times, inexplicably lost to me.

One evening, light suddenly blazed in the room, and before I could see, I heard Mother laughing and talking in a new, excited voice to someone. It was Daddy, longed-for and instantly familiar, who had returned, as I had known he would, from the other side of the world!

Before I could utter the cry of joy that was in my throat, Bess sat up in her crib and gazed at him solemnly. Slowly, her lips curved in her pleased smile. Raising her hand, the chubby index finger pointing, she said clearly, "My Daddy!"

Overcome with astonishment and disbelief, Mother and I watched Daddy leap to the crib and gather Bess up in a tumultuous armful, kissing her, rumpling her silky golden hair, and exclaiming, "Little Bess! Baby B!"

Turning joyfully to us and seeing our stunned faces, he demanded, "What's the matter? Is Baby B the only one who is glad to see me?"

Both of us tried to explain at once, and when he finally understood that those were the first words Bess had ever spoken, his pleasure knew no bounds. "It took her Daddy to make her talk!" he boasted over and over.

And always throughout this mostly unremembered time there was Mother. I cannot see her as she was then, as I can see Melissa and Annie and Mammy Jennie, nor can I recall any moment in which she emerged to dominate, however briefly, the unmarked days and nights. But she was all of the days and nights, the center and source of love and safety and well-being: the never-failing presence and gentle words, the glass of water in the night and the cool hand on a feverish forehead, the reader of fairy tales and teller of "when I was a little girl" stories, the answerer of questions and mender of broken toys, the comforter, holding me in her little golden-oak rocking chair and singing "Baa, baa, black sheep" in her strangely lovely alto.

There is a picture of her taken with me during this period—I wonder for what occasion, for she never cared to be photographed. The gaze of her lustrous eyes is calm and steady, but the young, hurt mouth, so piteously, determinedly firm, betrays her anguish and bewilderment, and when you look again at her eyes, it is as if they are shining with the tears she would not shed.

This was not the face she turned to me. I was her companion in misfortune, although I did not know it yet, but the face of the little girl beside her in the photograph, tousled hair caught back with tiny ribbon bows, is a happy one.

The Thirty-first Street bungalow—not ever to be confused with the Bungalow—was built in the late summer of 1904, shortly after Mother and Daddy were divorced. From the outside, it was rather charming: low, redwood-shingled, with a steeply sloping roof that came down from the dormered attic and over the front porch like a half-shut eyelid. On a street where most of the houses were tall and angular, with old-fashioned cupolas and gingerbread trimmings, it must have appeared very modern and up-to-date. It was neither; as a matter of fact, it was a singularly unsuccessful house in every respect, badly placed on the lot, badly planned and poorly heated, and far larger than we needed or Mother wanted.

I look back at it with a dislike which surprises me and which it does not merit—poor, homely, uncomfortable little bungalow. It is still there, appearing much smaller, of course, than it used to, and although I have passed it scores of times, I have never been able to bring myself to reenter it since we moved away fifty years ago.

Moved away? No, we *escaped* from it, from its gloomy rooms, from the houses that hemmed us in, from the illnesses we suffered there, from the loneliness, the anger, the heartbreak.

And yet we knew joy and laughter and beauty there, too, and small triumphs, and hopes that were not quenched until long after and elsewhere. When we left, it was with no promise or expectation of any change in our circumstances; nothing was yet decided or conclusive; in some ways, the worst was yet to come. But I do not like to think of how much more difficult it would have been to endure that worst in the bungalow on Thirty-first Street.

I came to know the bungalow slowly. It was divided into two parts: the "front of the house" and the "back of the house." At the beginning of our stay there we spent most of our time in the front part, which contained the living room and an adjoining bedroom, and the bathroom. The back part—two little bedrooms, a dining room-kitchen, a pantry and a laundry—was joined to the front by a small, completely windowless hall in the center of the house, an incredible cave-like space with five doors, including one to the linen closet, and a big old-fashioned telephone on a strip of wall betweeen two of the doors.

No, the bungalow was not a very modern dwelling, even for 1904. It was unheated except by the open fireplace in the living room and the coal range in the kitchen. From the ceiling of each room hung combination fixtures for gas and electric lights, the gas providing the steadier, more reliable, and much pleasanter illumination. In the always, even in the summertime, chilly bathroom was a marble washstand and an old-style high-tank water-closet; except that it was much smaller, it resembled the bathroom in Melissa's far older house.

There were good reasons why we should have lived almost entirely at first in the front of the house. Mother had sufficient furniture for the living room and one bedroom, and because it was late October or early November and the start of the cold and rainy season, the living room fireplace not only warmed both rooms but made them more cheerful. Bess and I were often ill that winter, I with colds and another attack of pneumonia, and Bess with croup and chronic earache, and warmth was essential.

I have a clear recollection from that time of feeling that our stay there was to be only temporary. Of course, I had never lived anywhere for very long; I was not yet four and this was my ninth home. The fact that we occupied only a portion of the bungalow, as if we were camping there, contributed to the illusion of impermanence. But there was another factor that strengthened the impression—a tiny hope that waxed briefly through a spring and summer, and then was abruptly extinguished.

My first memory of the Thirty-first Street bungalow is of Thanksgiving, which we celebrated, if one can use that word to describe the melancholy observance of what had always been a joyous festival in the Maddern home, soon after we moved in. After the dinner, which I have completely forgotten, I sat beside Melissa on the long window seat in the living room and listened drowsily while the Maddern women, Mother, Auntie Min, Auntie Florrie and Melissa, talked.

I remember Melissa very well that day. She was wearing a silvery-blue silk dress that rustled pleasantly whenever she moved, and she smelled of violets from the tall, green bottle of cologne that always stood on her dresser. It was the last time I was to see her, I think, for she passed away not long afterward.

With her usual animation, she was describing the shrubs, cuttings, rose-slips, bulbs and seeds she was going to give Mother for her new garden when I fell asleep with my head in her lap. I awoke to find the room filled with twilight except for the flickering flames in the fireplace, and Melissa was saying gently, "Try not to take it so hard, Elizabeth. Perhaps it may yet come out all right."

I don't recall what Mother said then, but her voice was tight and strained and I knew she was trying not to cry. Suddenly, Mother's grief, my longing for Daddy, the strangeness of the new house, the closing in of the gray November day were a weight too great to bear.

The aunts were sure that I wept because I had a stomach ache, Mother and Melissa thought I was merely tired, but Mammy Jennie, who had come the night before and helped Mother prepare the dinner, and who had been sitting quietly near the fireplace, carried me off to the kitchen where she soothed me with her never-failing magic, comforted me with warm milk and made me ready for bed.

It was an inauspicious beginning, but the sombre mood did not last. Tentatively at first, then quickening while the winter passed and spring moved gently into summer, a breathless, exciting happiness began to pervade the bungalow as, in small ways, our lives seemed to be meshing once again with Daddy's. He had taken a flat three blocks away and came to see us every few days. His Korean boy, Manyoungi, lived in our attic room, and for a while we kept two dogs for Daddy in our big backyard. Awaking at night, I would hear the murmur of voices through the partly open door. Sometimes Daddy and Mother were talking in front of the fire, sometimes it was only Daddy's voice and I could tell he was reading aloud to her, and sometimes they were laughing. It made such a pleasant sound, their voices and their laughter, that in a moment I would be asleep again.

Always when Daddy came to see us in the afternoon, he romped with us. As soon as we saw him coming up the walk, we would scamper to the front door, shouting our delight, hopping up and down, and raising our arms for him to lift us up as soon as he was inside. We scarcely gave him time to greet Mother, for the moment he put us down we would swarm over him and the romp was on.

Noisy, spontaneous, hurly-burly, the romps nevertheless had strict rules, the penalty for infraction being an immediate end to the game: no scratching, kicking, biting or hair-pulling, "be careful of the eyes," and more important than anything else, no tears, for Daddy would not play with cry-babies. For us, the aim was to make Daddy cry out, "I give up!" On his part, he was to fight us off and postpone the moment of yielding as long as possible.

I was four and Bess was two when the romps began and they were relatively mild and brief then, but as we grew older they lengthened and became more boisterous. From the start the rules were so rigidly enforced that I cannot remember, except as one remembers a tradition, any of the romps that were penalized for rule infractions. Fingers or toes accidentally stepped on, heads bumped, elbows skinned on the rough Axminster carpet, no matter; we would not cry.

Singly or simultaneously, we would rush him, growling fiercely, and the next instant be tumbled back with one sweep of his arms. Sitting on the floor, he would parry our lunges with lightning-swift jabs, knock our heads together, tease us and taunt us with high good humor until we launched a fresh attack. In the end, the fortress was stormed, four small legs clambered over him and four small fists reduced him first to shouts of laughter, then to prolonged fits of giggles, and finally the three of us sprawled on the floor, breathless and content. For that little while, he was wholly ours and we were wholly his, and the knowledge was good.

The vividness with which I recall the romps is a measure of their significance. I can still hear our shrill, little-girl shrieks and Daddy's deep-throated chuckles and giggles punctuated by tremendous snortings and blowings as he sought to recover his breath. I can see the geometrical pattern of the carpet, worked in dark green, gold and black. I can feel Daddy's sandpapery jaws and chin, sometimes rough enough to hurt when they brushed across our tender cheeks. And for a moment the Daddy-smell comes back, compounded of Bull Durham and shaving lotion and freshly laundered linen.

It was natural, of course, that our relationship with him at this time should have been largely physical. Because of the circumstances of our lives, however, the romps, except for hello and goodbye kisses and hugs, were our only physical contact with him, and we desperately needed that contact and its reassurance. He did not bathe us, or carry us off to bed, or spank us when we were naughty or touch us in any of the dozens of ways common to young fathers. He might have read to us or told us stories when he came to see us, he might even have taken us for walks, but he did not. And if the romps were wild, delirious orgies of laughter and squeals and shouts, leaving us exhausted and depleted, it was because they were all we had.

As I remember Melissa, I remember Manyoungi chiefly by his hands: small, slim, supple and very strong. He left his attic room in the mornings to walk to Daddy's flat before we awoke, but almost every evening he returned in time to play with us for a half hour or so before we were put to bed.

We did not romp with Manyoungi; we did acrobatics. We were timid and awkward at first and unable to follow instructions, but he was a patient and skillful teacher. One evening soon after the nightly games began, we sat together on the floor while he explained acrobatics to us. The words he used I have long since forgotten, but the essence remains.

"Do not think of your body, of your arms and legs and back and chest and head," he told us, and I hear again his clear, lightly accented voice. "Think only of what you want to do, and then all the parts of your body will move together as one without you telling them what to do."

He gazed seriously into our faces to see if we were following him. "It's just like when you walk," he went on. "You don't say to your body: now put your right foot forward and shift your weight so that it will be on that foot, then lift your left foot and place it ahead of the right one. Of course not!" He sprang up. "Look, I will show you the trick you liked last night, but first I will do it very slowly, as if I had to tell each part of my body what to do, step by step."

We watched him break up his trick into its separate movements, and it was as if he had become a puppet maneuvered by clumsy hands. "And now look!" he cried, and the trick became a lovely pattern sketched swiftly in the air, all the separate motions flowing together as one, and the whole visible for the moment that he held the dynamic final position. "Now let's try it," he invited, and we scrambled eagerly to our feet.

The evening sessions always ended the same way: first one, and then the other, we "walked up him." While he performed prodigies of balance, we grasped his hands—and how tightly we clung to them at first—and, our bodies horizontal, walked up his legs and thighs and torso; then, swinging to the vertical, we stepped lightly onto his shoulders and stood there, triumphant and unafraid.

How we adored Manyoungi! Esepecially on those days when Daddy had been unable to visit us, he brought Daddy to us. We would ply him with questions: did Daddy tell him about this, that or the other thing we had done? And, most important of all, was Daddy coming to see us the next day?

I had no understanding of "servant." I thought of Manyoungi as Daddy's friend, who helped him because he was so busy, and I was proud because he was my friend, too. And so I was puzzled because Daddy was not particularly interested in our acrobatic stunts, and on the rare occasions he came to the bungalow in the early evening he did not care to see us perform with Manyoungi. I was bothered, too, because when they did happen to arrive together and Bess and I were scurrying delightedly from one to the other (such riches, to have both of them there at the same time!), Daddy would soon say, "That will be all for tonight, Manyoungi." And although Bess and I would beg, plead and cajole Manyoungi to stay with us a little longer, he would immediately make his charming, formal goodnight bow to Mother and Daddy, and then a special one to us little girls, and go quietly upstairs.

That summer Daddy took Mother and Manyoungi and Bess and me to the Chutes in San Francisco. He showed us where to stand and watch, and then, without telling Manyoungi what to expect, Daddy had him take the front seat in a small boat. I saw the boat pushed into place and move slowly up a sort of track until it reached the top of the high chute, poise there a moment, then slide down the steep incline, faster and faster, until it leapt into the air and struck the water with a tremendous impact.

Watching the boat's terrifying descent, I saw Daddy grinning happily behind Manyoungi, but mostly I remember Manyoungi, his hands resting lightly on the sides of the boat, his face calm and impassive. But in the instant that the scene comes to full life again in my memory, I can see that his body, seemingly so easy and relaxed, is tense and alert for whatever it must do to meet the possible danger toward which he is being hurled. They landed safely, of course, in a great swirl and foam of water, and he was laughing heartily when he and Daddy rejoined us.

It was a good deal later that I began consciously to associate various incidents that had a common quality, and so embarked on the long search that would lead eventually to knowledge of the qualities themselves, but Manyoungi's impressive performance at the Chutes was, I think, the start. Manyoungi had been brave. And when Bess and I, no matter how difficult it was for us, observed Daddy's chief rule for the romps—don't cry when you're hurt—we were brave. And when Mother stopped the dogfight, she had been brave.

In some way, I do not pretend to know how, these three examples came together in my mind about this time, and the concept of bravery, and its name, sprang suddenly to life. The deeper understanding, that to be brave you must first be afraid, I was yet to discover, but even then I dimly recognized that there were differences in bravery. Daddy was brave, too. Had he not been with Manyoungi in that plunging boat, facing the same danger? Yet, for me, Manyoungi was, and remained, the hero of the episode.

Then, as she always was to be, Mother was the bravest person I knew. But she was more than merely brave. Not only did she demonstrate her extraordinary courage on countless occasions, but she frequently did what many brave persons fail to do: she kept others from being frightened at the same time. The dogfight was a classic example.

Brown and Yellow, in the prosaic way of small children, we called the two dogs Daddy asked us to keep for him. Brown, an Alaskan wolf-dog— really half-wolf, Daddy said—had been a gift, while Yellow was a golden-coated chow, a lost dog whose owner Daddy was eventually able to find.

During the several days that the dogs were together in our backyard, their instant, intense dislike for each other rapidly increased, culminating suddenly in a ripping, slashing, murderous fight. How it began, by what means it was finally ended, I cannot remember. Mother sent for help, and then, while Bess and I, terrified and crying, watched agonizedly through the window, she went into the backyard to see what she could do.

One of the dogs was fastened by a rope to the long clothes line that ran from the back porch fifty feet or more to the woodshed at the rear of the yard, and the battle raged up and down the length of the line. Commands from Mother had no more effect on the animals then turning the hose on them. Both warned her furiously away whenever she attempted to approach them.

She stood there, wringing her hands in helpless frustration, until her eyes fell on a stout clothes pole some six or seven feet long that had fortuitously been left leaning against the back porch. Grasping it, she ran swiftly to the fence, old-fashioned and well-built, with a wide stringer near the top. She was slim then, agile and strong. One moment she was climbing the fence, the next, it seemed, she had separated the dogs by well-aimed blows with the clothes pole, and miraculously maintaining her balance was able to keep them apart until help arrived.

But while she was still on the fence, a heroic figure against the sky, brandishing the long pole, speaking authoritatively to the dogs, she looked for an instant across the yard to the window where her two frightened little girls were standing, and smiled at us with such gaiety and triumph and reassurance that our fears fell away, our tears dried on our cheeks and we smiled and waved at her, sharing her triumph, tremulous with pride in having the bravest mother in the world.

One other incident gleams in my memory from that curious year, more significant in retrospect than it was then, for although we did not recognize it at the time, the shadow of what was to come briefly touched us on the afternoon of the first and only visit we were ever to make to Daddy in his own home.

Daddy underwent minor surgery in March and had to remain in bed for some days after he returned from the hospital. Longing to see us, he managed to persuade Mother to bring us to the flat. We were very excited and happy that we were going to visit him. Dressed in our best, we skipped beside Mother down Telegraph Avenue, talking incessantly. The sight of the unfamiliar house sobered us, but when we were inside the door, ready to run up the stairs and find Daddy, we were inexplicably kept back while first Manyoungi and then Grandma London talked earnestly with Mother. For a time it seemed that we were not going to see Daddy at all. Mother was very angry, while Grandma kept saying, "He wants to see them so badly, Bessie. And after all, she can't hurt them."

Finally, with great reluctance, Mother consented. "You take them up," she told Grandma and Manyoungi, "and stay with them all the time. I'll wait here."

Mystified, we followed our guardians up a dark flight of stairs and into a shadow-filled room. A small lamp glowed rosily beside the bed, and there was Daddy, his arms outstretched to embrace us.

Bess scrambled up on the bed, but a great constraint fell upon me and I could only stand beside him, smiling shyly, and nodding or shaking my head in reply to his questions, unable to utter a word of the many things I had planned to tell him.

A strange woman was sitting in a dark corner near the bed, staring at us. She did not speak, nor did Daddy introduce us to her, but her eyes did not leave us until the disconcerting visit was over.

I wondered about the woman who did not speak to us and only stared. When I asked Mother, she answered shortly that she was a friend of Daddy's, and then began to talk of something else. It was a long time before I knew who the strange woman was, and even longer before I knew her name.

It was in September, the first of that loveliest of months I can remember, that Daddy told us he was going away again in a few weeks and that we would not see him for a while. He had gone away before, to Korea, and returned; I had no reason to fear that he would not return this time. But even as my young senses were informing me of the slow waning of summer and the coming of change, I was haunted by a vague uneasiness.

Trees were yellowing and the Thirty-first Street gutters were beginning to fill with faded leaves that sailed through the air like tiny kites whenever the wind blew. The acacias along the sidewalks were dropping their scarlet and black seeds, and there were no more roses. One day we helped Mother shell the sweet pea pods which had been drying in the barn, scooping the small brown seeds into empty baking powder cans to keep until they were put into the ground after the first rains. The sun shone all day in the cloudless, deep blue sky, and the air had an exciting new fragrance that I could not define.

And yet I was often oppressed with a feeling of imminent loss, and in solitary moments was unhappily aware that, although we had been with Daddy so much during the past year, he did not live with us as the fathers of other children on the block did. We were different, and how passionately I did not want to be different. Many years were to pass before I learned that my growing confidence that year in the realization of my dearest hope, that Daddy would come back to live with us again, had not been merely the wishful thinking of a four-year-old little girl who longed for her father, but a very real possibility.

September merged into October, with skies of deeper blue, the sunlight more golden but less warm, the mornings sharp, dusk and the first stars coming early. Tangy smoke rose from smouldering piles of leaves in the gutters; when we awoke the lawn was sparkling with dew; the year was beginning to fold in on itself. Most of the time I forgot that Daddy was going away—east, he said (wherever that was), to lecture (whatever that was)—but suddenly, in the midst of play or on the brink of sleep in the evening, I would remember, and the unease would reawaken.

On the afternoon that Daddy came to say goodbye, he brought me a story book. We did not romp that day, and Mother and Daddy talked together, leaving us out, longer than usual and not happily. And then he hugged us tightly and kissed us many times and told us to be good girls until he came back. Noses pressed to the window, we watched him go down the walk and turn once and wave and blow kisses to us, and we waved and blew kisses back to him until the high fence next door hid him from view.

Desolate, close to tears, I turned away from the golden day into which Daddy had vanished and looked across the gloomy living room to where Mother was standing. She was staring, unseeing, over my head, but she must have noticed the small movement of my turning from the window and glimpsed my woebegone face.

Quickly, she picked up Daddy's gift. "Isn't it beautiful? Have you looked at it yet?"

Bess and I ran over to inspect the pretty book, the title and author, *The Golden Heart and Other Fairy Stories,* by Violet Jacob, stamped in gold on the light blue binding, and a brightly colored picture on the cover. She sat down in the "small" Morris chair, Bess and I perching on each arm, and together we pored over the illustrations.

"Will you read me some of it tonight?" I begged.

"After supper," she promised.

As she started to close the book she saw what we had missed before. "Look, Joan, Daddy wrote something here especially for you!"

"Read it to me," I said urgently.

And while my eyes traced the flowing script that I could not yet decipher, she read:

> *Dear Joan, my dear daughter—*
> *With a heart full of love,*
> > *from*
> > *Daddy*
>
> Oakland, California
> October 18, 1905

She put the book gently into my outstretched hands and I clasped it to me tightly. That night and for many nights thereafter it lay under my pillow while I slept.

THREE

Slowly, in subtle ways, our lives began to change after Daddy returned from the lecture tour early in 1906. Looking back, as I often did in ensuing years, I came to realize, sorrowfully and unwillingly, that our relations with him were never again the same as before he went east.

Recalling that time from my vantage point of today, it would be easy to report simply: this is the way it was, and this is the way I was; this is what I did and felt, and, although it took a long time, my attitude came to be thus and so. But such a recital would tell only the smallest part of the story, for it was not easy then; it was very painful, difficult to accept and adjust to, impossible to understand. Nor can I bring myself to dispose so readily of that embattled little girl, groping and confused, rejecting rejection without even recognizing it as such and never losing sight of her goal in a continuing situation that, superficially, constantly varied.

And today I can see what was hidden from me then. The enchanted world in which my babyhood had been passed and out of which I had been thrust so early—but not so early that I could not remember some of it—was closed to me forever. Though I might, and did, linger outside, peering through the barred gates, catching glimpses of Daddy now and then, dreaming confidently of the triumphant day when I would be welcomed back, I was never to pass through the gates again. Once and once only, they were to open wide to me with a welcome beyond my happiest imaginings, but entrance was at a price I could not pay. After that the gates were shut and signs were posted, reading "Keep out!" It was not really long before the signs came down, and the gates were not ever locked, I know now, but I could not be sure then; besides, there was no time left.

Mother felt the difference, I think, as soon as Daddy returned, and for a time Mother changed, too, becoming crisp, decisive, even assertive, who had never been so before and was not so again.

Daddy changed, Mother changed, our lives changed.

As I see it today, it was as if two forces were set in motion during the months after Daddy's return, a centripetal one which drew me ever more closely to him, and a centrifugal one which spun me further and further away from him. They alternated, depending at first solely on his physical presence or absence, later, on what occurred when we were together and on the letters I received from him and, finally, after his death, the ambivalence having long been established, they shifted back and forth as events set in motion the old responses.

Before he went east, Bess and I, like small sunflowers with faces turned always toward the sun, had focused on Daddy the most intense devotion of our young hearts. To be with him was supreme happiness and fulfillment; to be without him was joyous expectancy and planning for his next visit. As the change gradually took place, our devotion did not lessen, but in the time between his visits new interests began to develop. I learned to read and write, for instance. The feeling of impermanence about our stay in the bungalow faded; we spread out until we were no longer camping in the front of the house, but occupying and living in all of it, with the attic for play on rainy days and the backyard in good weather. People became important. We began to have friends whom we visited and who visited us; some of them were old friends of Daddy and Mother's, others were new and did not know Daddy at all.

It was good, I suppose, instinctive and healthy, but it was sad, too, for implicit in it was the compulsion to grow out and away because Daddy was setting us aside; we had to grow or perish.

It was during this period, also, that I became sharply aware that, somewhere beyond the bungalow, Daddy had a whole other life that did not include us at all. This knowledge was incredible at first, and I fought against accepting it in every way I could, but it pushed past all my defenses, my furious resentment, my futile efforts to ignore it. Eventually, I came out of the long struggle with little else but pride and a fierce determination not to betray my deep and bitter wound to anyone, least of all to the one who had inflicted it. How inexorably I was ruled by Daddy's maxim, "Don't cry when you're hurt," and what singularly tearless children Bess and I were!

Coincidental with the slow forging of this protective armor was my recognition and acceptance of an unspoken challenge from an unknown rival. Little by little, I grew certain that in that other life of Daddy's there must be someone for whom I was being set aside, a usurper of my role as unquestioned and sole possessor of Daddy's love and interest. Willingly, even graciously, I had shared my possession with Bess and Mother, but in my imperious five-year-old heart I had not doubted that Daddy was completely my own.

I seem to have been essentially a reasoning child. Already it was fairly clear to me that nothing happened without a cause, even when that cause was invisible. When I finally accepted the painful fact that my place in Daddy's life was no longer a very large one, I began to seek the reason for my diminished status. Apparently it never occurred to me to blame myself, and I am grateful for whatever was the cause of that, since I escaped thereby the anguish of what we came to know years later as an inferiority complex. Instead, I was obscurely angry.

From the start I reasoned that my place must have been taken by some person. Then, from a quickly hushed word here, a hint there, slowly there began to appear the shadowy figure of a competitor who lived and had her place in Daddy's other life.

Against this threat, when suspicion later became certainty, I was to marshall all my resources and resolution. By the time I was seven, my yearning for the father I was somehow losing had shaped my confident plans. How well I remember them! I would grow up as quickly as I could and make Daddy proud of me; I would be beautiful and accomplished; I would read and study and learn everything important; I would sing and play the piano and speak languages. And never, for one instant, did I doubt that I would succeed.

Thus did I start the long preparation to meet head-on the shattering events to come. And thus, beneath the pride that armored my hurt, was nourished the will to excel. But how difficult it must have been, I think, for that little girl who was I to have competed, year after year, with an unknown rival who for long was nameless, and for even longer faceless.

Bess and I were wildly happy to see Daddy on his return. As the year progressed, however, he came to the bungalow less frequently than the year before, and he was usually in such a hurry to keep appointments that he seldom stayed long. And so, during that year when everything was changing, the dear familiarity of Daddy's presence dimmed. We were still too young to remember him vividly during the lengthening intervals between his visits, so that whenever we saw him there was a little diffidence to overcome, a little shyness, and, though concealed by me at all costs, a little reacquaintance to be made before we could be at ease with him again. At the same time, there was a conscious effort on our part to be and look our very best, to entertain him and make him laugh, to so ensnare and enchant him that he would not pull out his watch so soon and say, "I have to run along now. There's a man I must see downtown."

The tensions that arose at this time were to mark our relationship to the end. Our expectancy before his arrival used to reach a pitch that was nearly unbearable. Faces and hands scrubbed, wearing our prettiest dresses and hair ribbons, we would run into the living room to watch for him at the window. Either we were ready for him too soon or he arrived later than planned, for almost always there was an agonizing wait before he finally came past the high fence next door and turned into our walk. Then, whether it was rainy or fair, we would fling open the front door, and hiding our unsureness with noisy bravado, we would dash pell-mell across the porch and down the steps to greet him. Everyone laughed and talked at once; only Mother, smiling in the doorway and leading the way inside, seemed calm. And how sweet it is to remember that in those days Mother and Daddy always kissed when he arrived and later when he left, exchanging this brief, affectionate caress over the heads of the little girls, clamorous and wildly excited on his arrival, clinging and reluctant to let him go on his departure.

As soon as he was inside, Daddy would settle himself in the "big" Morris chair (the "small" one was always for Mother), and Bess and I would perch precariously on each side, our arms around his neck. Mindful of Mother's instructions, we tried earnestly to sit still and wait until they had finished talking before we monopolized him, but it was impossible. Our excitement leapt up from moment to moment as spontaneously and irrepressibly as twin geysers. We wriggled and twisted on the narrow arm rests, clutching frantically at Daddy to keep our balance, then, suddenly, with no intention of interrupting, we would burst into their conversation to tell him something from the small hoard of happenings we had been saving for him for days, sometimes for weeks, and with which we hoped to astonish and delight him.

In seeking his attention, Bess and I were never rivals, but fellow-conspirators, constantly helping each other, nor did we regard Mother as a rival, for she helped both of us. The compelling wish to win him back, to make him our own again, had for long tacitly united the three of us and governed our behavior.

The moment Bess and I longed for finally came, sometimes at the peak of our importunities, sometimes after we had won his attention and he had patiently and lovingly listened and responded appropriately with amazement and delight to all we had to tell him. With a sudden whoop, he would sweep us from the chair, and together we would tumble to the floor and into the romp.

In that year of change, the romps changed, too. They grew rougher and noisier, and pillows, the big, feather-light, velvet ones from the window seat, were added, along with an extension of the old, strictly observed rules to cover their use. But as the year advanced, the magic the romps had once possessed, of communication and closeness and belonging, grew less and less powerful. For me, they no longer filled the void of Daddy's absence or expressed the love and trust that formerly flowed so freely between us.

All the preceding year he had been physically close to us. Even when we did not see him for several days, we knew that he lived nearby, and although it was a fading memory now, we also knew that once we had actually visited him.

Then, suddenly, he was no longer there. He had moved, he told us one afternoon soon after he returned from the east, to his ranch in Glen Ellen, which would henceforth be his home. Whenever he came to Oakland, however, he would be near us, for then he would stay in a house on Twenty-seventh Street, just off Telegraph Avenue, which he had recently bought for Grandma London, and where Mammy Jennie would live, too.

This is an odd memory. It has an odd clarity, for one thing, having been so little used in all these years that it has the freshness and newness of yesterday. On my endless journeying back to the memories of happier days, the paths I made around it, avoiding it, were well-worn. I knew it was there, but I used merely to glance at it without pausing and hurry on. And this memory is also odd because, now that I have picked it up and am looking at it, I am at once that little girl meeting the first severe test of her conditioning, and myself watching her pass it.

He had moved, Daddy said. Now, truly, he had gone away, and he would not come back except once in a while—I grasped no more than that from his announcement, and it was overwhelming. But it appeared that something was expected of me, that I must make some response.

"What is a ranch, Daddy?" I managed at last. "And where is Glen Ellen?"

"It is in the country," he explained, and it was easy to see that he was excited and glad about it. "A lot of land, very beautiful, with many hills and fields and trees. And Glen Ellen is a tiny town about seventy or eighty miles from here."

I wondered hopelessly what was seventy miles, and forbore to ask; learning the answer would not lessen my anguish. Not ever again to fall asleep secure in the knowledge that Daddy was only three blocks away . . . not ever again to dream of walking those three blocks by myself, some day when I was a little older, to pay him a surprise visit . . . not ever again . . .

But my conditioning held. I did not say I was glad for him, although I was because he seemed so happy; I did not beg him not to go so far away from me, I did not cry. Instead, I asked—and hearing myself ask it astonished me so that I remember it still, "What kind of trees grow on your ranch, Daddy?" It was the best I could do, and perhaps he understood.

"There are oaks and redwoods and madrones," he told me. "But there are also fruit trees, apples and plums and prunes, and many kinds of grape. . . . And do you remember Brown Wolf, the dog you and Baby B used to call Brown?"

"He had a big fight with Yellow," Bess contributed solemnly.

"That's right. . . . Well, Brown Wolf has been up on the ranch since I bought it last summer. You can imagine how happy he is to be there with all those acres to run around in."

Last summer, I though bleakly, he bought it last summer, and he didn't tell us about it until now.

Daddy was rummaging in his pockets. "I've brought something for you. Look!" He pulled out a half a dozen small puzzles: two twisted pieces of heavy wire which seemed hopelessly entangled but slipped easily apart when held in the right position; the brightly colored picture of a clown inside a round, glass-topped case, with tiny balls that rolled helter-skelter, but if you tipped the case and held it just so, the balls would finally fit into little holes and make the clown's bulging eyes and the buttons down the front of his costume; and there were others which I have forgotten.

We were instantly enthralled, and it was not until Daddy had left and we were having our supper that I remembered the ranch. I tried to picture it, to comprehend that puzzling term "seventy miles," and could not, nor was Mother very helpful.

What was a ranch? I wanted to know. Was it like a farm? (There were many farms in my story books.) How many blocks were there in a mile? What was seventy? Could I walk seventy miles, maybe, when I was a little bigger? And finally, after a long silence, I asked, "Do you think I will ever go to Glen Ellen and see Daddy's ranch?"

She looked at me, startled. "I don't know," she answered, then added with unwonted harshness, "probably not."

During the following days I tried to reconcile myself to the fact that Daddy had gone to live so far away, and that from then on we would not see him often. Why? I wondered, and could find no answer. Nevertheless, I began to make plans, the first being to learn how to write as soon as possible so I could send him letters, and surely he would answer them. As for the seventy miles, I would solve it somehow, later.

But a week or so afterward came a second and more devastating blow. Although incomplete, this is an easily evoked memory, rich in details recorded by all five senses, but its significance lies, of course, in what is missing from it. Dominating the moment when the blow fell, so that I cannot recall feeling pain or outrage or incredulity, or anything at all, is an absurd, childish fantasy.

It was a dismal day of pouring rain, I remember. The grey sky pressed heavily on the rooftops and telephone poles, and the sound of the wind-driven rain was everywhere as it furiously assaulted the windows, gurgled down the drain pipes, and even fell with angry hisses on the glowing coals in the fireplace, on the floor in front of which Bess and I were happily coloring. Mammy Jennie had come to spend the day with us and had brought us a rainy-day gift from Grandma London, a box of crayons and a coloring book apiece.

In the kitchen, Mammy Jennie was baking apple pies and Mother was ironing. The murmur of their voices came to us faintly, and the thump of the iron, and sometimes the different thump when Mother placed a cooled iron on top of the range and clamped the wooden handle onto a hot one. When Mammy Jennie opened the oven door to look at the pies, their spicy fragrance mingled with the rich odors from the soup pot simmering on the back of the stove.

Suddenly, quick footsteps sounded on the front porch, then a tattoo of knuckles on the window, and we looked up to see Daddy, rain streaming from his hat, grinning at us gaily.

Our shouts of joy and surprise brought Mother and Mammy Jennie to the living room. How excited we were! It was one of the very few times Daddy ever came to see us without first telephoning. We all helped to get him warm and dry, hanging up his dripping overcoat and hat, settling him comfortably in the big Morris chair in front of the fire. Bess and I succeeded in untying the wet laces of his "low-cut" shoes and placed them on the hearth, then put one of the pillows from the window seat under his feet. And a moment later Mammy Jennie and Mother brought in freshly brewed coffee and apple pie still warm from the oven.

It was fine, it was like a party, it *was* a party, with guests and refreshments, and everyone laughing and talking. Mammy Jennie, sitting in the fireplace corner, scolded Daddy for wearing such silly shoes and no rubbers when it was raining so hard, and he scolded her back for worrying about him. Bess and I showed him the pictures we had colored and he admired them extravagantly. Outside, the wind-lashed rain beat steadily against the bungalow but we did not hear it anymore—only the laughter and the voices we loved most in the world filled the enchanted half-circle in front of the fire.

And there my memory of the scene halts, with Daddy beginning to tell us his great news: he was building a boat, and as soon as it was completed he was going to sail around the world and be gone for seven years.

I remember thinking: that's impossible, you can't sail *around* the world—the world is square! And instantly, in my mind's eye, I saw a vast cube with sharp edges and precipitous sides, floating in a pale blue, cloud-etched sky that stretched everywhere forever. The sharp edge was the "jumping-off place," and if you traveled far enough to stand there and peer over, you could look straight down the enormous flat side of the world, or gaze into the limitless, cloud-filled void beyond and above and beneath.

I have no idea of the source of this fantasy; as far as I can tell, it leapt into being at the moment of Daddy's announcement. Also, I know that I understood perfectly that the world *was* round. Mother had explained it to me, and had shown me a large globe not long before in Smith Brothers' bookstore downtown, pointing out where we lived in California, and then, turning the globe slowly while a bright blue ocean passed beneath her finger, where Manyoungi had come from in Korea. Nor did my brand-new idea of the squareness of the world do violence to the acknowledged concept of its roundness. Both existed side by side in my mind without conflict. But for years afterward I was to search for the "jumping-off-place," and never climbed a hill, seeing the empty sky beyond and above, without a burning hope that this, at last, would be it, and that when I reached the top and stood carefully near the edge with all the winds of space blowing past my ears, I would be able to look down and down the flat-sided earth, and up and out into the blue foreverness.

Perhaps it was because I thus fled into fantasy to keep from hearing more of the coming seven-year voyage around the world that the remainder of this warm, firelit memory is ragged and confused, or perhaps because the grown-ups behaved so unaccountably and did and said things I could not understand. The dismay and tension evoked in all of us for different reasons were sufficient, certainly, to distort everything that followed Daddy's shattering announcement.

What did we say, I wonder? When I try to remember, I see only my square world sailing majestically through space. How long I was bemused, I don't know, but when the scene comes back again the grey day was darkening to dusk and beyond the half-circle of firelight the room was full of shadows, and Daddy was saying, "No time for a romp today, girls. I must be off."

He took out his watch, pressed the stem that magically raised the cover and held it near the fire so that he could see the time. The case was open only briefly, but in that moment Mother and I saw that the little photograph of Bess and me which he had taken with him to Korea and had carried ever since was no longer inside. Before the cover snapped shut I glimpsed the face of a woman, teeth showing in a wide-lipped smile and hair elaborately arranged on the top of her head.

Mother said something in a low, shocked voice. And suddenly Daddy was cross, reaching for his shoes and not letting us help him to put them on, taking his coat from Mammy Jennie and forgetting to thank her. Then he kissed us goodbye, but not Mother this time, and was gone.

The silence that always followed Daddy's departure was sometimes rich and glowing with shared happiness, sometimes sad and sometimes irritable, almost angry, torn with frustrations and contradictory emotions. That day, the silence in the gloomy room was massive; neither the roar of the wind and the rain outside nor the sputtering of the fire within could prevail against it. And then Mother and Mammy Jennie did what they rarely did—talked over our heads. It was not done deliberately; they had forgotten we were there.

"Oh Bessie, Bessie," Mammy Jennie sighed.

Mother said roughly, "We planned it, every bit of it. You were to go, too—remember, Jennie?"

"I remember. But seven years!" She shook her head in disbelief. "Isn't that what he said, Bessie? Why, I'll never live that long!"

I looked at her in alarm. She appeared neither sick nor any older than usual, but just the same as always, bright-eyed, unwrinkled, erect and vital.

"And what will his mother say?" she went on worriedly. "She won't like it, she won't like it at all."

"It won't make any difference whether she likes it or not," Mother told her. "She has no more to say about it than you have, or I have or Joan and Bess have. Now it's only . . . only the other," she finished bitterly.

"But seven years!" Mammy Jennie protested again.

Seven years, I echoed to myself. The familiar words had lost their meaning. What was seven years? This was a great deal more difficult than seventy miles. After all, seventy miles could finally be made into a certain number of blocks, even if it were a million or more, and you could see a block with your eyes and walk it with your feet. But seven years! I was five years old, and that was a very long time, so long that I could remember only a part of it. Seven years, then, would be much longer than I had been alive! I strove to understand, remembering that just as there were blocks in a mile, there were months and weeks and days in a year, but it was like trying to pick up a length of running water and hold it in my hands.

A log broke softly in the fireplace with a small shower of sparks and a flicker of new flames.

"How dark it is in here!" Mother exclaimed, startled. "Turn on the lights, Joan, while I build up the fire."

And after that I remember only that the room became bright and cheerful again, that we unexpectedly had our supper in front of the fire and that when Bess and I were ready for bed Mother read us more of a wonderful new story about a boy named Mowgli who lived in a forest that was called a jungle. Absorbed in his adventures with Baloo and Grey Brother and Bagheera, whom I loved most of all, I forgot the seventy miles and the seven years and the great square world. But as Mother was tucking me into bed, I remembered one last enigma.

"Who is that lady?" I wanted to know.

"What lady?"

"The one in Daddy's watch."

She did not answer right away, and when she did her voice was queer. "That," she said slowly, "is the Beauty."

Mystified, but too tired to wonder any more about anything, I fell asleep.

Deep beneath the surface of our lives change was at work and enduring patterns were forming, but on the surface, this year was marked by a rhythmic ebb and flow of activity. Long, quiet periods when the days slipped past softly, one after the other, differing only by weather or season, were interrupted from time to time by extraordinary events that signaled the start of wonderfully exciting periods which subsided very slowly.

Thus, I awoke in the grey dawn of an April morning to thunderous noise in a crazily lurching world. The next instant Bess was thrust into bed beside me, and I opened my eyes to find Mother bending protectively over us.

The noise increased, outside and inside the house, culminating in a tremendous crash overhead as if a giant hand had slapped down hard on the attic floor, and followed by a fine snow of plaster dust. Outside, there was a torrent of sound as many heavy objects fell together a great distance for a long time. Then the fluted glass chimneys on the madly swinging electric fixture in the middle of the ceiling began to fly off and shatter against the walls.

I looked up at Mother in wonder. She was very alert and aware, but obviously unfrightened.

"It's all right," she assured me confidently. "This is an earthquake, a bad one, I think, but we'll be safe. There's nothing to be afraid of. Just stay where you are."

"What is an earthquake?"

"I'll explain it to you later. It's very interesting. . . . Move over a bit, so I can pull the covers over your little sister. That blessed baby, she's still sound asleep!"

Slowly, although, as it always happens during an earthquake, catastrophe seemed imminent until the very end, the noise and the strange deep shudders diminished. There was a moment of complete silence, then, from across the street, arose a crescendo of terrified screams.

"That's surely the sick people in the hospital," Mother said quickly. "They're frightened, of course."

She turned to the window and raised the blind. "Oh! Put on your slippers and come here . . . you'll want to see this."

Across the street, but on the corner, facing Telegraph Avenue, was the East Bay Sanitarium, a large, four-story-and-attic wooden hospital. At the end nearest us had stood a huge brick chimney. Now most of it sprawled in heaps on the ground in a slowly settling cloud of brick and mortar dust.

"Did you hear them falling during the earthquake?" Mother asked.

I nodded; that had been the torrent of sound. Simultaneously, we remembered the tremendous crash overhead at the height of the earthquake, and Mother hurried up to the attic to discover what it had been.

"Several bricks fell out of our chimney," she reported a few minutes later, "and I suppose there are some more outside on the roof—nothing serious, though. But the really big noise was that old walnut bedstead that was leaning against the chimney. It fell flat down on the attic floor!"

While she was dressing and helping me with the buttons I could not reach, she began to explain about earthquakes, what caused them, what happened when they occurred and what to do and what not to do while they were going on: "Never be excited or frightened, and never run outside where falling bricks and timbers might hit you. If it is a really violent quake, go to the nearest doorway and stand there until the shaking stops. A doorway is the safest place in a house during an earthquake. And if you're outside, get away from buildings. The middle of the street is the best place."

Quietly, simply, she stripped the experience of its unreality and terror and fitted it into the familiar category of natural phenomena, along with the wind and rain and thunder and lightning, rarer than any of these, possibly more dangerous and certainly more interesting, but not under any circumstances to be feared, because fear made people do foolish things, and it was not safe to do foolish things during earthquakes.

It was her way, to the very end of her life; it was her way of life. To her, the physical world was neither malign nor mysterious, but essentially orderly and law-abiding. She believed implicitly, therefore, that if you understood what was happening, the natural law that was being obeyed, you would not be afraid, and if you were not afraid, you would be able to use your intelligence and common sense to save yourself and others from harm. What an enemy of fear she was, all ready to attack and put it to rout by searching for its cause. In our house, strange noises were always investigated, especially if it was night, and under her tutelage, darkness, which torments so many children, became for us a different and strangely beautiful dimension in which we learned to "see" with our fingertips and to move through with confidence.

One's first earthquake is unforgettable; almost always some residue of how one felt during its progress persists through all subsequent repetitions of the experience. And so to this day I find those sometimes ephemeral, sometimes enduring, but always unexpected and startling convulsions of the seemingly solid earth, awesome, sobering, intensely interesting and a little exciting because of their ever-present potential danger, but never frightening.

The first half-hour of that 1906 earthquake, in which understanding and acceptance of the phenomenon followed so closely upon the event, thus remains distinct in my memory, whereas what happened afterward is, for the most part, submerged in the continuing excitement which lasted for days. Some time during that first morning Daddy telephoned from Glen Ellen, which, for me, was marvel piled upon marvel, to see if we were safe, and told Mother he had just learned that San Francisco was afire. There was much coming and going all day. Grandma London and Mammy Jennie and various aunts and uncles came to see us and exchanged experiences. Toward evening, with a friend of Mother's whom we called Uncle Charlie, we walked to the top of nearby Orchard Street hill, from which we could look across the bay and see the red glow of burning San Francisco against the darkening, smoke-filled sky. That night, probably because of persistent rumors that there were also fires in Oakland, we slept in the living room as close as possible to the front door.

At intervals during the next few days the slowly subsiding tremors of the earthquake recalled the astounding violence and din of the first great shock, but the center of attention was already shifting from the earthquake itself to its chief disaster, the fire. Earthquake stories began to pall; their variety was limited and after a while they all began to sound alike. But eye-witness accounts of the fiery death of San Francisco, even at second- or third-hand, were thrilling. Listening to friends and neighbors relate what they had seen or heard, or to the newspaper accounts which Mother read aloud to Mammy Jennie, I could see the flames, feel their heat, was blinded and stifled by the smoke. Clutching my own most prized possession, *The Golden Heart*, I helped people save what they could before abandoning their homes, and with them fled to safety before the advancing fire. My vocabulary increased. I spoke knowingly of "refugees" and "dynamite" and "heroism," and paraded my treasury of new adjectives and superlatives on every occasion.

Daddy had managed to reach the burning city on the afternoon of the earthquake and had remained there throughout the three days of its agony. He described this experience to us soon afterward and, listening raptly to his vivid words, I shared his sadness that so much of the city he had known since boyhood was gone forever, although all that I actually remembered of it was the Chutes.

It was perhaps a fortnight after the fire that Uncle Charlie, Mother, Bess and I took the train and ferry across the bay. From the Ferry Building, I gazed in wonder at a blackened, desolate city. Heaps of rubble and fragments of tottering walls and chimneys stretched away on each side of the widest street I had ever seen, and far up into the hills. Was smoke really still rising from those ruins? I do not think so. But for days I had listened to descriptions of the holocaust, ashes had fallen in our garden and the sun had shone redly through the smoke that drifted across the bay. I am sure that I added the smoke to those ruins for verisimilitude, and have remembered it so ever since.

There is a fragmentary memory from the weeks following the earthquake which bears no relation to that event except proximity in time, and has survived because it was the beginning, for me, of a long and wonderful acquaintance with the woman I knew first only as Cousin Minnie. There was also another cousin, Cousin Emily, in the big country house in Ben Lomond where we visited them for several days, probably in May. Cousin Emily I can remember from that time because of a snapshot of her standing on the lawn, slim, blonde, lovely, but I never came to know her very well.

The Cousin Minnie of that visit I cannot see in my mind's eye, but she is sitting on a bench in the garden, talking with Mother, and I keep interrupting until Cousin Minnie says firmly—and did anyone ever speak so quietly with such authority?—"Go sit on the lawn, Joan, and look for a four-leaf clover."

I was entranced; I had never heard of a four-leaf clover! From then until the end of our visit I looked for a four-leaf clover every day, and at last, when I was beginning to doubt their existence, triumphantly found one. I remember that Cousin Minnie was as surprised and pleased as I was.

And then came the horse and buggy. Undoubtedly, conversations between Daddy and Mother, lengthy correspondence and persuasions preceded their arrival, but of these I knew nothing. Suddenly, we had a horse and buggy.

At Mother's request, although she had been familiar with horses from childhood, care had been taken to find a staid and elderly horse that would be easy for her to handle and care for. Our horse's name was Bess; she was quiet and gentle, and in every way seemed to meet Mother's specifications.

What a happy time that was, and how our horizons expanded! In those days one did not have to drive very far from Oakland to be in the country, and it was to the country we invariably drove in the shining black surrey. Often, Grandma London or Mammy Jennie and sometimes both of them accompanied us, and we would be gone the whole day, taking our lunch and picnicking under the trees along the way.

It must have been early summer when our trips began, for I remember the young green of willows edging the winding dirt roads, and the silver-rippling grass in the fields, where horses and cows grazed among clustered poppies and blue lupine. Bess and I discovered wild flowers we had never seen before and Mother told us their names: butter-and-eggs, cream cups, baby blue-eyes; later there were dusty-pink hollyhocks and flamboyant godetias. Sometimes, among the more common hedge roses, we found the tiny rosy blossoms of the sweetbriar whose delicate leaves were as fragrant as spice, and we learned to look in shady places for minty yerba buena, gold-back ferns, and the small, dark-red wild strawberries that tasted so much better than the large domesticated kind.

I did not realize until now, as I write, how well I can recall those leisurely drives—the gentle creaking and swaying of the surrey, the jingle of Bess's harness and the lovely rhythm of her hooves along the yielding brown roads and across the frequent low, wooden bridges; the sweetness of the breeze across the fields and the pungent smell of tarweed as the summer advanced; the undulant flight of flocks of birds and the heart-troubling song of the meadowlarks; the golden sunlight streaming over the hills and valleys and orchards that moved slowly past.

Even Grandma London became cheerful on these drives, and she and Mammy Jennie would recount incidents that had occurred when they were younger. Listening, I would superimpose the imagined landscapes of far-off Ohio and Virginia on the rolling California hills, and try to picture the young girls Grandma London and Mammy Jennie had once been. And watching Mother, sitting very straight, the reins easy in her hands, speaking with gentle authority to the horse from time to time, I was very proud.

Not long after we acquired the horse it was necessary to change her name. A horse, a mother and a little girl, all named Bess, were at least one Bess too many and frequently made for confusion. For days we debated a new name for Bess the horse. Meantime, a comfortable barn, generous feeding and plenty of rest were miraculously altering her. Her years fell away, her eyes brightened, her coat shone, her gait quickened. More and more often, at the end of a day in the country, she chose her own pace home, trotting briskly while Mother held her in with taut reins. One afternoon, half-amused, half-exasperated, Mother scolded her, "Not so fast, Bess! Have you forgotten you're an old lady? You're acting like a colt!" And so we named her Baby in affectionate derision of her pretensions.

With the coming of autumn and colder weather, Baby had little to do. She grew restless in the small paddock in the backyard and began to give Mother so much trouble during her morning grooming that it was finally necessary one day to fasten her to one of the big swing posts. This apparently outraged her, for she tried at once to pull free, and when that failed she began to rear and kick angrily. By afternoon, however, she seemed to have recovered her temper. Mother harnessed her without difficulty and, leaving Bess at home in Mammy Jennie's care, we set off for the dancing school I had recently joined.

Rain which had been threatening all day began soon after we arrived. Baby had been securely tied to the hitching post and blanketed, but Mother chose a seat near a window from which she could watch her. Absorbed in the dancing, I did not see Mother suddenly get up and run outside, but at the end of the class, while she hurried me into my hat and coat, she told me that Baby had broken loose and started for home. Mother had caught her before she reached the corner and brought her back. Everything would be all right, she assured me, but I could tell she was uneasy about the drive home.

Baby was standing quietly when we reached the surrey. She turned her head and gave Mother a long look, twitched her ears, and then pawed impatiently. Mother put me in the back seat and showed me just how I was to hold on tightly with both hands if it became necessary—although, of course, it wouldn't be necessary. Baby was motionless until Mother was seated and took up the reins, then, without waiting for a command, she bolted. Gripping the reins with both hands, Mother tried to hold her in, but Baby had evidently made up her mind: she was going home, and fast. I hung on for dear life, sliding and bouncing on the slippery leather seat, and loving every moment of it. I had never dreamed of such speed; it was wonderful!

Dusk had come early because of the rain. Lighted houses flashed past as Baby tore up Grove Street, rain blew in on us and from moment to moment we were drenched with icy water from the puddles struck by Baby's flying feet. We took the turn into Thirty-first Street on two wheels and thundered halfway down the block before she slackened her pace, then turned, just barely on four wheels, onto our driveway and straight into the barn. I remember that she halted so suddenly that I slid helplessly off the seat to the floor and Mother, looking back and not finding me, had her only moment of panic during the entire episode.

"Now that we're safely home," she told me when she had assured herself that I was unhurt, "I can say that I wouldn't have missed it for worlds, but never again! I wonder what got into that horse?"

What had got into her, of course, was only her youth. We had aptly named her Baby. The quiet, elderly mare we had first known had actually been an unutterably weary, cruelly overworked and mistreated youngster, but her appearance of age had been so convincing that no one had bothered to check it or even to look at her teeth.

When Daddy heard our dramatic account of the runaway, he decreed that Mother was not to drive Baby again; he sent her up to his ranch and promised to get us another more reliable horse. As it turned out, he never did. The building of his boat, and later the voyage itself, intervened, and after his return we could not bring ourselves to remind him of his promise.

At first we desperately missed Baby and the escape from the bungalow she had made possible, but when spring returned the following year Mother showed us another way to get near, if not quite, to the country: we learned to walk. In time, we walked everywhere, tirelessly, happily, and the wild flowers we brought back brightened the gloomy bungalow, even though they had been picked in empty lots at the edge of the city and not in the far and lovely hills.

FOUR

What a crowded, vividly remembered year that was! Perhaps five-year-olds are more aware of everything that happens around them and to them, and even of themselves, than when they were younger or will be a little older. In my memory, the events of 1906, whether significant or not, have a clarity and continuity that later memories often lack. And there is a kind of radiance about them that later memories also lack, for this was the last of the enchanted years.

The earthquake, the drives in the country, Daddy's visits, all too brief and infrequent, the dancing class and finally the never-to-be-forgotten Christmas—these were the hills and mountains of that year, but in the wide, quiet valleys between them I was deeply absorbed, first, in learning to read and write, for my determination to accomplish this as soon as possible had never wavered, and, second, in my first conscious effort to discover and identify myself in relation to people and places and events, and to time itself.

The earthquake had at once become a date-point for people in the Bay Area. "Before the earthquake," they said, and "after the earthquake," but these were East Bay residents; San Franciscans, of course, always said before or after "the fire." For me, however, the earthquake had a special significance: merely through having shared the experience with others, I unexpectedly found my place in time. When Mother or Daddy, or Grandma London or Mammy Jennie told about something that had happened before I was born or when I was too young to remember, it might be and usually was interesting, but it was never quite real. Because I had had no part in it, it was as if it had never happened. But the earthquake was different. It had been *my* experience as well as theirs, I could speak of it out of my own knowledge, and remembering it, I could feel it and hear it and see it again.

I relished this sense of belonging, this identification of myself in time. For me, "after the earthquake" meant *now*, the wonderful, urgent *now* of childhood. And there grew in me a great desire to recapture the "before the earthquake" part of my life which I had somehow carelessly let slip into oblivion. It did not seem a difficult task; all I had to do was to remember. Confidently, I turned then to *Joan, Her Book* to evoke the past, studying the pictures, not merely looking at them as I always had before, reciting the captions, which I could not yet read but which I had long since learned by heart, and earnestly questioning Mother, Mammy Jennie and Grandma London.

The device failed me. No matter how hard I tried, I could not remember; the forgotten past was irrecoverable. I stared at the pictures until they wavered and swam before my eyes: the tiny baby on the pillows, the slightly larger baby laughing—and crying immediately after, the little girl stopping the rocker, taking her first steps, riding on Daddy's bike—was this really I, if I could recall nothing of these occasions? The captions said that the baby and the little girl were Joan, and that was my name, so it must be true, but I was deeply dissatisfied. Only when I looked at the pictures near the end of the album, the ones that had no captions, was I sure; the little girl sitting in a well-remembered poppy field, watching Daddy fly his kites, was certainly I.

My excursions through the album and my persistent questions did, however, solve some of its mysteries. The "squeaky pig"—why, of course, it had been merely a rubber toy, and the "Purple Cow Man" was a friend of Daddy's who had written a poem about a purple cow and whose real name was Gelett Burgess. The poem did not make any sense, but I liked it immensely. Perched on the back fence where I could see into three backyards besides our own, I used to chant it solemnly under my breath or shout it like a challenge to the sky. As for the magical picture in which the full-rigged ships sailed across Mother's lap toward my outstretched hand, Mother said it was a "double exposure." This was equally mystifying, but suspecting that it was a reasonable explanation, I would not press her further. How could I relinquish "the earth and its fullness, the sea and its ships," which, on that long ago day I could not remember, had been almost within my grasp?

One day, searching the album with my new awareness, I recognized the "small" Morris chair in a picture of Mother sitting in it, sewing. I recited the incomprehensible caption:

> *Behold the Mater before she was the Mater. What is it that she worketh so busily upon?*

and took the album to Mother. "Mater," she explained was another word for Mother, and what she had been working upon were baby clothes for me. And the chair, I wanted to know, was ours the very same one? Enthralled, I listened then for the very first time to the story of how Daddy became a writer, of how poor he had been and how hard he had worked to succeed; of how he and Grandma London had lived in a tiny cottage, where day after day and night after night, he sat at a kitchen table in a small bare room and wrote and wrote, scarcely stopping to eat or to sleep; and of how, at last, the magazines began to buy his stories, and though they brought little at first, there came a day when all the bills were paid and he had enough money left over to buy something he had always wanted—a comfortable chair to sit in while he read. And that was the "small" Morris chair.

How proud I was of him! How I loved him! I ran over to the chair, touched it gently, rubbed my cheek against its velvety cushions. "And now it's *our* chair," I said happily, looking at it with new eyes, this most tangible link with a past I could not remember, and finding it very beautiful and elegant, and certainly the most comfortable of all our chairs.

My efforts to pierce the curtain that hid the past had not been successful, but I abandoned them without regret, for midway I had made a great discovery: Joan was I, I was Joan. When I stumbled upon this simple statement the effect had been overwhelming. I had found myself, I knew who I was! A flood of new ideas, new questions, followed this discovery, ideas and questions that I lacked the words to frame. One line of inquiry was open: names.

My name was Joan; I had never been called by any other. Bess's name was Bess, but she had also been called Baby B, and, for a while, Sunny Jim, because she was such a happy, smiling baby, and now she was acquiring yet another name, Buster, because of her Buster Brown haircut. Mother was Mother, of course, although I had called her Mamma when I was younger and still did once in a while, and Daddy was Daddy, but they called each other Bessie and Jack. Manyoungi, however, had always addressed Daddy as Master and spoke of him as Mr. London, while Mother had a variety of names: Bess, Bessie, Elizabeth, Lizzie, though this was rare, Auntie Bess, Aunt Bessie, and Mrs. London. I was especially curious about that name London, for it seemed to belong not only to Mother and Daddy, but to Bess and me, and to Grandma as well, but not to anyone else.

Names were very important, I was sure, and I wished they were not so confusing. There was also the problem of uncles and aunts. Some uncles were "related," like my uncles Henry and Will and Bob, who were Mother's brothers, and other uncles were also related, but a little differently, like Uncle Ernest, who had married Mother's sister Florrie. But how, then, explain Uncle Charlie, who was not related at all, who was a friend? He was a "courtesy" uncle, Mother said, which explained nothing, though I liked the sound of it. Aunts were complicated in the same way as uncles, except for Aunt Eliza, who was complicated in still another way, for she was not Daddy's sister but his stepsister. All that I knew about stepsisters I had learned from fairy tales, and that knowledge did not help me to understand why I called her, first, Aunt Lylie, and later Aunt Eliza.

Manyoungi's name provided endless diversion. Was it really a Korean name, I wondered, or was it a foreign way of calling him "Young Man?" When I asked Mother, she said she thought it was probably Korean, and what sounded like "young" and "man" meant something quite different in the Korean language. Daddy could have told me, I am sure, but I always forgot to ask him. Best of all would have been to ask Manyoungi himself. I planned to do this, but the opportunity never came. We had scarcely seen him since he had left our little attic room to live on the ranch in Glen Ellen, and when he came to see us one day in the autumn of that year to tell us he had left Daddy's service and was going away, we were so sad at the thought that perhaps we would never see him again that to ask him the meaning of his name did not occur to me.

And then there was Mammy Jennie.

Gone beyond recall is the slow accretion of knowledge, impressions and emotional responses that fused in a blazing moment of insight some time during that year and determined me never to call her *Mammy* Jennie again. I loved her deeply, with the same quality of devotion I had for Mother, but with this difference: I was fiercely protective of her as I did not have to be of Mother. I had not forgotten, nor would I ever forget, the cruelty and scorn that the blackness of her skin had called forth, in a word that had no meaning for me, from the boys in West Oakland.

Like most small children, I paid scant attention to speech whose key words were unfamiliar. But when a conversation concerned myself or people I loved—and how quickly a child is aware of this—I was instantly alert. Relying on an instinctive appraisal of tone of voice, facial expression, a briefly illuminating gesture, I came to know the value of many words long before I knew their meaning. When I had first heard the epithet "nigger," I knew from the boys' voices alone that it was a hateful word intended to hurt. Forever afterward I would not permit it or the equally offensive "darkie" to be applied to any Negro without an immediate protest, and I am sure that my angry rebukes embarrassed many thoughtless grownups before I learned to temper my indignation. I remember that I even rejected "colored," although Mammy Jennie used it herself, because it was not honest. There were many colors, I argued; I myself had seen numerous red- and even purple-faced men and rosy-pink-faced ladies; but when people said "colored," they meant only black or brown.

Tenuously linked with these unlovely terms and with Mammy Jennie were two more words whose meanings I did not know. One was fine, but the other was an ugly-sounding word, always pronounced with a hard emphasis on its long a, and with its end spat out quickly, as if the speaker was eager to get it out of his mouth and be done with it: slavery.

Ours was a house in which the Civil War was often recalled by grownups. Grandma London used to tell how, when she was young and lived in Ohio, she made lint for bandages from soft, old linen sheets and handkerchiefs, and of dancing with Union soldiers home on leave. But it was Melissa Maddern who, through Mother, dominated these talks with her uncompromising abolitionism. Nearly a hundred years ago, Mother told us, Melissa's Grandfather Bowman had embraced the belief of a fellow Virginian named Thomas Jefferson that all men were created free and equal, and had freed his slaves and moved north to upper New York State, where he had fought against slavery to the end of his days. There was another man they talked about who seemed to have been the most important of all and whose name they spoke softly and with love— Abraham Lincoln—and it was he who had freed the slaves. It was very confusing to me, for I did not know what slaves were, except that they had lived in a place called the South and that Mammy Jennie had incomprehensibly been born one. But out of the talk about the Civil War I did learn the values of two key words: "slavery" was ugly and bad, but "freedom" was a fine word.

Days of pondering over the names of various people had brought me at length to Mammy Jennie's name, and for the first time I noticed the uniqueness of "Mammy." Only Daddy and Bess and I called her so; Mother and Grandma London said simply Jennie.

"Why do we call you Mammy Jennie?" I asked her the next time she came to see us.

I recall almost every detail of that conversation. She was sitting in the small Morris chair, her hands busy as always, shelling peas perhaps, or stringing beans, and I was on the floor at her feet. But the memory is surcharged with emotions whose sources I cannot truly name or place.

She was mildly surprised at my question. "Why, child, I guess it's because your Daddy has always called me that."

"Then why don't Mother and Grandma?"

"Because . . . well, they're grown up, you see, and so they call me Jennie."

"Daddy's grown up," I argued.

"Yes, but he has always called me Mammy Jennie, ever since he was a baby."

"But," I protested, "that's not what . . ."

In her eagerness to help me she did not wait for me to finish. "It must be the 'Jennie' you're wondering about. That's not my real name, of course."

"It *isn't*?" This was so astonishing that for the moment I was sidetracked.

"No. I guess you would call it a nickname. My real name is the same as the state where I was born—Virginia."

"Virginia!" It was a beautiful name, but when I thought of it as being her name and of people calling her by it, it did not seem to belong to her.

"When I was young," she went on, "they called me Ginny. Then when I grew up and came West, well, California people just never seemed to say Ginny as they did in the South. They called me Jennie, instead, and that's the way it's been ever since. . . . Is that what you wanted to know?"

I shook my head. "No, that's not it. It's why Daddy and Bess and I call you *Mammy* Jennie. Is Mammy a name, too?"

"It's not a name, exactly . . ."

"What is it, then?" I urged. "What does it mean?"

Her face cleared. "Oh, now I understand! Well, I can tell you about that. In the South, little colored children always called their mothers Mammy. And when a colored lady took care of a white child, was his nurse, you know, that little girl or boy called her Mammy, too. I took care of your Daddy when he was a little baby, so he has always called me Mammy Jennie, and then I took care of you and Bess, too, when you were babies."

I was silent for a long time while the words I needed slowly came together in one last question. "Didn't they ever call a white lady who took care of their children Mammy?"

"I don't believe so," she said puzzled. "Leastways, I never heard of it. Besides, I don't think I ever knew of any white ladies in the South who took care of other people's children. It was only us."

Why had my question been so significant to me? Why was her answer so overwhelming? Was it the way she had said, "It was only us," not bitterly or resignedly, but merely stating a fact? I do not know. But I *do* know that for a moment I was swept by anger and outrage completely beyond my comprehension, and, in the midst of it, I knew that I could never use the name Mammy again.

She was watching me, worried because she felt my distress, but, not understanding its cause any better than I did, was unable to comfort me. I scrambled to my feet and her arms went out to me in the old way. Hugging her fiercely, I whispered, "I love you! I love you so much!" and kissed her smooth cheek.

But, I pondered later, if I was not going to call her *Mammy* Jennie any longer, what was I to say? I could not call her Jennie, for that was for grownups. Then it came to me: if there were "courtesy" uncles, there could be "courtesy" aunts. She would be Aunt Jennie.

I don't remember if any questions were asked about the change or if I volunteered an explanation. Daddy continued to call her Mammy Jennie, but for both Bess and me, she was Aunt Jennie from then to the end of her days.

And sometimes during my long preoccupation with names, I used to wonder about the Beauty. To a child who moved familiarly through the world of fairy tales, this name was rare, but not especially unusual. There was the Beauty in *The Beauty and the Beast*, for instance, one of the first fairy tales Mother had read to me. But I did wonder who was this Beauty who had usurped Bess's and my place in Daddy's watch. Mother had spoken her name only that one time, Daddy never. Some instinct forbade me to ask either of them about her, or even Grandma London or Aunt Jennie, and although I often listened while they talked about various people, that name was never mentioned. After a while I forgot about her, and only at long intervals would the mysterious Beauty briefly enter my mind.

That year, to my intense satisfaction, I began to read and write. Under Mother's skillful guidance, learning to read was effortless, but only my inflexible determination to write letters to Daddy mastered my stubborn, uncooperative fingers.

Throughout my childhood, Montessori was a household word. Madame Montessori, Mother called her, and for a while I believed they were old friends because Mother spoke of her so often and so warmly and knew so much about her ideas.

"Why doesn't she come to see us?" I asked Mother once.

"Oh, she doesn't live in this country," Mother said. "Her home is far away, in a country in Europe called Italy."

"Does she write you letters?"

"Oh no!" She realized at once my misapprehension. "I don't know her, but I have read many books and articles about her, and some she has written herself. She is a very wonderful person. Think of it! She's just a few years older than I am, and yet when she was only twenty-four she became a doctor. Doctor Maria Montessori, the first lady doctor in Italy!"

"A doctor? A real doctor—like Dr. Wright? She takes care of sick people?" I was amazed; in my experience, all doctors were men.

"Indeed she does!" Mother seemed as proud as if it were her own achievement. "But her real work is helping teachers to teach better so that children can learn more easily and quickly and enjoyably. It's the way I'm teaching you—the Montessori method."

Mother was an extraordinary teacher, gifted beyond most in this particular channel of communication, as all her later years were to show, and undoubtedly she would have been so if she had never heard of Madame Montessori. Nevertheless, her adaptation of the Montessori theory and practice was a personal triumph. I was her first Montessori experiment and the results pleased us both.

I learned to read "by sound," finding it tremendous fun, and impatient only with the silliness of the stories in the little dark red primer, my first school book. For a time I merely sounded the letters of the words, making no attempt to pronounce them or to discover the meaning of those that were new to me. It was during this period that Mother said to Daddy one day, "Did you know that Joan is only one short step from reading?

"Nonsense!" he scoffed. "She has probably memorized her stories from hearing you read them to her."

Mother's professional pride was stung. "All right," she challenged, "try her with that magazine you brought with you, and you'll see what I mean."

Frankly skeptical, he opened the magazine at random and invited me to read with him. Trembling with excitement at the thought of showing him my accomplishment, I began to sound the letters of the words which were almost totally unfamiliar.

"What on earth does the child think she's doing?" he demanded after a moment. "This is nothing but gibberish!"

"Listen more carefully," Mother said firmly.

Suddenly he perceived the shape of the words under the unaccented sounds of the letters and he shouted with delight. "She's really doing it! She *can* read! Bess, you're wonderful, and so is Joan!"

How pleased and proud we all were, and how deeply satisfied I was that the first sure step toward the goal I had set myself had been taken. But after this I was more impatient than ever with "Mamma, see Baby. Baby, see the cat" and similar exercises in the primer. So ardently did I long to be able to read the books Mother read to me that I shall always remember the moment, only a few months later, when, for the first time, I read a complete sentence, word by word, in a real book.

In our nightly reading aloud we were nearing the end of *The Jungle Book*, and had reached the point where Mowgli had found his mother. "Joan," Mother said unexpectedly, "here is something I think you can read yourself."

I scrambled up on the arm of the small Morris chair and looked where Mother's finger pointed. Slowly, and with a sense of greeting friends encountered in an unfamiliar place, I read: "She gave him a long drink of milk and some bread, and then she laid her hand on his head and looked into his eyes."

At last I could read!

Writing, however, was a different matter entirely. It seemed impossible at first to find a way to hold my pencil, not comfortably, for that did not matter, but efficiently. It and my hand refused to cooperate. When I watched Mother write, her sharply pointed pencil ran eagerly across the page, apparently not even waiting for her orders, and forming the clear, open letters precisely and beautifully. But in my hand, the same pencil behaved abominably. The point promptly broke, of course, then, resharpened, instead of carrying out my wishes, it made monstrous loops and crooked lines that were either too tall or too short, all the while watching for an opportunity to escape, either by rolling across the table or flinging itself out of my hand to the floor. But I kept at it, stubbornly pushing my enemy into some semblance of the letters and words I was trying to copy, filling page after page with ugly markings that horrified and enraged me.

Sometimes I despaired of ever learning to write, then, panic-stricken because Daddy would soon be sailing away and I must be able to write him letters during those seven years, I would return to the battle, grimly resolved to conquer. Perseverance finally brought me out of the "pushing" stage into the "drawing" one. The first letter I wrote to Daddy no longer exists, but in the second one, on which he himself rubber-stamped the date, October 13, 1906, the text is obviously drawn, not yet written.

Here and there it is evident that the pencil won a skirmish, but for the most part the margin of victory was mine:

> *Dear Daddy,*
>> *Why did you not write me*
> *a letter?*
>> *Mamma said you were too busy.*
>> *Lyly printed a letter for*
> *Irving. He does not know I can write.*
>> *Bess and I send you a big*
> *kiss and a hug.*
>>> *Your loving little girl,*
>>>> *Joan*

I wish I could see that long-vanished first letter. It had been so great a triumph for me, freighted with such hope, that I could not believe he would not answer it immediately. The second letter betrayed how deeply I felt about it. I did not reproach him for failing to reply, I rebuked him, and in the same breath indicated that, although Mother had found an excuse for him, I would have none of it. Having made my position clear, I am sure that what I wanted to say next was "Daddy, see what a wonderful thing I can do!" but my pride would not permit it. I must have pondered a long time before I found the way to draw his attention obliquely to my accomplishment by pointing out that Aunt Eliza's son, Irving, who was a few years older than I, still had to have his letters printed for him and did not even know that I could write my own.

Thus began a correspondence that was to continue for ten years, and for much of that time was to be our only means of communication. I entered upon it exuberantly, confident that it would keep us close to each other, no matter how far or for how many months or years at a time he would be away from me, but long before the end even this was to fail us; worse, our letters became weapons with which we drew heart's blood from each other.

The year was drawing to a close. Daddy's boat was nearing completion, he told us excitedly; soon he would be setting forth on his seven-year voyage around the world. I pressed for mastery over my pencil more fiercely than ever, and little by little it began to yield. My third letter to him, rubber-stamped as before, November 28, 1906, is surprisingly legible, and "written," not "drawn." He had brought us more puzzles, and I reported, "Buster and I have lots of fun with the puzzles," and proudly announced that I could make all of them "except the owl." Then, sadly, because I had been fond of him, I told of the death from diphtheria of a little boy we had known from the Bungalow days. Finally, I wrote the really important paragraph.

At the dancing class and on the street downtown, I had discovered as the winter set in, that little girls were wearing fur muffs and tippets—the most beautiful, the most delectable and instantly the most desirable objects I had ever seen. My longing for a set of my own grew until it possessed me wholly. I talked of it by day and dreamed of it by night. That Mother was unable to gratify my wish was difficult to realize, but it did not dim my hope that somehow the impossible would be realized. One morning a happy thought occurred to me. "I'm going to ask Daddy," I announced.

Mother looked doubtful. "I don't believe you should. Furs are expensive, and Daddy's boat is costing him a great deal of money right now. Perhaps later would be better."

But I was determined. "I'll write him a letter."

And so the letter which began so gaily with the puzzles ended with an urgent plea: "Daddy, will you get Buster and I a muff and fur? We like to have a brown one. All the little girls have them." At the last moment my courage had failed me and I asked for only one set, which Bess and I could share. For days afterward I waited for the mailman, my confidence slowly ebbing, but no answer came.

There is always one Christmas that shines most brightly in the memories of childhood, with a special wonder and magic that sets it apart from all others. The Christmas of 1906 was that Christmas for me.

The pre-holiday weeks were a kaleidoscope of gleaming displays in the downtown stores, crowded streets, bell-ringing Santa Clauses (all of them brothers of the real Santa Claus, Mother explained for Bess's benefit, for I was pretty sure about the Santa Claus myth by that time), Salvation Army lassies in the bonnets I so admired shaking their tambourines, package-laden people scrambling on and off streetcars, and everywhere, Christmas carols and fragrant Christmas trees and wreaths, starred with scarlet berries. At home, there were secrets and the tantalizing imminence of surprises, and then, a few days before Christmas, a sudden quickening of anticipation triggered by Mother as she drew a veil of deepest mystery over a new and stupendous secret. We clamored for hints, but she was obdurate. I guessed reasonably, I guessed craftily, I guessed wildly; Mother's only reply was, "Wait and you'll see!" On the day before Christmas, Aunt Jennie arrived, and she was gay and smiling too. I was immediately certain that she shared the great secret and would not tell it no matter how I badgered her, but the knowledge did not keep me from trying.

At intervals all that day Bess and I explored the bungalow from front to back, finding everything as always, with no sign of holiday preparations except a big bowl of holly berries in the chilly living room, Christmas greens on the mantel and a fire laid in the grate. Secretly relieved that we had found no clues, for the suspense was intoxicating, we would run back to the warm kitchen to caper about, turn somersaults and pester Mother and Aunt Jennie with more questions.

In the middle of the afternoon came the first break: Mother asked us if we could do something very important to help her. Hopping and skipping ecstatically, we agreed to do anything, anything! All right then: both of us were to go to our room, lie down and take a nap. Bess did not understand, but I knew at once that the big surprise was very near, was, in fact, to be that very evening, on Christmas Eve, rather than on Christmas Day. I exchanged a quick glance of comprehension with Mother and caught Bess by the hand, crying "Oh, let's take a nap!," as if it were a rare privilege instead of something we always resisted.

Bess, who was just four and who had trotted everywhere after me all day, fell asleep at once, while I, certain that I would not be able even to close my eyes, followed suit moments later. When I awoke it was almost dark. I lay still, savoring what was to come and aware that something had changed since I had gone to sleep. The house felt different, as if it had all come alive and was humming happily to itself. The bright little room off the kitchen had been our bedroom since summer, and through the closed door I could hear Mother and Aunt Jennie talking in low voices and the kettle singing on the back of the stove.

After that everything happened quickly. We ate our supper, were sponge-bathed in front of the stove and helped into our party dresses, speechless now, content to be borne along on a tide that was sweeping us faster and faster toward unguessed wonders. While she was brushing our hair Mother told us the last and hardest thing we had to do before the surprise, and that was to stay in the kitchen with Aunt Jennie for just a little while—and to sit quietly and not muss our dresses.

If I had been one of the grownups waiting in the living room that Christmas Eve, I would have seen two little girls enter from the dark hallway, hand in hand, a-tiptoe and breathless with expectancy, and watched them stop when they were fairly in the room and look and look with eyes like stars.

I remember that long, lovely, wholly perfect moment. The room was lighted only by the leaping flames in the fireplace and a multitude of small, rainbow-hued wax candles burning steadily and proudly on every branch and twig of a glittering Christmas tree. There was Mother, standing tall and beautiful in the firelight, and near her was Grandma London, nodding and smiling, and in the big Morris chair—it could not be, but it was, it was!—Daddy, leaning forward, laughing, his arms open wide for us. And amid shouts of "Surprise! Surprise!" and "Merry Christmas!" we flew across the room to him.

Because this is the earliest Christmas I can remember, it has always seemed that we performed what became our Christmas gift ritual for the first time that night. Sitting on the floor beside the tree, Mother picked up the presents one after the other and gave them alternately to Bess and me to carry to the persons for whom they were intended. There were packages of all shapes and sizes, some small and surprisingly heavy, some large and feather-light, and all were beautifully wrapped in white tissue paper and tied with bright red ribbon.

For Bess and me, there were dolls and books and toys, the building blocks we loved through all our childhood, brightly colored beads for stringing, packed in round wooden boxes with perfectly fitting lids, and a little red chair for each of us. And finally there were two identical packages, large and flat, one for Bess and one for me, which we opened last of all.

Carefully, I untied the broad satin ribbon and the paper fell away to reveal a plain, white box. Daddy was sitting on the floor between us. "Take off the cover, Joan," he prompted, and turned to help Bess with her package. Under the cover was smooth tissue. With trembling fingers, I folded it back, and sat utterly still, for there it was, more beautiful than any I had ever seen, a muff and tippet of grey and white squirrel.

I am sure such moments come only once or twice in a lifetime; more could not be endured. There, beneath my eyes, beneath my hands, the impossible had materialized, the dream, misty and remote, become tangible.

But there was more. Under Daddy's guidance, Bess was folding back tissue to disclose a muff and tippet like mine. Each of us had her own; we would not even have to share! The room, the bungalow, the world swung gently, just a little, and I knew a brief, pleasant vertigo. And then Daddy was saying, a little anxiously, "Do you like it, Joan?"

I had no words then, nor have I now, to tell him how dear my wish had been, how incredible was its fulfillment, how far beyond mere joy was the ecstasy I felt. "Oh, Daddy . . ." I managed and could say no more.

It did not occur to me that the gift was from him, or from anyone. It *was*, and that sufficed. But the surprises within the all-encompassing surprise of the gift itself were like the nested boxes-within-boxes the Chinese used to make, and the last of these told me the giver.

"Try it on," Daddy urged.

Reverently, I lifted the muff and placed the silken cord around my neck, and then the tippet so that it nestled softly against my cheek. Undirected, my hands found their way inside the satin-lined muff, and I drew a long breath of supreme content. Then I spied, deeply embedded in the fur at the top of the muff, the tiny golden jaws and catch of a coin purse. My hands flew out of the muff to open it; inside, gleaming against the creamy chamois, lay a five-dollar goldpiece. Instantly I knew that the gift could be only from Daddy, for ever since I could remember he had carried those exquisitely fashioned golden coins in his pocket, along with others that were larger, in a slim cylinder of softest leather which he called a miner's poke.

My memory of that moment is as confused as I was then, caught in a maelstrom of emotion far too large for me. I could only sit there, unable to speak, and gaze at him with adoring eyes. I do remember, however, finding time in the midst of my turmoil to savor the completeness of the gift—he had thought to place a coin in the little purse—and to recognize the triumphant confirmation of my faith in writing letters.

Nothing marred the perfection of that fabulous Christmas. Daddy did not pull out his watch and say, "I have to run along now, girls," so that we would stand at the window, the Christmas glory dimming behind us, and sadly watch him disappear into the darkness on his way to that other life of his in which we had no part. Instead, after he had inspected and admired all our gifts, and even read to us bits from our new books, he announced that if we would get ready for bed, he would help us hang up our Christmas stockings for the next morning's surprises. Mother and Aunt Jennie undressed us in front of the fire and got us into our nighties and slippers, and then Daddy carried us, a double armful, to our room. The stockings were carefully fastened to the little round knobs at the foot of each bed, so that we would not have to run through the cold house in the early morning to get them from the fireplace, and Daddy helped Mother tuck us in. Then he held us very close and kissed us goodnight. "Merry Christmas, girls!" he wished us from the doorway, and from the far edge of sleep we called after him, "Merry Christmas, Daddy! Merry Christmas!"

The three months that followed the wonderful Christmas were not happy ones for any of us. The sailing of Daddy's boat, the *Snark*, was postponed time after time because of incredible and expensive delays, which have been described by others and by Daddy himself far better than I can. At the time, certainly, I knew little of the circumstances and understood none of them.

Perhaps, although it is debatable, the voyage itself had not been ill-conceived, but the preparations for it, the building of the little ship, its outfitting and manning, were so badly executed as to be beyond belief. While, out of my later knowledge of the facts, I find it possible to wonder what mischance trapped Daddy in a circle of thieves and incompetents, it is utterly impossible to understand why he was unable or unwilling to recognize them as such and send them packing. Suffice it to say that the *Snark*, planned to be built for some seven thousand dollars, cost thirty thousand to complete, and then was barely seaworthy.

At times he raged incontinently against the least of the offenders, tradesmen, suppliers of goods and materials, who considered him fair game because those he had placed in authority apparently did so. Sometimes he was so sad and chagrined that, listening, I could not believe he was voluntarily embarking on this strange voyage, and even felt a tiny hope that he might break free and not go away at all. Sometimes, too, he would be all anticipation and enthusiasm and eagerness to be off, so that we, who had come so close to him in his anger or sorrow, were again thrust away and shut out. But most often during his brief, irregular visits he was tense and irritable, unable to sit still for long, given to restless floor-pacing and sudden, abrupt departures.

At such times Bess and I found it difficult to hold his attention for very long, if we had been able to capture it at all, for that was not easy. The once-joyous visits, the romps, the sharing of hoarded secrets and surprises had now become painful intervals during which we sat apart from him in unhappy silence, listening uncomprehendingly. Only Bess found a means of self-expression during those dreadful half-hours. When boredom or despair could no longer be endured, she would begin, solemnly, meditatively, to turn somersaults—a curious, solitary performance which demanded and received attention from no one and brought her peace.

Daddy's moods were never predictable. Mother, indignant, might exclaim, "Jack, they're cheating you! It's outrageous!" He might reply despondently, "I know it, I know it, but what can I do?" Or he might blaze at her, "You don't know what you're talking about! It's the earthquake and fire that have sent prices sky-high. And what do *you* know about building boats anyway?" After a lengthy recital of grievances against the man he had chosen to captain the *Snark*, Mother would suggest reasonably, "Perhaps you should get someone else. Eames is only a bay sailor, I think you said, and has had no experience in taking a boat beyond the Heads." Daddy might shrug wearily and change the subject, or irritably remind Mother that *her* knowledge of ships and sailing was nonexistent, or he might laugh uproariously and proclaim, "He's as preposterous as the whole idea of the voyage, but it'll succeed, you'll see! And Eames will learn!"

Sometimes, when he was in an especially gloomy frame of mind, he would worry about our safety while he was away, fearing housebreakers and similar marauders. Mother might have pointed out that our safety would be no more precarious if he were half the world away than if he were on the ranch in Glen Ellen, but she forebore to do so. Instead, she reassured him and tried to comfort him.

Distinct in this confused time is the afternoon Daddy telephoned from the Piedmont Baths, Oakland's large indoor swimming pool, to persuade Mother to bring us there to meet some old friends. Had it not been for Bess and me, I am sure she would have refused. We had heard much from Daddy about the Piedmont Baths—many times he promised to take us there some day and teach us to swim—so that when we understood from Mother's end of the conversation what Daddy was proposing, we set up such a clamor to go that Mother, caught between Daddy's urgings and our entreaties, had no choice but to assent.

What a surprise it was! One moment we were in the entry of an ordinary building, the next we had stepped through a doorway into a place unlike anything I had ever seen before. New sounds and smells assaulted my senses. Hollow shouts and cries, mingled with crashing water, echoed and reechoed in a vast vaulted space and eddied upward through warm, moist, queerly scented air toward a dimly seen glass roof. The broad expanse of water at our feet was in constant turbulence, so that wavelets edged the pool in running scallops. At one end, people flung themselves into the water from a bouncing board, others leapt from the sides, emerging in the midst of roiling, churning water with only their heads and swiftly moving arms and shoulders visible.

Several strange men swam over to where we were standing and, clinging to the edge of the pool, looked up at us. Some of them nodded and smiled and called greetings to Mother. I wondered where Daddy was, then one of the unknowns called my name in a half-familiar voice, and when I turned to look at him I saw it was Daddy, but a Daddy so changed and different that I could scarcely believe it was he, even after he ducked his head under the water and reappeared with his hair smoothed back from his eyes.

To my astonishment, all the strangers knew me and called me Joan without being told it was my name. They said they had not seen me for a long time, and marveled that I had become such a big girl. I was overwhelmed, speechless, and though I had a burning desire to be at ease and conversational, the best I could do was to answer their questions, generally in monosyllables.

They asked me how old I was, and when I told them I was six, they wanted to know if I was going to school yet. I told them no, but this seemed so inadequate that I made a desperate effort and managed to add that I could read, and write letters, and do arithmetic, which made them laugh, though it did not seem funny to me.

Then a tall, thin man pulled himself out of the water and sat down on the tiles near me, hugging his knees against his chest and regarding me with friendly curiosity. His face was very beautiful, unlike any face I had ever seen; I was reminded then, and always thereafter, of the drawings of woods folk and fauns in my fairy tale books. Almost I knew him, but when I reached for the flickering memory, it vanished.

"You haven't changed much, you know," he said at length. "Do you still run away?" In his voice was remembered laughter, and I was sure that I would recognize him at any moment. "We used to sit in the poppy field together, you and I, and watch your Daddy fly kites," he went on in the same easy, comfortable way. "You were so small and the poppies so tall they used to cluster around your ears." He leaned toward me, smiling, but serious, too, as if this were important to him. "Do you remember me now? You used to call me Jawdge."

And for an instant, the poppies and the deep, sweet grass with the wind brushing it to silver and the larks singing overhead and Daddy and the kites came back to me, and the tall, thin man with the beautiful face—Jawdge—was there, too. "I think so," I told him uncertainly.

He put out a long, narrow hand. "Let us shake on it then," he said gravely, "for we are two friends who have met again after long absence, just as we shall do often, I think, in time to come."

I shook hands with him solemnly, feeling very important because he had remembered me, and, because he had wanted me to remember him, experiencing for the first time the heady sensation that I, Joan, was interesting to him.

I could hardly wait until we started for home to ask Mother, "Who was that nice man who talked to me?"

"He is your Daddy's best friend," she told me. "Did you remember him? He was our neighbor when we lived in the Bungalow. His name is George Sterling, and he writes very beautiful poems."

A poet! I thought ecstatically. How was it, I wonder now, that this had such significance for me at the age of six? Except for nursery rhymes and Stevenson's verses for children, I had little knowledge of poetry.

But my delight could not have been greater had it been a plumed and armored knight, or the masked prince in *The Golden Heart* who had appeared and sealed a pact of eternal friendship with me.

It had been very fine and exciting to meet Daddy's friends and receive their flattering attention. During the next few days I went over each detail, lingering with special fondness on the image of the poet and savoring every word of our conversation at the edge of the pool. But my pleasure was ephemeral; the luminous scene faded, leaving me with a baffling dissatisfaction, which, during those last weeks, became an inseparable part of my growing apprehension over Daddy's imminent departure.

This was the time of the immense popularity of Buster Brown and Mary Jane in the Sunday funny papers, and like many of our contemporaries, Bess and I wore our hair in the styles made famous by these characters—Bess, the Buster Brown bob and bangs, and I, Mary Jane's big ribbon bow on the top of my head. Once a month Mother took us to Tisch's barber shop for expert trimming.

Tisch's, under the old Central Bank at Fourteenth and Broadway, was the finest barber shop in town. I remember it as very large and bright and fragrant, with a long row of chairs in front of a mirrored wall, against which were gleaming white basins and shelves laden with shaving mugs, piles of sheets and towels, and an endless variety of bottles and jars. Because languages were part of the plan I had made for my life, I was especially pleased that the white-jacketed barbers spoke French and German to many of their customers and crisply accented English to the rest of us.

Sitting on a board placed across the arms of the big barber chair, my head bowed forward and a little to one side, and shivering whenever the cold shears touched my neck, I watched one morning the slow, graceful ritual of hot towels being performed on a man stretched out in the chair beside mine. Light-footed as a dancer, the barber moved back and forth between basin and chair, hands never still, simultaneously removing one towel and replacing it with a freshly steaming one without once revealing an inch of the customer's face. The ritual completed, the barber raised the chair-back and the man sat up.

"Daddy," I cried.

"Well, Joan," Daddy said, pleased. "And where is Baby B?"

"Here I am, Daddy," she called joyfully from the chair on the other side of his.

Everyone was laughing and talking at once, including all the smiling barbers, and then, a few minutes later, Daddy was waving goodbye from the doorway and hurrying up the steps to the street on his way, as usual, to keep an appointment. Unhappily watching him leave us almost as soon as we had discovered him, I felt again empty, cross, dissatisfied. How long it was before I was able to admit and understand my childish resentment that I occupied so small and casual a place in Daddy's life, that we met his friends more or less by chance, that we encountered him being shaved at the barber shop by purest accident. How stubbornly I clung to my wish for him to be a real father, to be present, where I could see him and touch him and talk to him at will.

Finally, in April, Daddy came to say goodbye. The ship was ready at last and he was sailing the next day.

He was excited and happy and eager to be off, and at the same time he was sad, reluctant to leave us, and curiously worried about our safety during the long years he expected to be away. His gaiety was infectious, so that I grew excited, as if I, too, were to sail through the Golden Gate the next day on a fabulous seven-year voyage around the world. (The vision of the great cubed world, cloud-wreathed in space, was still compelling, but it coexisted as always with the round globe in the bookstore with its azure oceans and sprawling, multicolored continents.) When he grew sad because he would not see us for so long, and begged us to write him often and urged Mother to send him snapshots of us every few months, I was sad, too, and thought dismally of the eternity that was seven years, and how, when he finally returned, I would be—oh, incredible!—thirteen years old. But he was too sad and we could not bear it, so we fell to comforting him as best we could until his emotions came full circle and he was gay and excited again.

"I shall send you curios from all the places I visit," he announced.

"What are curios, Daddy?"

His eyes fell on the big brass-studded chest he had brought to Mother from Korea. "*That* is a curio, the chest, made in Korea by Koreans, and different from all other chests in the world, except other chests made by Koreans." He looked helplessly at Mother. "You'll explain it to them later, Bess?"

"Of course. And we'll get books from the public library about the various countries so they'll know something about the faraway places your letters will come from. . . . And I've thought of something else, Jack: when they're available, why not get little dolls dressed in the native costumes? The girls would love them."

"Fine!" he agreed enthusiastically. "Good idea . . . I'll remember that."

I matched his moods as they swung erratically from joy to sorrow and back again, but when, abruptly ignoring Bess and me, he spoke nervously and even irritably to Mother about his fears for us, I could not follow him. He seemed obsessed with the idea that marauders would break into the bungalow, rob us, harm us.

"Jack, you're being silly," Mother scolded him gently. "We shall be perfectly safe here, just as we have always been. Besides, who on earth would want to rob us? We haven't any valuables.

But his fears would not be allayed, and again and again he returned to the subject.

He kept looking at his watch but could not bring himself to leave us, sitting stubbornly in the big Morris chair with his arms around Bess and me. When at last his departure could no longer be delayed and he was beginning his farewell admonitions and promises, he drew from his overcoat pocket a bulky parcel, wrapped in heavy brown paper and tied with twine, and held it out to Mother.

"Here, take this. Don't argue with me about it, just put it in a safe place where you can get it easily if you ever need it. I would never have a moment's peace if I thought you and the babies were here alone without a weapon for protection."

I shall never forget the expression on Mother's face. "Oh no!" she whispered. "A weapon . . . oh Jack, not a revolver!"

"A revolver—loaded and ready for use."

"No, please, Jack, no!" She backed away, desperately trying to control her rising panic. "I assure you," she went on, her words tumbling over each other, "we don't need it, really we don't. And you know I could never bring myself to . . . even touch it. Please, oh please, take it away with you!"

But his determination to leave the weapon with her was as inflexible as her refusal to take it. In the end, he placed it on the Korean chest and turned to the door.

And so our final goodbye kisses and embraces were exchanged in an atmosphere of terror and exasperation on the part of our parents, pierced suddenly, for me, by the realization that now Daddy was really going away from us for so long that it might as well be forever.

Through a mist of tears I watched him stride out into the lovely April twilight, stopping, as always, before the high fence next door shut him from view to turn and wave and blow kisses, and then he was gone.

FIVE

It seemed a long time that I stood there at the window with Bess after Daddy was out of sight, aware of the darkness gathering outside, the lights in the hospital across the street beginning to shine through the trees and the aching emptiness growing in and around me, but it was really only a moment. Daddy could not have reached the corner before Mother was shooing us into the kitchen, and in a voice that brooked no argument, bidding us stay there until she told us we might come out. Ignoring our questions, she went to the telephone.

If she had tried to divert us from our sorrow, she could not have been more successful. Intrigued, and awed by the urgency in her voice, we stood together in the doorway, watching and listening.

She spoke briefly over the telephone, asking Uncle Charlie to come to the bungalow as soon as he could. Then she flung open the door to the linen closet and proceeded to empty every one of its shelves, piling sheets and pillow cases and towels and spare bedding in a great heap on the dining table. This was a bewildering Mother; certainly she had never done anything like this before. When our curiosity could no longer be contained and we asked why she was taking everything out of the closet, she replied sternly, "I'm going to make this house safe for us to live in."

Uncle Charlie arrived as she was clearing the last of the shelves. We heard the murmur of their voices in the living room, then Uncle Charlie's chuckle and Mother's sharp "Don't laugh at me . . . you know how I feel about such things!" and his gentle rejoinder, "Of course I know, Bess . . . no one better than I."

Still in the kitchen doorway, we watched them come into the hall, Uncle Charlie carrying the package Daddy had left on the Korean chest.

"Put it on the top shelf, please, as far back as you can reach."

And when this was done, she locked the door of the linen closet, leaned against it and sighed in relief. "I'm going to hide this key," she announced after a moment, "and no one but myself will know where it is."

The long, emotion-packed afternoon and the sharing of Daddy's excitement over setting out on his voyage had finally produced in us little girls a sort of euphoria, which, combined with Mother's unaccountable behavior in connection with the revolver, kept us hysterically gay until bedtime. Nothing was quite real any longer; everything was very funny, and we laughed and laughed. Both of us wept before we finally fell asleep, but our tears were not for Daddy, I think, but for ourselves, who could not find our bearings in a suddenly topsy-turvy world.

Our elation ebbed swiftly, and there ensued a bleak, featureless interval that I recall only with the greatest effort. My resolution to win back my place in Daddy's life and the small successes my plans had thus far achieved could not prevail against a leaden and terrible sense of abandonment. Numb with despair, desolate in a house of desolation, I escaped, as I had often escaped before, into pneumonia, welcoming the oncoming drowsiness, yielding to the pain or skirting it with careful, shallow breaths, recognizing in pleurisy only the beating wings of an imprisoned bird. Yet, as soon as I was convalescent, I began once more to plan my campaign, which had now become more difficult than I believed possible.

Slowly and painfully, I made myself realize that Daddy was gone and that I was not going to see him again for years and years. Then I tried to rebuild my confidence that he would return some day, and that when he saw me again he would be proud of me and love me more than ever, but this was a more difficult task. In the end, I merely hoped it would be so. Lying in bed, I thought of the letters I would write him, the letters I had counted on for so long to keep me close to him, but when I was well again I was reluctant to undertake them. What was there to tell him, far-voyaging to strange new places and adventures, that would interest him and make him remember me?

Especially in the first weeks after Daddy left, his revolver seemed to dominate the bungalow, and its menace never entirely lifted during all the time it was there.

The linen closet, you will remember, was in the tiny hall with four doors, not counting the door to the closet; it was not possible to go from the front of the house to the back without passing through it; and the telephone was there. Unwittingly, Mother had communicated her horror of firearms to Bess and me, but because we had no experience with guns other than the Fourth of July cap pistols of the neighborhood boys, our bogus fears were light-hearted and exciting. We used to dash through the hall shrieking in mock terror at the thought that the gun might, just might, go off accidentally, and often after we had been put to bed for the night, we used to frighten each other deliciously with such suggestions as, "Suppose there was another earthquake . . ."

The linen closet remained locked until Daddy returned from his voyaging. When, at Mother's request, he lifted the never-opened package from the top shelf, he teased, "I imagine you'll feel much safer now without this?" And she answered in all sincerity, "I certainly shall."

That Mother, so brave in every way, should be terrified of firearms mystified me. It was Uncle Charlie who finally explained it, for he as well as Mother had been present on a fatal summer afternoon many years before when a group of young people were admiring a newly acquired revolver, and one of them had been killed by the "unloaded" weapon.

Out of the physical and emotional trauma that followed Daddy's departure, Mother emerged at last to bring order and beauty into our lives once more. It was a difficult time in her own life. Too long denied by her passive acceptance of Daddy's wishes and desires, her inner need for direction and purpose was at last asserting itself and demanding to be met. Restless, dissatisfied, she floundered badly for a while, seeking, considering, rejecting, tentatively accepting, but determined to rebuild her shattered life.

Pinned on her bedroom wall beside her mirror was a copy of Henley's *Invictus*. I used to read it aloud to myself when I was a little older, shivering at the thunder of the words . . .

> *Out of the night that covers me,*
> *Black as the pit from pole to pole,*
> *I thank whatever gods there be*
> *For my unconquerable soul!*

. . . and dimly comprehending what it meant to her.

A few years earlier she had received a small legacy from her parents. She had planned to keep it for emergencies, but now she dipped into it recklessly. While I was ill with pneumonia Bess had been tormented by croup and earache. Also, although she did not speak of it to us, Mother had been frantic with worry over Daddy. When the newspapers began to report that the *Snark* was overdue in Hawaii and probably lost with all hands, she could endure no more. "We must get away from this house!"

she cried desperately. "We'll go to some place in the country where the sunshine will make you little girls well and strong, and where there will be no telephones and no newspapers!"

Although the *Snark* finally reached Hawaii in May, Mother's resolve did not falter, and our own great travels began—to Patchin in the Santa Cruz Mountains, and to Los Gatos; later to Carmel-by-the-Sea; the middle of the summer found us in Camp Meeker near the Russian River; and in September we stayed at an enchanting farm in Kentfield where green-gold bellflower apples hung from every bough in the fragrant orchards. There had never been a summer like it, nor would there ever be again.

That was the year that Uncle Charlie began to play an increasingly large role in our lives and that Ella became a member of our household, but for Bess and me, it was most especially the year we had Glen.

He had come to us early in the year, before Daddy went away, a two-month-old puppy, not only a gift from Daddy but the son of Brown Wolf himself. As soon as he was released from the small, wooden crate in which he had traveled by express from Glen Ellen, he had leaped about, cavorted, run off in all directions, jumped into our laps, rolled over on his back, gulped water from the bowl Mother had brought him, wriggled, twisted, sniffed at everything—all so swiftly that, watching him, our vision seemed to blur—and then he had sat down suddenly with absurd dignity, ears alert, tongue lolling, and gazed at us long and thoughtfully. Speechless with wonder and joy, we returned his gaze, giving our whole hearts to him instantly and irrevocably.

His decision about us was reached more deliberately. Almost as if he foresaw the burden which his compulsion to take full responsibility for our safety and well-being would impose upon him, he weighed the matter carefully while he made the rounds once more, regarding each of us soberly as we stroked his head and spoke our love and welcome. Then he stretched himself out at our feet, gave a deep sigh and went to sleep. We were accepted.

Even then, as a puppy, dignity and intelligence were his outstanding characteristics. Short-haired, golden-coated, white-breasted, with unusually large and well-spaced eyes, he bore little resemblance to Brown Wolf, except perhaps for his deep and powerful chest. But when Daddy came to see us not long after Glen's arrival, he showed us how his fur rose on his neck and back—his hackles, Daddy said—whenever he confronted anything unfamiliar which he felt might be dangerous. "This happens with many dogs," Daddy explained, "but with Glen, it's different . . . it's the wolf in him."

"Will he be wild and fierce?" we asked anxiously, and, remembering Buck "leaping gigantic among his fellows," "Will he run away when he gets big and join the wolves?"

"Oh no!" Daddy laughed. "He loves you too much already to want to leave you. Buck went back to the wild . . . remember? . . . only because he had lost his master. And Glen has too much civilized dog in him ever to be wild or fierce. But some day, perhaps, something may happen that, just for a moment, will bring out the wolf."

Daddy gave us a special leather collar for Glen to wear as soon as he was large enough—special because a brass plate was riveted to it bearing the legend: PROPERTY OF JACK LONDON, GLEN ELLEN, SONOMA COUNTY, CALIFORNIA. "It will help to get him back if he ever strays or is lost," Daddy said. We put the collar on him every day to see how much he had grown since the day before, and finally, fastened in the first hole, he was able to wear it. At once, it seemed, his dignified posture ceased to be absurd. He was still a young dog, and for a while longer behaved like one, but from the time he began to wear the collar his innate calm and poise were manifest.

Early he assumed guardianship over Bess and me. We soon learned that it was useless to question his authority or challenge his rules. We used to argue with him sometimes, pointing out the unreasonableness of his restrictions. He would listen patiently but would not yield an inch. Climbing fences, stepping off the curb into the street, wandering out of sight of the bungalow—these were dangerous and therefore prohibited. When we attempted to defy him he would pull at our skirts, gently, but firmly and persistently, until we gave up. If we walked decorously side by side, with him just behind us, he would permit us to go all the way to the corner, but no further. At such times, passers-by, children, even other dogs did not distract him, but when horses trotted down the street he would stand quite still for a moment, ears pricked, and follow them with longing eyes. He loved us devotedly, but horses he loved with single-minded passion.

How pleased he was when we elected to play in the safe backyard, where he forbade only fence-climbing, and where he could stretch out on the sunny walk while we took turns in the hammock or swing or could sit with us and our dolls in the sandbox and share our tea parties. And if, while we were thus safely occupied, the milkman came around the side of the house to the back door, stopping to fill Glen's pan from the big milk can, he felt free to go off with the milkman and run happily beside the horses for an hour or so along the route.

Glen loved Mother, Bess and me and all horses; the milkman was his friend; he treated Grandma London, Aunt Jennie, Uncle Charlie and the family doctor with grave courtesy; Ella he ignored; with strangers he was polite but aloof. When I recall all the beloved dogs in my life since Glen, he stands out as the only one who was balanced, calm and poised, never nervous or worried, always and under all circumstances reliable. He even had that rarity in a dog, a sense of humor. Mother and he shared private jokes, we suspected, at our expense, and the four of us laughed together on many occasions.

One night at the peak of our illnesses after Daddy had gone away, Bess's attack of croup became so alarming that Mother called the doctor. "I shall leave the front door off the latch," she told him, "so don't ring the doorbell, but come right in."

All that I actually remember of that night is being awakened by confused shouts in the front of the house, quickly followed by low-voiced, excited speech. But the story that Mother and, later the next morning, Dr. Wright told us was so vivid and dramatic that even today I find it hard to believe that I did not witness what occurred.

Glen habitually slept on a low stool beside the fireplace. I can see him lift his head, listening, as the horse and buggy came down the quiet street that night and stopped in front of the bungalow, followed a moment later by footsteps along the walk and up onto the porch. He did not bark; if he growled, it was so deep in his throat that no one heard. Soundlessly he moved into the hall, and as the door opened he sprang for the doctor's throat. Some sixth sense must have given the man a split-second warning; simultaneously he dodged and shouted, "Glen! Down, fellow!"

Glen checked his leap in mid-air and fell to the floor in a graceless heap, overcome with embarrassment and shame. His chagrin and desire to make amends for his error were agonizing. He stood nearby, tail between his legs and ears drooping sorrowfully while Dr. Wright treated Bess, then when she had begun to breathe more easily, the doctor turned to him at last, stroking his head and praising him in unmistakable tones for his watchfulness and care in protecting his household. Glen's joy and relief, and our pride in him when we heard the story, knew no bounds.

At last I had something to tell Daddy! "Glen is the most wonderful dog in the whole world," I wrote to him, "and the most civilized!"

But Daddy, replying from Hawaii, was not yet ready to cancel out the wolf entirely. "Wait," he counseled. "Perhaps Glen will never meet a situation which calls forth his heritage of the wild. But if he does, you will see."

When our travels began, Glen of course accompanied us. On the very first journey, to Patchin, we discovered that riding on streetcars and trains affected him strangely. A little surprised to be on leash, he walked sedately to the corner and, on command, mounted the steps of the streetcar. Although it was a new experience, he behaved with his usual calmness until the streetcar got underway. Then, nose pointing upward, he began to howl, a long, low, bone-chilling sound that nothing could stop. For the first and the only time, we thought he might be frightened and sought to comfort and reassure him, without effect. It was clear that he was not frightened but in the grip of something nameless that none of us, and he least of all, understood. When we left the streetcar at First and Broadway the howling ceased as suddenly as it had begun, and Glen trotted at the end of the leash, interested in the new sights and smells, and unperturbed as usual.

"He's very gentle," Mother told the baggage man on the train. "I don't believe he'll give you any trouble, except . . . well, he may howl a little." And she was right. When we retrieved him at the end of the trip, the baggage man reported that Glen had howled almost all the way.

Patchin was lovely and wild and lost in the folds of the wooded mountains. It was early summer; azaleas bloomed along the creek banks and tiny meadows and copses were rosy with sorrel and starred with blossoms. Real Christmas trees, minuscule, middle-sized and some that were incredibly tall, grew everywhere. We learned to call them redwoods, to recognize the different oaks and to distinguish and name correctly the madrones and manzanitas. The little green rosettes on the slender branches of the hazel bushes, Mother explained, would become the nuts we always found in our Christmas stockings. The blackberries were just beginning to redden, but ripe wild strawberries gleamed in every clearing.

Best of all was the meadow that sloped away from the farmhouse. There, lying on my stomach in the midst of the poppies and lupine and sorrel that grew in the lush, deep grass, I watched ants, intent and tireless, seeking I knew not what on far-flung solitary expeditions or in long caravans endlessly passing each other in opposite directions, dragging great burdens along the aisles between the towering grass-stems and communicating mysteriously in brief encounters with their fellows.

A flight of Monarch butterflies came to the meadow one day, dipping and rising on fragile, gloriously painted wings as they moved from flower to flower. A wish grew in me to catch one and hold it for a moment in my cupped hands. I was sure it would be easy to scoop one up as it clung, wings slowly opening and closing, to a swaying blossom, but always, at the last moment, it would evade my cautious hand and flutter out of reach. And then I remembered the saying that you could catch a bird if you put salt on its tail. If a bird, why not a butterfly? In the kitchen I appropriated a tablespoon, filled it with salt from the wooden box near the stove, and returned, full of confidence, to the meadow. For a long time I pursued the elusive Monarchs, but it proved as difficult to place a bit of salt anywhere upon them as to capture them with my hands.

Mother found me, hot, perspiring, exasperated, running back and forth across the meadow. "Whatever are you doing?" she called. And when I told her, she did not laugh, but looked so distressed that for a moment I thought she was going to cry. "Oh, Joan," she said, "that's just a saying about putting salt on a bird's tail."

"It isn't true?"

She shook her head.

"Then why do they say it?" I demanded.

She sat down in the grass and drew me to her. "Let me see if I can explain it. . . . You see, if a bird would let you come near enough to put salt on its tail, you wouldn't need the salt at all, for you could catch him quite easily with your hand."

And suddenly I understood. Almost as if I could see it, what the words of the saying seemed to mean fell away and the real meaning was revealed. I was immensely pleased. "It's like a riddle," I exclaimed happily, "or a joke!" After that, I tested every saying I heard and treasured those I found with two meanings fitting closely together like "philopenas" in an almond shell.

And it was in the meadow, lying on my back on a day when snowy cloud-masses spread like vast continents in the bright blue sky, that I found a way to be with Daddy, sailing with him along the coasts of cloud, exploring bays and inlets, running before the wind on wide traverses, skimming past chains of islands on winding stretches of blue and from the deck of our tiny ship viewing the ever-changing, billowing mountains that rose, mountain piled on mountain, behind the undulant edge of beaches and cliffs.

Glen's joy at being in the country was boundless. Not since his earliest days on Daddy's ranch—and then he had been too young to roam far from his mother—had such spaciousness of field and woods been available. Almost immediately it was evident that he considered the country far safer for Bess and me than the city, for he relaxed his vigilance and indulged in long explorations, returning only at intervals for a perfunctory check of his charges. Transcendent among all the pleasures of his life in Patchin, however, were the horses. His periodic reappearances at the farmhouse, we were sure, were as much to see if our host, Mr. Hall, was saddling his horse or hitching up the team as to assure himself of our well-being. When he could run with the horses, even though he might be away for hours, Glen was apparently willing to trust Providence to look after us.

An unseasonable rainstorm swept over the mountains one evening, heralded by spectacular thunder and lightning, the first Bess and I had ever experienced. We fell asleep in the din of rain pounding on the roof and trees thrashing in the wind, and awoke to a glittering morning and air that tingled with wild, sweet scents of wet earth and crushed leaves and blossoms.

Late that afternoon the Halls invited us to ride into Alma with them in the big wagon. They had planned to be back well before dark, but an unexpected delay occurred, and it was dusk when we finally started for home. Perhaps because he believed it would save time, perhaps because he had lingered overlong in Alma's one tavern, Mr. Hall decided to take a shortcut, a little used road which, he assured Mother, would save several miles.

In the woods it was completely dark. The road was rough and steep and full of sharp turns, and so narrow that branches constantly scraped along the sides of the wagon. Glen trotted far ahead, returning to the wagon from time to time and then disappearing again. Sometimes, where the road passed a small clearing, we could see the white tip of his tail glimmering in the darkness. It was on a particularly black stretch of road that we heard him barking as he ran toward us, sharp, high barks, and when he reached the horses he began to leap up at them, still barking, until he brought them to a stop. Each time that Mr. Hall urged them forward, Glen halted them again.

"What's the matter with that fool dog?" Mr. Hall demanded angrily. "We've got to get home!"

He reached for the whip, but Mother intervened. "Glen never does anything without a reason. I think he's trying to tell us something. Why don't you get out and look?"

Grumbling, Mr. Hall got down from the wagon, lit a lantern and followed Glen down the road into the darkness. A few moments later we heard him shout, "Good dog, Glen! Oh, good dog!" We heard him running back, and before we could even see him, he called, "Your dog has probably saved our lives, Mrs. London! The whole road is gone up ahead there, just fallen away into the ravine, and a good piece more is likely to go at any minute. We've got to get out of here right away!"

When the wagon was finally turned around and we had started back to the main road, he told us that all the preceding year slides resulting from the big earthquake had been common throughout the mountains. "That piece of road back there would have gone out this next winter for sure, but last night's rain brought it on ahead of time. . . . That's a wonderful dog you've got. You wouldn't consider selling him to me, would you?"

"Never!" came simultaneously from the three of us.

And another letter telling of Glen's prowess and of our love for him went across the ocean to Daddy.

After Patchin, the sleepy little town of Los Gatos, with its neat houses and picket-fenced gardens, seemed tame and prosaic. Even the orchards and vineyards on all the surrounding hills looked as if they were brushed and combed every day. It was full summer now and very warm; in the evenings the air was heavy with the winey odor of ripe fruit. We took long walks, picked wild blackberries in the hills, waded in the sun-dappled creek and sometimes, while Mother sewed on the shady porch with Glen stretched out at her feet, Bess and I played endless games of jacks or cut pictures out of old magazines.

Los Gatos was not very interesting, but we must have liked it well enough, for whenever Mother asked us if we wanted to go home to Thirty-first Street, we begged to stay longer. The vacation was accomplishing what Mother had hoped for. Her pale, languid little girls were tanned golden-brown, bursting with energy and had actually gained weight. She was so encouraged that, to my delight, she began to talk about letting me go to school soon.

We had been so content to remain away from home that when at last we took the train for Oakland I think we were all surprised to discover that we were looking forward to seeing the bungalow again. Alas, our pleasure was brief. We had forgotten how gloomy it was, how shut in by other houses. Although its strangeness wore off in a day or so, we were not happy to be back.

Scarcely a fortnight after our return, Mother suddenly proposed, "Let's go away again!"

Bess and I danced for joy. "Yes, oh yes, let's!"

"Where would you like to go?"

"Patchin! Los Gatos!" we shouted.

"No, let's go to some place new—maybe to the ocean this time. What about Carmel-by-the-Sea?"

Carmel-by-the-Sea! Was it possible? Daddy had spent a few weeks there just before the wonderful Christmas and had described it to us: the sand white as snow, the wind-twisted cypress, the ruined mission. Now we would go there ourselves!

And it was at Carmel that it happened at last.

Oakland was grey and melancholy under a foggy sky the morning we left, but in Monterey the sun was shining and a crisp breeze was ruffling the bay into whitecaps. Monterey was exciting and foreign and different. Screened by blossoming oleander and jasmine, the balconied, pink and white and blue and pale gold houses were like pictures in a book of fairy tales with their tiled roofs, huge iron-bound doors and barred lower windows. How wonderful, I thought dreamily, to live in one of those houses in this enchanting town.

We rescued Glen from the baggage car ("Your dog certainly doesn't like trains," the baggage man said. "He kept howling in the queerest way . . .") and then found the stage that was to take us to Carmel. It was a high, old-fashioned vehicle drawn by four horses, with seats for the passengers at the very top.

"Oh, you've brought your dog!" the stage driver lamented. "That's too bad."

"What do you mean?" Mother asked. "Aren't dogs allowed in Carmel?"

"Oh sure. It's not that, but there's a big black dog that's been killing other dogs, especially if they're smaller. And your dog is still a puppy. He'll probably be killed, too. What a shame!"

Bess and I clutched Glen in alarm, but Mother reassured us. "I'll tell you what we'll do, girls. Glen will ride in the stage with us to Carmel, and while we stay there we'll always keep him on leash. Besides, I am sure we'll be able to find many places where it will be safe for him to run free."

Riding on the top of the stage was very fine. Behind us were fishing boats and the bay; ahead was the great sweep of dark green, pine-forested hills beyond which lay the ocean and Carmel. Surely no modern conveyance imposes such intimate participation in its movement as the old-time stage. The springless seats assured that when it lurched and swayed over cobbled streets, you also lurched and swayed in perfect unison, and when, harness jingling rhythmically, the horses trotted briskly along a smooth sandy road, you could capture the heady illusion of flying past fields and trees.

Glen was a restless and unhappy passenger. He did not howl as he did on streetcars, but his eyes kept begging us to let him out to run with the horses. In those days, the only way over the hill was up a long, steep grade that was a challenge even to the early automobiles. The stage moved ever more slowly as it climbed the hill until the four horses were merely plodding. Just before we reached the top and when we were already craning our necks to see what was on the other side, Glen's yearning to be free overcame his wish to obey. Before we could stop him he leaped to the ground. He looked back up at us as if expecting us to share his pleasure. In vain, we pleaded, cajoled and commanded. Good-humoredly ignoring us, he caught up with the horses, frisked happily about them, then, as the stage began to move more rapidly on the downgrade, he matched his pace to the horses, running like an outrider at the side and a little ahead of them.

"I'll stop at the edge of the village for you to catch him," the stage driver told Mother. "There's no danger before then, and it won't hurt your dog to run a little."

We were still some distance from Carmel, however, when an enormous black dog bounded into the road, saw Glen instantly, walked a few steps toward him in a curious, stiff-legged way, then stood still, waiting.

The driver brought the stage to a halt and reached for his long whip. "I've never seen him this far out of town! I'll do what I can," he promised. "But what a shame, what a shame!"

We sat, frozen, unable to speak, and watched.

Glen was wagging his tail in his usual friendly fashion as he moved toward the black dog. When they were a few yards apart, the big dog suddenly crouched to spring. Glen stopped short, and we saw the ruff spring out on his neck and back as his hackles rose.

There was a moment when we, the driver standing with the whip coiled and ready, the horses and both dogs were utterly silent and immobile. Then, with a convulsive movement, the black dog turned away and, crawling on his belly, disappeared into the underbrush.

The tension broke. We were laughing and crying at the same time, and Mother kept saying over and over, "Glen, oh Glen!"

The driver turned to us, open-mouthed. "What happened? What did he do?"

No one knew. Glen trotted back to the stage, looking up at us, and it seemed as if he was as puzzled as we were.

By nightfall, apparently everyone in Carmel had heard about Glen's mysterious victory over the black dog. Mother let us sit on the porch of our cottage for a little while after supper. From time to time people strolled past, calling a friendly good evening and asking, "Is that the wonderful dog we heard about today from our stage driver?"

Except for the yellow lamplight that spilled across the porch as far as the nearest branch-tips of the encroaching pines, it was very dark, and though the night was quiet, it was not silent. Dogs barked occasionally. Several times I heard in the distance the cheerful ring of a bicycle bell. Not far away someone was playing a piano, boldly and beautifully. And above my head, unceasingly, the sound of the wind walking through the tops of the pines and the long, slow surge and crash of the breakers on the nearby beach filled the sky.

After a while Mother took Bess in to put her to bed, and Glen came over to sit beside me on the low step. I put my arm around him and he kissed me briefly on the cheek, and we sat there together for a long time, listening to the unfamiliar sounds and smelling the new smells. I shall never forget that first evening in Carmel.

The next morning came the discovery of the beach, vast, empty of people, uncluttered except by driftwood, the dazzling white sand like soft, white sugar and breathtaking treasures of shells and gleaming pebbles at the curving tide-edge. We ran in and out of the surf, squealing as the icy water curled around our ankles. Glen barked at the waves, chased sea-birds, dragged and worried long strands of kelp up and down the beach, then lay down at last near us.

Bess and I, building a city in the sand, and Mother, engrossed in a book, did not notice when Glen rose and trotted off to investigate the man who had come over the low dunes and was walking toward us, so we were a little startled when he called, "Hello! I thought I'd find you here."

This time I knew him instantly—Daddy's friend, the poet . . . "Jawdge."

"I heard that a Mrs. London, two little girls and a remarkable dog had arrived," he announced, "and I was sure they were my Londons."

He sat down beside us on the sand, hugging his knees, and when the greetings were over and we had learned that he was living now in Carmel, he looked at Glen. "That must be the remarkable dog. Apparently I passed his inspection back there. He was perfectly friendly, of course, though in a dignified way. Where did you get him? What is his name? And, for heaven's sake, tell me what really happened yesterday. The village is agog!"

All of us tried to answer his questions at the same time, but somehow he understood. "The son of Brown Wolf!" he murmured, and when we had finished the story, he gently rumpled Glen's ears. "I knew your father, Glen—a great dog."

"What do *you* think happened?" Mother asked. "I was watching closely, and I know Glen didn't touch that black dog."

George studied Glen for a moment, then exclaimed softly, "The wolf . . . of course, that must be it!"

I remembered at once what Daddy had said, but before I could speak, George continued excitedly, "Don't you see? The civilized killer—and he's a dangerous brute—met a dog that is part wolf. At the instant Glen sensed his imminent peril, all that is civilized and gentle and friendly in him fell away, and the wolf-snarl of his savage ancestors rose in his throat, terrifying the killer-dog and sending him crawling to safety. . . . What a story . . . worthy of your Dad himself!"

We listened breathlessly to his explanation, then turned in wonder to Glen. Under the spell of the poet's voice—I remember that goose-bumps were prickling my arms—I was sure the wolf-signs would be plainly visible. But Glen, regarding us benignly and wagging his tail in recognition that he was being talked about, was the same as always.

"That might be it," Mother said. "It isn't any stranger than what occurred. And Jack has always maintained that something of the sort might happen some day."

George was triumphant. "Then that settles it!"

Late that afternoon, with Glen on leash, we set out for the village grocery store. As soon as we were observed, people scattered; in a moment the sandy paths were empty. A small boy yelled, "Look, there's the wolf-dog!" In vain, we explained to everyone we could that Glen was a kind and gentle dog who would hurt no one. Until the end of our stay, our strolls through the village were done in solitary grandeur.

Many weeks later, in reply to the letter I had immediately written him, Daddy enthusiastically confirmed George's theory. Thereafter, we believed it implicitly. Who knows? As Mother said, it was no stranger than what had occurred.

And so the summer passed. Letters from Daddy were brief and infrequent, and perhaps because the bungalow was full of memories of him, we were happier when we were not there, but I do not believe that was why we went away. After I had recovered from the first, overwhelming sense of loss, I learned to miss him less poignantly. The Patchin fantasy of sailing with him in the sky-seas among the clouds was often a happy escape in moments of loneliness, and in the end became a pastime I loved for its own sake. And there were books to read, and dolls and games and Glen to play with and always an irrepressible sense of well-being, for I was stronger and in better health than I had been since we left the Bungalow four years before.

No, it was Mother who decided our goings and comings. Perhaps at breakfast, or while she was watering the lawn after supper, she would say unexpectedly, "Wouldn't it be nice to take another trip? Let's go north this time." Eager to be off, she would be packed and ready to start the next morning, then after a few weeks away, she would be as eager to return.

Coming home became pleasanter, too, because after a while it was no longer lonely. Sometimes Uncle Charlie met us at the train, and always he took us to dinner the first night. Dining out was still a novel experience for me. The brightly lit restaurants, the snowy tablecloths and gleaming silver and glassware, the swift and graceful waiters, the subdued clatter of dishes and the hum of conversation—all were endlessly fascinating. I was careful to remember my table manners and covertly watched others to see how they lifted their forks or buttered their bread. I learned the

French or German names of many dishes, discovered that most elegant of desserts, Charlotte Russe, and became sophisticated about finger bowls.

It is more than forty years since I last saw Uncle Charlie, but I remember him best and most distinctly from the earlier time when he was so much a part of our lives. My memory of him is warm and friendly, and I am glad, for I have learned to trust the judgment of children about older people. His dark brown hair, just beginning to turn grey at the temples, was crisply curly, and he had the merriest brown eyes I have ever seen.

His hands were magical; there seemed to be literally nothing he could not make or do with them. Anything in our house that was broken—and for Bess and me this meant especially our toys and dolls—miraculously became whole again and like new. He understood the mysteries of electricity and locks on doors. And in his spare time he made beautiful bowls and trays and candlesticks of burnished, hammered copper and brass, and sometimes of shining silver. Transcending all these marvels, however, and making the memories of him I most cherish, was his gift of music.

One Sunday afternoon in early autumn Bess and I were in the attic playroom, building a house of blocks for our paper dolls. A storm was brewing. Wind blew across the roof in noisy little gusts, whining softly from time to time, and when I first heard the sound I thought it was the wind. In a lull, I heard the sound again, a single note that melted into another and another, each separate and whole for an instant and wondrously round and full, but in their progression becoming a new whole, a flowing line of sound that I recognized as a fragment of music.

But what was making it? The only musical instruments I had ever heard were pianos and violins; neither could produce such sounds. After a brief pause the music began again, and now it was purposeful, clearly stating something, not calmly but very surely, and not stating it so much as somehow calling it, for it seemed to be reaching me from a distance, though I was sure it was in the bungalow.

Tiptoeing so as not to miss a single note, I went down the stairs and opened the door into the kitchen. Uncle Charlie was there, sitting on a straight-backed chair, his slightly puckered mouth against the end of a long, slender tube which coiled around and around itself to frame the intricate center of a gleaming golden instrument and continued past and down to flare into a wide opening through which flowed the music I had been hearing.

I stood quite still until he had finished. Then he saw me and smiled. "You liked it?" he asked in his friendly way.

"Oh yes! But what is it, Uncle Charlie? What makes the sound?"

He laughed and shook his head despairingly. "I doubt if I could explain that to you, for it's very complicated. But this is a horn, a French horn. It makes very beautiful music, but you should really hear it when it is being played with other musical instruments . . . you know, as in an orchestra."

At sight of the blank look on my face, he placed the horn on the kitchen table, bade me bring up a chair and began my first lesson in music.

It is odd how much I remember of it after so many years, but he was a patient and graphic teacher. When, for instance, he told me that what he called the body of the horn, the coiled tube, was actually over seven feet long, he rose and paced off seven feet on the floor so that I might grasp it more clearly. He showed me the strangely named crooks and the slide, and did his best to explain how they worked. He told me why his horn was called a wind instrument, and had me watch how his lips vibrated against the mouthpiece as he blew on it. And then he described an orchestra, arranging the salt and pepper shakers, the sugar bowls and knives and forks and spoons in a half-circle around his gold watch, which was the conductor, to show me where the strings sat, and the woodwinds and the brasses, and to one side at the back he placed a plate of walnuts for the drums and cymbals and other devices which I came to know later as tympani.

"Do you know why they call this a horn?" he asked once. "It is because long ago men learned to make a good sound that carried a long distance by blowing through the hollowed-out horns of animals like cattle or buffalo."

"Oh, I remember!" I interrupted eagerly. "In my nursery rhyme book there's a picture of Little Boy Blue's horn, and it looks just like a cow's horn."

"That's right," he nodded. "But the first horns were used long before Little Boy Blue . . . thousands of years ago."

"You mean, when there were cave men?" I asked, awed.

"I wouldn't be surprised. They've always been used in wars and when men went hunting, and I guess there never was a time when there weren't any wars or men didn't hunt. You see, it was easy to get lost in the wild forests in those days, but they could always call to each other by blowing their horns."

He picked up his instrument and began to play again; the lesson was over.

During the next few years I listened often to Uncle Charlie's horn. Sometimes I heard its call when I was playing outside, and I would close my eyes and instantly be in a forest of ancient oaks, lost, but found now because I had heard the horn. I have an impression that he played frequently with groups of other nonprofessionals who met in each other's homes to make music together. Every few weeks he would begin work on new numbers, but always he ended his practice sessions with two or three of the horn solos he liked best of all. They were also the ones I liked best, and after a while I could hum them through without a break. Many years later when I began to hear symphonies and operas, I recognized over and over again passages Uncle Charlie had played. And listening to those we had both liked the best as they rose out of the richness of a full orchestra to introduce a theme or reiterate a motif, I would see again the salt and pepper shakers and sugar bowl, the knives and forks and spoons and the plate of nuts grouped around Uncle Charlie's watch on the kitchen table.

Ella came to live with us during that summer of our great travels, after Carmel but before Camp Meeker and Kentfield. She made her home with us for two or three years, and after she went away we never saw or heard from her again. Bess and I neither liked nor disliked her, which is probably why we remember so little about her. In my letters to Daddy that survive from those years her name does not occur. I am not even sure of her status in our household. She "helped" Mother, but she did not "work" for us. In those days, of course, many unmarried women, without family and unwilling to take a job, used to manage in this way, helping around the house in exchange for room and board until they found husbands. I wonder if Ella found a husband; we never knew. Aunt Jennie, who had always been scornful of her, said after her sudden departure that she hoped Ella had not gone off with someone else's husband, but Mother quickly interrupted with her usual "little pitchers have big ears," and Aunt Jennie would say no more.

Ella was French, spoke French fluently, but English without an accent, so if she had been born in France, she must have come to America as a child. Later, when I was studying French in high school, I used to wonder how she spelled her last name; it could have been Moujé, or Moujais, or even Mougeais. She was a fresh-complexioned, big-boned young woman with slightly slanted eyes—green, I think, although they may have been blue—tan-colored hair and a long nose, oddly turned up at the tip. She sewed beautifully and cooked superbly, but as I look back at that time now, I see that her chief value was her physical presence in the bungalow. Not only did Mother have another adult for companionship, but because Ella, especially at the beginning of her stay, usually preferred to spend her evenings at home, Mother was free to accept invitations to dinner and the theater and to visit friends, which she did, often with Uncle Charlie.

In nightgown and slippers, Bess and I used to sit on Mother's bed and watch her dress for these occasions, admiring her "best" corset cover, handmade of fine embroidery, its fullness gathered together by baby ribbon run through tiny eyelets and tied in a bow in the front, and the long taffeta petticoat that rustled when she put it on over her head. It was the era of the shirtwaist, a style that was especially becoming to Mother. There was one of alice-blue silk with a deep yoke of creamy lace that I shall always remember; it hung for years afterward, unworn, in her clothes closet.

She coiled her long, thick hair, still blue-black except for the broad white band in the center, on the top of her head, fastening it with curly hairpins made of bone and adjusting it at the back and sides with small curved combs. Last of all, she pinned her little silver watch to her shirtwaist, touched her temples and ears and wrists with violet scent, and she was ready for our inspection. She looked very beautiful to me, standing there tall and slender, with shining eyes and pink cheeks, but I would not give my approval until she had slowly turned around so that I might see if the hem of her skirt was even and her petticoat did not show.

Then Uncle Charlie would arrive, and Bess and I would be tucked into bed, with Glen mounting guard on the floor between us, and in the midst of laughter and cries of "Have a good time!," they would be off.

We were allowed to look at our books for a half-hour or so before Ella put out the light, and even then we were permitted to talk to each other if we did so quietly. The two best-loved games of all our childhood had their origins in that little while before we fell asleep: "Let's start with the same word" and "Let's imagine." We played the first when we were still very wide-awake. Choosing a word at random, we would let our minds race at top speed, silently, from the first word to another and another for about a minute. Sometimes it was Bess and sometimes it was I who broke the silence, asking suddenly, "Where are you?" In turn, then, we would retrace aloud the lightning-swift associations that had led us so far and to such different ends from the words we had agreed upon.

"Let's imagine" was the game for going to sleep. It had no rules, although it was based on a tacit courtesy that obliged each of us not only to listen attentively to the other's fantasies, but also to limit our discourse when it was our turn to build and people our castles in the air. Usually we created the same imaginary scene or experience, each making her special contribution to the whole, but sometimes our needs of the moment were so unlike and required expression so urgently that we spun separate fancies, still aloud and in turn, dreaming thus on two levels simultaneously, participating in one and observing the other.

In the game, all that we wished for came true. We were back in Patchin or on the beach at Carmel. We lived in a pink house in Monterey. I went to a real school, could speak French as fast as Ella did to her friends over the telephone, and German like Lily Mason, and I could play the piano. It was Christmas, with a glittering tree that touched the ceiling and hundreds of presents heaped beneath it. We had a horse and buggy and rode again through the far and lovely hills. We took long journeys on trains, and Glen was with us, not in the baggage car. We had a coaster, a tricycle and roller skates. And always, and always, Daddy was with us, on our journeys, on our rides through the hills, in our house, living with us. For this was the biggest wish of all, and we always made it come true.

From the time we were very small and went downtown with Mother, we sometimes met people on the street or in a store who would stop and speak to her. They loomed over Bess and me—tall, trousered legs and, more often, bulky triangles of broadcloth or silk—saying "It's nice to see you again" and "How have you been?" From far above our heads their voices would float down to us: "So these are Jack's little girls!" and they would lean over and smile at us and ask questions that really did not need to be answered. After a moment they would say goodbye and walk away, and I could never remember what they looked like. With painful distinctness, however, I recall that Mother, usually so confident and friendly, was constrained and ill at ease at such times, and would move away from these encounters so briskly that Bess and I had to skip to keep up with her. "Who was that?" I would ask, and she would reply, dismissing the subject, "A friend of your Daddy's."

Now that I was older, I began to wonder about this. There was the mysterious lady who had sat silently in the corner and looked at us the day we had gone to see Daddy in the flat on Telegraph Avenue. She had been a friend of Daddy's. There were the men we had met at the Piedmont Baths who were Daddy's friends. Except for George, the poet, who was also my friend, all these and the ones we met on the street were not our friends, but Daddy's, and I wondered why this was so.

For a long time our visitors had been aunts and uncles, and Grandma London, and Aunt Jennie and Uncle Charlie. There was Lily Mason, whom Mother had known since they were little girls together, and Birdie Fennell, with whom Mother had gone to night school, and a few others, but we had seen these only infrequently. But now it was different: we had many friends. Some of them were new, like Mrs. Morrow, the jolly lady with the curly grey hair whom Bess and I called Aunt Edith, and beautiful Mrs. Codding, and the Sweezeys, in whose house there was always music and flowers, and others whose names I can no longer recall. Most of the new ones were Uncle Charlie's friends who had now become ours as well, but there were old friends, too, who, for a mysterious reason had not come to see us for longer than I could remember. "Oh Bessie, we should have known!" they used to say at first. "We never should have believed her!" It was a long time before I knew what they meant.

All of the old friends had also been friends of Daddy's: the Austin Lewises and their four children, Jim and Ida Reed and their two, and Frank and Madge Atherton. Frank and Jim and Daddy had been school-boys and best-friends together; Austin had known Daddy since before he became a writer. And three of the beautifully named Lewis children, Aylen, Hesper and Saxon (Hope had not yet been born), had actually come to my first-year birthday party at the house on Bayo Vista and their pictures were in *Joan, Her Book*. What a satisfying link they made for me with the beloved past I could not remember!

But if the Lewis children momentarily brought the past closer to me, in all the other ways it was retreating, being obscured and overlaid by a present far different from anything that had gone before, and by an imminent future that promised even greater change. Daddy, somewhere on an unimaginable ocean, was moving further and further away as the passing weeks and months nibbled without noticeable effect at the enor-mous total of seven years of weeks and months that I knew would have to pass before I saw him again. And while the distance he was placing between us lengthened, I was being caught up and whirled away into a new life in which, for the first time, it seemed he would play no active role. He did, of course, and very soon, but this was something else that I did not learn for a long time.

The new life was very wonderful, filled with friends and visits, a happier Mother than I had ever known and, for me personally, freedom from illness and the growing certainty that I would really go to school at the beginning of the year. This immediate future was perhaps the most wonderful of all. Not once during all my childhood was I to forget the grand design I had made to regain my one-time importance to Daddy. Now, certain features of the design were beginning to be real. Going to school was one of them. And surely, I thought, with so much music in our house, I would soon learn to play the piano. Finally, I found in Ella a willing, though casual teacher of French, so that I was acquiring a store of nouns and verbs and phrases, and could sing endless verses of "Savez-vous planter les choux?" and "Sur le pont d'Avignon."

Then, across the beginning-to-be-happy winter fell a heavy shadow: Glen was lost.

We had gone to a Saturday matinee at the Orpheum with Uncle Charlie, and afterwards to dinner at the nearby Gas Kitchen. When we reached home Glen was not there, nor had he returned when we awoke the next morning. A dozen times during that long Sunday we thought we heard him at the door and ran to open it, but always we were mistaken. On Monday, Mother placed an advertisement in all the Oakland papers, with special mention of the brass plate on Glen's collar and offering a generous reward. The milkman and the iceman and the other drivers who knew Glen were asked to watch for him along their routes, and Mother began her daily calls to the city pound.

It is always the same when you lose a beloved animal, unless the end comes swiftly and without warning. When they fall ill, when they stray and you cannot find them, your confidence, which seems so strong and sure, slowly ebbs until only hope is left, and as the hours and days drag by, hope, although it springs up wildly at the tiniest change, the faintest rumor, fights a losing battle with fear and foreboding.

Our confidence was in the brass plate on Glen's collar that so plainly identified him and in the advertisement that contained our telephone number. Bess and I were in bed but not asleep when the first answer came. Barefooted, we ran into the hall and waited breathlessly while Mother talked on the telephone with someone who had seen Glen. But that had been on Saturday, for the man who called was a janitor at the Orpheum, and after the theater was empty that afternoon he had seen a dog, exactly matching Glen's description, who was obviously hunting for someone. He had run swiftly through the theater, nose down, sniffing as if he was following a scent. The janitor had called to him, but the dog had paid no attention and had finally left the building.

We were sure that this dog had been Glen. The description tallied, and his appearance at the very theater we had attended that afternoon made us even more certain. We could only guess that, unnoticed by us, Glen had seen us get on the streetcar, followed it into town and had eventually picked up our trail, for we had walked the three blocks from Broadway to the theater. Why, we asked each other agonizedly, hadn't he waited for us to come out? Where did he go when he left the Orpheum? And where was he now?

"If we only had Baby and the surrey," Mother fretted, "we could drive around and look for him." And the next day and the next, although a cold November rain had set in, she left us with Ella and walked for hours along streets that led away from the theater, looking everywhere and questioning everyone she saw.

There were no more answers to the advertisement. The rain fell drearily, endlessly, and each evening when we looked at the empty cushioned stool by the fireplace, we tried to feel sure that somewhere Glen was warm and dry. Our hope now was in the milkman and the iceman and the others whose horses Glen had loved to run with, and in Glen's own intelligence. If it had enabled him to follow us to the theater, surely, surely, it would bring him home.

Friday came. Ella had just left to spend the afternoon and evening with friends when the second and final answer to the advertisement came over the telephone. Mother had great difficulty understanding the man. Finally, it was agreed that she would meet him in town as soon as she could get there. She bundled us into coats and rubbers and left us with Mrs. Kendall, who lived in the big house on the corner. From the windows on the wide stair landing we watched Mother waiting in the rain until the streetcar came.

Yes, it is always the same when you lose a beloved animal—the first wild disbelief, the aching throat that only tears can ease, the recurring incredulity that time after time fiercely rejects and denies the unbearable loss.

I remember, as if it were a long journey, leaving Mrs. Kendall's sitting room where I had talked with Mother on the telephone, stumbling along the dark hall and down the steep backstairs and coming into the brightly lit kitchen where Bess and Mrs. Kendall were awaiting my news with expectant, hopeful faces. And later, at home, I remember listening to Mother tell of meeting the man who had telephoned, a longshoreman, a foreigner who could not speak much English but who understood everything so well that he needed no language at all. He had found Glen that morning, lying near the railroad tracks on First Street where he had been struck and instantly killed by a passing train.

"He was so kind," Mother said. "He told me that he, too, had lost dogs he loved, so he knew—with his heart, he said. . . . He wouldn't take even part of the reward, though I tried to persuade him. And . . . and he brought me Glen's collar. . . ."

She took it from her handbag and laid it on her lap, the collar that had been too large for so long, the brass plate shining and unblemished.

We wept then, and because Glen without his collar was unthinkable, we knew with a terrible finality that he was gone.

It is always the same. You grieve, you remember; sometimes you think you hear a familiar bark or at dusk you are sure for a moment that you see a flash of golden brown across the lawn. Then, as the days and weeks pass, the grief loses itself in the love that has not changed, and, even if you are not quite seven years old, you begin to understand dimly that death, like birth, is inseparable from life, and that love encompasses the whole. One day Mother said, "If there is a heaven for dogs, there must be horses there, too. Glen would like that." And always afterward I thought of Glen in the deep, flower-starred grass of some celestial meadow, running joyously with the horses he loved.

SIX

Starting school was an event of such tremendous importance to me that even now I fancy I can feel again my excitement and wonder and deep satisfaction on that January day in 1908 when Mother enrolled me in Miss Merriman's school.

All through the autumn and the beginning of winter my luck had held; I had not been ill, even with a cold. How many decisions were dictated when I was a little girl by whether I was well or ill, and if well, was I likely to remain so. Old- and new-fashioned remedies were used in those pre-vitamin days to hasten my various convalescences: small glasses of port wine before dinner; codliver oil; beef, iron and wine, scraped raw beefsteak, lightly salted and spread on thin pieces of bread. With the promise of going to school as a reward if I remained well, I cooperated eagerly, shuddering over the despised codliver oil but relishing the thimbleful of port and the raw beefsteak. My health also dictated the choice of a private school, which Mother neither approved nor could really afford. Two public schools were fairly near the bungalow, but Mother feared lest I catch cold while walking the several blocks each way on rainy days. Miss Merriman's school had a horse-drawn bus which gathered up the smaller pupils every morning and returned them at noon.

The preparations Mother made for the start of my formal schooling emphasized its private importance to me. Never before had I had so many new clothes, from the skin out, at the same time. Mother and Ella made two woolen dresses for me and a warm coat, and two or three full-skirted school aprons of white, cross-barred muslin, of which I was inordinately proud until I discovered that none of the other girls wore them. There were also new shoes and ribbed black stockings, ferris waists, white panties and flannel petticoats, mittens, rubbers and umbrella, and a small, well-remembered wicker basket for mid-morning snacks.

The weeks, even the Christmas holidays, crept slowly by; I did not "come down" with a cold or anything else; finally, soon after the new year began, I entered school.

I used to like to think that the few years I spent in the private school were, on the whole, pleasant ones. I was very fond of round, rosy-cheeked Miss Mira, as everyone called Miss Merriman, and I adored Miss Diehl, beautiful and gentle, from the moment I saw her. They were excellent teachers, and I was an excellent pupil, as any child prepared by Mother should have been, even without my determination to excel. My mind, well-nourished from babyhood, was trained to learn with a minimum of effort and a maximum of interest and enjoyment. I was placed in the third grade and progressed with no difficulty.

And yet, when I seek my reasons for thinking that these were pleasant years, I find only a handful of happy memories. I was intensely interested in everything I was taught. Penmanship and drawing I labored over conscientiously, learning to write at least legibly and to draw not at all, but the rest of the basic curriculum of those days—reading spelling, arithmetic and geography—was easily mastered.

I remember especially the keen joy of becoming familiar with numbers and the arithmetical processes, addition, subtraction, multiplication and division. This was true magic, instantly responsive when summoned, trustworthy, able as nothing else to bring order out of chaos. I was never to go far beyond the anteroom of the great temple of mathematics, but with my first step within its portals, its pure beauty filled me with reverence.

I also remember with affection the French teacher we had for a time, a spare, energetic little spinster, who used to trot into the classroom crying gaily, "Bon jour, mes enfants! Comment vous portez-vous ce beau matin?," and we would shout back, "Bon jour, m'amselle! Très bien, merci, et vous?" Then she would place her flat wicker satchel on the desk, and out of it would come, one by one, marvellously detailed colored prints of gardens and houses and rooms full of furniture, and stores and farms and zoos and ships, and the game of "Qu'est-ce que c'est que ça?" would begin. We learned hundreds of nouns and adjectives, but, alas, few verbs.

I remember rehearsing, with joyful anticipation, a Christmas play in which a toy shop came to life. I was to be the queen of the dolls and sing a song whose words and tune I have never forgotten. My tarlatan ballet skirt and ruffled bodice were ready, my borrowed French bonnet was ready, I was ready, but I caught a cold the day before the performance. An understudy took my place and my theatrical début was postponed.

Happiest of all is my memory of the creek. In the second term, when I went to school the whole day, I was permitted to walk home alone in good weather. My way led, if I wished—and I always wished—along a shallow, tree-shaded creek. The banks were steep and high, but it was not difficult to scramble down to the water and walk along the edge, hopping from side to side on stepping stones, peering hopefully into occasional pools for the fish that were never there and, the next spring, scooping up pollywogs to see their blackness, like wriggling commas and apostrophes, against the palm of my hand. It was a place of enchantment. Yerba buena and ferns grew on the banks in the shade of tall oaks and bay trees, and bright green cress wherever the water was almost still. As the season advanced the pollywogs grew legs, turned green and became frogs, leaping up inches from under my feet and swimming energetically across the tiny stretches of deeper water. Black water snakes and beautiful little garter snakes slid silently into the pools as I approached, and brown, orange-bellied salamanders, which we called water-dogs, posed utterly motionless for an instant, then flashed across the rocks and vanished.

Was this little creek, perhaps more beautiful in my memory of it than it really was, the origin of that love of brooks and streams and all shallow running water which was to recur again and again in my early efforts to write stories and in my letters to Daddy? I remember, and remembering, can almost recapture the special fascination they had for me and the inexpressible delight I took in exploring them, but I do not know why this was so.

But I do know why that particular little creek is so lovingly remembered, and why it and the handful of happy scenes come so readily to mind. I never really deceived myself at the time; certainly I cannot do so now. Those pleasant memories of first going to school—fragmentary, indistinct, ragged-edged from being torn out of context, worn from over-use and significantly lacking in association with the season of the year and the weather, unlike almost all my early memories—these were the materials of the frail barrier I reared against the pain and bewilderment of harsh experiences which I could not understand and did not want to remember, and which I have never been able to forget. As sharp and clear as if it had occurred yesterday is the most revealing of all my memories of going to Miss Merriman's.

Like a picture in *St. Nicholas Magazine*, I see us, four little girls, standing at a corner near the school on a showery April afternoon, waiting for the streetcar I can take only when it is cold or raining, although the others can take it every day. We are dressed much alike: bulky rubbers half cover our black, high-button shoes, and our long winter coats hide all but an inch or so of our ribbed, black cotton stockings. Each of us is carrying an umbrella with a carved bone handle, but Sally's is of shining black silk, while ours are cotton. Everything of Sally's is nicer than anyone else's, for Sally is one of the "rich girls." (How ardently I admired her at first and hoped foolishly that we might be "best friends.") I am eight, the youngest and smallest, and Sally, beautiful, imperious and unkind, is eleven. Beth is a new girl, but Ellen I know very well because our mothers are friends and we often visit each other's homes.

Suddenly, although indifferently, as if it did not really matter to her, and in the haughty tone I know as well as I do the question, the one the "rich girls" like best to ask, Sally asks Beth, "What does your father do?"

Beth does not understand. She is a plump, good-natured girl who moves and speaks slowly. "Do? What does my father do?"

"How does he make his living?" Sally explains impatiently.

"Oh. He's in real estate."

"You mean, he sells houses and lots and things like that?" How ignoble she makes it sound!

But Beth is unperturbed. "That's right." And then, feeling perhaps that good manners require a similar interest, she asks politely, "And what does your father do, Sally?"

"He's a very important man . . . an attorney."

Sally does not elaborate, and I know she is displeased. She looks around for a more satisfactory target. Inside, I feel myself beginning to cringe. Oh, let it not be me! If only the streetcar will come! But it is Ellen who is the next victim.

"Anyway," Sally continues loftily, not looking at anyone in particular, "I think it's much nicer to have a father who sells real estate than one who has to poke around in people's dirty old cellars reading gas meters."

Beside me, Ellen stiffens. She is very pretty, with shining golden hair and blue eyes, and somehow cool and remote—like a snow princess, I always think. She is my closest friend at Miss Merriman's, but not very close.

"My father does not read gas meters." Ellen's face is scarlet with anger, but her voice, emphasizing every word separately, is like ice.

"He works for the gas company, doesn't he?" Now Sally is enjoying herself.

"Certainly."

"Well?"

And I? I know that Ellen's father does not read meters, that he has a big office in the gas company building downtown, because I once went there with Ellen, but I do not come to the aid of my friend. I stand there, silent, rejoicing that Sally's victim is Ellen and not I. And seeing the streetcar come over the top of the hill and start down, I feel relief flooding through me to the tips of my fingers and toes. This time I have escaped.

That night, lying wakeful in bed, I faced and named the unease that had haunted me ever since I reached home, and naming it, felt it expand like an evil genie erupting from a bottle and overwhelm me. I was ashamed, bitterly ashamed, not of my cowardice, but because I had failed a friend. I knew that I should have spoken up, taken Ellen's side, defied Sally to do her worst; instead, I had not only cravenly kept still, but I had even been glad that Ellen was the persecuted one instead of me. I squirmed inwardly, sought excuses to ease my anguish, but the burden of humiliation could neither be shifted nor shared.

Long ago this memory ceased to distress me, but I was never able to forget it. Its viability served two purposes: it kept vivid and alive the painful lessons that were forced upon me from my very first day at Miss Merriman's and it strengthened my awareness of Mother's unyielding, almost fanatical insistence upon loyalty in friendship which had been deeply impressed upon me at an early age. Years later, when facts I had not known previously were revealed to me, I understood at last the excessive scorn and anger that disloyalty always provoked in Mother, and with this understanding, much else that had long been obscure became clear.

If I had entered school a decade or so later, or if, entering when I did, it had been a public rather than a private school, I might perhaps have escaped the searing revelations of my contemporaries concerning myself, my circumstances and my status. But if such an escape, in whole or in part, had occurred, or even if the manner of revelation itself had been kinder, I do not believe it would have materially altered either what was to happen to me thereafter or the way I was to meet the many assaults upon my faith and my pride. Too much was inescapable.

With my first step across the threshold of Miss Merriman's school, the shadow of a world-famous name fell upon me, and simultaneously, I, who had so lately discovered myself, lost my separate identity. I had been Joan; henceforth, for year after year, I would be Jack London's daughter. For a brief moment only, at the beginning, the public recognition of this relationship was pure joy. I was astonished and immensely pleased that my schoolmates and teachers, who had never seen Daddy, knew who he was, had read his stories and even knew he was sailing around the world in a little boat. It was a heady experience to realize for the first time that I was the daughter of such a famous man, and in all innocence, I basked in my new importance, but not for long. What had been given with one hand was ruthlessly torn away with the other.

I did not receive the full course of instruction all at once, but it was begun on the very first day, and continued for months with endless variations on the single, fundamental theme. From my schoolmates I learned that being the daughter of a famous man, in my case, meant nothing at all. My parents were divorced, and I did not live with my famous father, but with my mother. Apparently, divorce was a disgrace under any circumstances. The circumstances of the London divorce, however, were notorious because everyone had read about them in the newspapers, and that was very bad. Rewarded by the effect this produced on me, they joyously pursued their quarry. In time it became a sort of liturgy of persecution, perfected from day to day as new conclusions, implications and comparisons rose with impeccable logic out of the original premises.

My father had left us and gone away and married someone else. That showed, plain as plain, that he did not love us, for no one went away from people he loved. We probably did not even interest him very much, who was a great writer and very smart, or would he now be sailing further and further away from us on his long journey around the world? *Their* fathers would never do such a thing. *Their* fathers loved them. *Their* fathers were home every night, and bought them pretty clothes and lovely toys, and on Sundays they all went visiting together, riding in their horses-and-carriages or in their new automobiles.

What did I say? What could I say? Outraged, I tried to fight back at first, hotly denying the incredible assertions, fiercely defending myself and Mother and Bess, and even Daddy, against the insidious, slippery arguments, and got nowhere. My mother and father *were* divorced, weren't they? Well? He *did* have another wife, didn't he? He *did* expect to be gone on his trip for many years, didn't he? Did I have lots of pretty clothes? Did we have an automobile or a horse-and-carriage? Well?

And so, helpless, frustrated, I learned to be silent, no matter what they said. I would have learned not to cry when their thrusts went deep, even if I had not long before mastered that discipline. After many errors, I learned to evade my tormentors at recess times and lunch hours, but not pointedly, for that would have triggered a fresh assault. And seeking to rebuild my shattered ego, I comforted myself, thinking: wait until the report cards come out and they'll see how much smarter I am than they are! My scholastic triumph was very real, as I had known it would be, but very brief. Adroitly, they made of it a two-edged sword and turned it against me. "Your father can't sign your report card, can he?" they said. "Why, he won't even see it!" And when, throwing caution to the winds, I pointed out my uniformly excellent marks and bragged a little, they delivered the *coup de grace:* "Why shouldn't you get good marks? Look who your father is!"

Who were "they"? They were four or five little girls, the prettiest, the best dressed, the gayest in the school, all of them from wealthy homes. In the midst of my misery, how I admired and envied them! They were so sure of themselves, so confident of their opinions, so certain of their right to dominate all the other little girls. (The few boys did not count; they and the girls ignored each other.) If Sally and her friends pronounced something to be thus and so, it was accepted without question. When they stated flatly that divorce, especially the one that involved me, was shameful and hinted that somehow it was my own fault, there was no dissent. In many ways, I was a made-to-order victim; besides, I was a novelty, the first and the only "divorced" child in the school.

I had no inkling then, nor would I have understood if I had, that their crushing judgments and opinions were parrotings of their parents, who, in turn, parroted the opinions and prejudices of their time and class. No religious or moral principle prompted the condemnation of divorce by the wealthy middle class, only Mrs. Grundy, wielding the last of her fading power and due shortly to vanish from the social scene. In a few more years I would not have been a novelty.

But how did it happen, I wonder, that I understood, from the very first moment, the meaning of the attack on me? How did I know what "divorce" signified, who scarcely knew what marriage meant? When and how had I learned that Mother and Daddy were divorced and that Daddy now had a second wife? I do not know. Mother had not explained these matters to me and they were not discussed in my hearing by relatives and friends. Because I can recall no interval of incomprehension between my first shock and surprise at Sally's attack and my violent denials of the charges and insinuations, it may well be that understanding had followed closely upon attack, not in any dramatic revelation, but in an instant's synthesis of the hints, ambiguous remarks and fragments of mysterious conversations I had overheard for years.

Did I believe their assertions or accept their judgments? Of course not! The facts were inarguable, but I passionately rejected all else. I *knew* Daddy loved me; nothing else mattered; and my confidence in the bright future toward which I was striving did not waver. Nevertheless, a small seed of doubt had been planted in me, so deeply that I did not know it was there and even refused to recognize it later in the sick uneasiness I felt during and after the crises that were to arise in my relations with Daddy.

Side by side with my unyielding resistance to the persecutions of Sally and her clique was a stubborn refusal to confide my difficulties to Mother. My motives were mixed. Perhaps it was only that to tell Mother would have been crying when I was hurt, it would have been tattling, it would have been not fighting my own battles; perhaps I sensed that it would have worried and saddened her, and that in any case there was nothing she could do to help me; finally, and this is certain, there was my stiff-necked pride which forbade me to show myself to anyone, even to Mother, as humiliated and despised. Once only, in a moment of great tension between Daddy and me, I tried to put the bitter memories of this time into words, but he overrode them with counter-memories from his own childhood which mine had evoked, and perhaps his were the more bitter.

And so the creek, an allure even to a carefree child, was for me a brief but total escape from everything. Once down the steep bank, there was no school, no Mother or Daddy, no Joan. For a timeless interval I wandered in another dimension, merging myself wholly with the life and growth of the creek, belonging there with the ferns and the watercress, the wind in the tops of the trees, the frogs and snakes and salamanders, the murmuring, endlessly flowing water.

At first, with Daddy so forcefully brought to mind every day at school, I tried hard to recall him clearly, see him again in my mind's eye, hear his voice and laughter, feel his bristly chin against my cheek, but with small success. He had been gone for nine months. After my last sight of him, standing on the sidewalk in the April twilight, blowing kisses and waving goodbye to us, had come our great travels, the life and death of Glen, the exciting preparations for starting school and school itself.

His letters, moreover, had been few and short, and told nothing of the wonders of his trip or the strange places he visited. The only one that survives from the first summer of his voyage is typical:

July 11, 1907
Honolulu, H.I.

Dear Joan:—

Thank you for your nice letter. I am glad you like it at
Los Gatos. I am waiting till I get to countries where the dolls
are different. They are just the same in this place as at
home. Bye and bye I'll get them. Lots of love and kisses.

Daddy.

The large framed photograph of him, formally posed and over-retouched, did not help; it had hung in the same place on the wall for so long that it had become as impersonal as a piece of furniture. A smaller picture, enlarged from a camera-shot made by Mother not long before they were married, was better, for his hair was tousled, and he was lighting a cigarette, cupping the match in his hands and squinting one eye against the smoke as he always did. At best, however, it was an indistinct figure of him that emerged, and I was not comforted.

Late one night, two or three weeks after I had started school, I was roused from sleep by Mother's hand on my cheek and her voice saying softly, "Wake up, Joan. See who is here."

"Who?" I asked sleepily, trying to make out the figure standing beside her in the dimly lit room.

Then, incredibly, Daddy moved nearer and sat down on the edge of my bed. Even as our arms went out to each other and I felt the solid reality of him, I did not believe it. Either I am dreaming, I thought confusedly, or, like Brunhilde on the mountain or the Sleeping Beauty in her tower, I have been asleep for a long time and the seven years have passed and Daddy has come back to me from around the world!

"How is my girl?" he asked in the old affectionate way, and suddenly I knew, whether it was dream or reality, that there were many things I must tell him, about Glen, about Uncle Charlie's wonderful music, about being seven years old now and going to school, and most urgent of all because I had not realized it until that moment, how terribly much I had missed him.

The words would not come. "I'm fine," I managed at last, and took a deep breath before trying to begin my recital, but he did not wait.

"I haven't been able to get the dolls you wanted," he said, and explained, as he already had in the letter, that the dolls in Honolulu were the same as those in Oakland. "We're in Pepeete now, though," he went on incomprehensibly—and again I was sure I was dreaming, for people always said crazy things in dreams—"and when I get back I'll look for the native dolls."

He pulled the familiar gold-dust sack from his pocket, poured coins into his hand and slipped one of them under my pillow. "Here, this is for you . . . to get something you want."

He rose and went over to where Bess was still deeply asleep and put another coin under her pillow, and stood there a moment, looking down at her.

"Good night, Baby B," he murmured, and to Mother, wonderingly, "How they have grown!"

"They should have," she said. "It's been nearly a year."

"It's late, I must go." He held me close and kissed me goodnight. "Sleep well, dear Joan, and happy dreams!"

In the morning, only half awake, I remembered the strange and wonderful dream, going over it in my mind so I could tell it to Mother and Bess. When I came to the part where he had put a coin under my pillow, involuntarily I slid my hand under it, and instantly came fully awake, for my fingers touched something that had not been there when I had gone to sleep. Flinging the pillow aside, I saw it—Daddy's own coin, a five-dollar goldpiece! So it had not been a dream at all, he had really been there!

Answering my excited questions, Mother explained that Daddy had returned to take care of some important business, but would stay only a few days and then take a steamer back to the island where he had left his boat and continue his trip. When would he come to see us? I wanted to know; would he come that very day, or maybe the next? To my intense disappointment, it appeared unlikely that he would have time to see us a second time, but he had told Mother he would try. I kept hoping, marshalled my thoughts as I used to do before his visits, so I could tell him all I had been unable to when he sat on my bed in the middle of the night, but we did not see him again. The evening before he sailed back to the South Seas he telephoned to say goodbye, and after that there were only brief letters and occasional small curios, and once, a pearl, and a cat's-eye apiece for us little girls.

As the months passed he grew less and less real. His infrequent letters that neither described his experiences nor evinced interest in what I was doing failed utterly to bridge the space and time that lengthened steadily between us. In the end, they seemed to bear almost entirely upon the dolls he was never able to find for us, until we were all heartily sick of them. "I wish I had never thought of the idea!" Mother exclaimed finally in exasperation.

For a while after his unexpected return and immediate departure at the beginning of 1908, I made a valiant effort to keep up my end of the correspondence, planning my letters carefully, relating everything I thought, and hoped, would interest him (and concealing, perhaps even from myself, my true feeling toward Sally), and chiding him for writing me so seldom.

(March or April, 1908)

Dear Daddy,

I have not heard from you for seven weeks. I have had a cold. And Bess has not. Uncle Charlie made us a coaster. And Bess can steer very well. I have finished the Third reader and am in the Fourth. I like reading very much. I know how to play on the piano a little. I wish you would let me take real lessons. . . . I know a girl and her name is Dorothy Dukes. Her Daddy is a doctor. We have French every Monday and Thursday and Friday. . . . There is a little girl named Sally. And I like her. Next term Bess is going to school.

Your little
girl Joan

A few months later I made a supreme effort:

(Summer, 1908)

Dear Daddy,

Did you get our letters? Mamma and I wrote.

I am going to send you my promotion card. After you look at it please send it back because I want to keep it. The doll has not come yet. Are not there any dolls at the other islands you have visited?

Bess is very proud of her first new tooth. Mrs. Kendall gave us three little banties. And one hatched out three little babies. The milkman gave us a rooster. I got two dollars and eight cents and Bess has got 71 cents. The cats eyes and pearls came and I like them very much.

I have just to save 75 cents more to get my little sewing machine. Mamma takes us very often to Sunny Cove. And I go out up to my neck and duck my head right under the water. Uncle Charlie is teaching me to swim but Bess just likes to wade.

Daddy, if you cannot get real dolls can you not get our American dolls and have some native dress it like they dress?

Mamma, Bess and I send lots and lots of love and kisses.

Your little
girl Joan

This letter crossed one from him, the first in a long while. The envelope was so bulky I was sure it would contain the long letter I had been hoping for, but the bulk was a tropical leaf he had pinned to the bottom of the single small sheet:

Fila Harbor, Efate Island
New Hebrides, June 17, 1908

Dear Joan:—
    This is a banyan leaf. Ask Mamma to tell you about
the banyan tree. All its branches become roots, you know,
whenever they reach the ground.
    With lots and lots of love,

Daddy

P.S.—In all these islands they do not have dolls.
Daddy

I think I must have given up trying after that, not deliberately or all at once, and not even with any special awareness that the one means of staying close to Daddy I had counted on for so long had failed me. I still wrote to him, but the letters were composed more dutifully than gladly, and they were mailed at longer and longer intervals. It is significant that Daddy did not save any of these later letters.

Many years were to pass before I learned that Daddy's mysterious return to California on business had also, and perhaps even especially, involved a matter of utmost importance to Mother and Bess and me. I did not know, for instance, that several hours of harsh argument between Daddy and Mother and Uncle Charlie had preceded my awakening to find Daddy inexplicably beside my bed, or that a cherished plan which would surely have altered the lives of all of us had been fatally blighted on that February night.

How or when I learned that Mother and Uncle Charlie were going to be married, I cannot remember. Evidently, it was knowledge gently imparted and happily received, for I do remember how pleased Bess and I were at the prospect. We had known him for a long time and regarded him with genuine affection. Looking back, I can appreciate now how patient and understanding with us little girls he was, who had been a bachelor for so long, how generous with his time and skills on our behalf, repairing our toys and making new ones, how he lightened the tedium of bed-rest after our various illnesses, playing games with us and reading aloud. Although Ella was there to look after us, we were almost always included in his invitations to matinees and dinners afterwards at restaurants, expeditions to San Francisco and the Alameda beaches, visits to relatives and friends. And always between him and me was the bond of the music we loved.

Search my memory as I may, I can find no hint of resentment that, by becoming Mother's husband, he might usurp Daddy's place in my life. The concept of "stepfather" in connection with him seems not to have occurred to me; Daddy was Daddy and Uncle Charlie was Uncle Charlie, separate and distinct forever. Only after I grew up did I recognize that in many small and endearing ways he was, for a brief time, more of a father to us than Daddy would ever be.

The one barrier that might have made it difficult, if not impossible, for me to accept this coming change had already crumbled. The bitter knowledge of Daddy's remarriage and his departure on the long voyage around the world had destroyed my long-held dream of an eventual fairy-tale ending to my separation from him. During the few years when the marriage seemed certain, though never really imminent, I did not relinquish that dream, but set the broken pieces aside, as if I knew that later it would be formulated more realistically.

For me, the most exciting part of the marriage plans was the new house Uncle Charlie was going to build for us. Evening after evening, he and Mother would sit at the big, square dining table discussing, then sketching, and finally drawing, floor plans. Even today, I never see graph paper without recalling the blue-squared yellow pad, the ruler and the row of freshly sharpened pencils spread out on the white tablecloth. "These are windows," Uncle Charlie would say, pointing to meticulously ruled double lines. "And here . . ." and the pencil tip would touch a tiny line drawn at an angle, "is the door to the kitchen." Sometimes they laid out the garden they would make around the house, the lawns in front and in back, the fruit trees with rows of vegetables in between, a group of silver birches here and, there, against the fence, massed flowering shrubs like those that had grown in Melissa's garden.

Almost every Sunday in good weather we walked over to look at the lot, already purchased, where the house would be built. It was on Jean Street, not far from the eastern tip of Lake Merritt, on a slope overlooking what was then called Pleasant Valley but has long since become Grand Avenue. A creek meandered down the little valley and there were still a few small farms. The lot was large and nearly level, with a sweeping view of the hills, and was covered during the spring and early summer with wild grasses and scattered poppies. One unforgettable day I found, for the first and the only time in my life, trembling grass growing there.

Frowning intently, Uncle Charlie would pace off the rectangle the house would occupy, marking the corners with whatever was at hand, a stone, a twig, a clump of wild mustard. "The walk will curve this way. . . . Here is the porch, and this is the living room, with the windows facing the hills. . . . Back here, with French doors going into the garden, are the little girls' bedroom and study and bath. . . ." (French doors! I had not the faintest idea what they were, but if they were French, they would be elegant.) And then he and Mother would survey it all contentedly for a long time before they turned to the equally absorbing pastime of reaffirming or altering their garden designs. It became so nearly real to me that sometimes I could almost see the house standing amidst its lawns and plantings, and if I closed my eyes, there we would be, living in it.

Why, I asked myself a thousand times before I reached some understanding of the mystery, did not this marriage take place? Once, in the last of the years we were to spend in the dreary bungalow, I recalled the pleasant house that was to have been built on Jean Street and asked Mother what had happened, why she had not married Uncle Charlie. She tried to explain, giving various vague reasons, none sufficient of themselves, only the total seeming to have any weight, but still I did not understand.

"Your father was very angry about it," she said at length. "And when he is angry, you know, he is very unpleasant and even unjust."

"But why didn't you get married anyway?" I protested. "*He* did!"

She shook her head. "No, I couldn't have done that."

"But why was he so angry?" I persisted.

She did not answer right away, and then she said softly, "I don't really know. He seemed to have a strange idea . . . well, I'll tell you about that when you're older. I kept hoping that he would come to see it differently after a while, and I persuaded Charlie to wait, but it wasn't any use. Finally, I realized that it wouldn't be fair to you little girls, or to Charlie either, to take a step your father disapproved so violently, so I told Charlie I could not marry him."

I remembered the fun we had always had together, and how happy Uncle Charlie had been when he was with us. "Wasn't he very sad about it?" I asked. "Didn't he try to make you change your mind?"

"He was sad about it," she answered simply. "And he did try for a long time to persuade me differently, but I couldn't agree. . . . He married someone else, you know, not very long ago, and the night before he was going to ask the lady to be his wife, he telephoned me for the last time. . . . Well," she sighed, "perhaps it was for the best, I don't know."

Lying before me are two documents, handwritten by Daddy in February, 1908. By themselves, they cast more shadow than light on what was involved in that stormy interview between Daddy and Mother and Uncle Charlie. A third pertinent document is missing, the agreement signed by Daddy and Mother at the time of their divorce. Why it was not among the letters and papers carefully preserved by Mother over the years, I do not know. Both of them mentioned it on occasion, and a copy must surely be among Daddy's private papers, but these, of course, have never been available to me.

If I have ever read this agreement, it was so long ago that I do not recall any of its terms, but I know that Mother regarded and referred to it as her "community property settlement." As far as I can make out, however, no real property was settled upon her. Apparently, Daddy had merely agreed, not to give her, but to provide her with, a home for herself and Bess and me. Construction was begun on the house on Thirty-first Street soon after the agreement was signed, but it is certain that Daddy retained title to this property; in the three wills written by him of which I have knowledge, two in 1905 and one in 1911, he made disposition of the bungalow, which he would scarcely have done if it did not belong to him.

In this same agreement, there appears to have been, in addition, mention of certain twenty-year endowment insurance policies, one on Daddy's life and two for smaller amounts on Mother's, the premiums on which Daddy agreed to continue to pay. Many years later these policies were to be the subject of bitter disagreement between them, Daddy insisting that he should receive all the endowments upon maturity of the policies. More than this I do not know. It seems clear, however, that the home and the insurance policies were substantial items in the agreement entered into at the time of the divorce, and that Mother, with no head for legal technicalities and complete trust in Daddy, sincerely believed these to be the community property which became hers with the signing of the agreement. One may ask reasonably: if these were not her share of their community property, what was her share? Surely, not merely the two Morris chairs and other odds and ends of household goods, and a few books!

Nevertheless, it was upon Mother's misapprehension of these matters that Daddy seized when she wrote him in Tahiti to announce her coming marriage, and it was his method and manner of attack which contributed to the ending of these marriage plans.

With Mother's letter in the accumulation of mail that awaited Daddy's arrival in Papeete had been communications indicating that the management of his financial affairs had been left in poor hands. He immediately altered his plans, left the *Snark* in Papeete and caught the next steamer for San Francisco. I do not believe, however, that the prime motive for his precipitate return was either the need to take care of these business matters or to settle the disposition of the bungalow. I suggest that there may have been a third and compelling reason.

The first document lying before me was the end product of the lengthy, often acrimonious discussion which took place on the fateful evening when I awoke to find him beside my bed. Dated in Oakland, February 1, 1908, it is an agreement signed by Daddy in which he promises to sell the bungalow to Mother for a specified cash sum upon her marriage to Uncle Charlie.

It is evident that either Daddy had convinced Mother that the bungalow was not in fact a part of her community property settlement or, what was more likely, she had remained unconvinced but refrained from argument. During all the years I knew her, she detested arguments about anything, but especially about financial matters, and almost invariably yielded rather than permit a dispute to be prolonged.

The second document is a letter written from Papeete a fortnight later, carefully conceived though carelessly composed, and containing certain interesting corrections and alterations. The large, barely legible handwriting sprawls across several half-sheets of paper.

"Dear Bessie," it begins, but lines have been drawn through "Bessie" and "Mother-Girl" written above, and it is signed "Daddy-Boy." He has been thinking of his agreement to sell the bungalow to her, he writes. (Each of the three times he refers to the bungalow, he has first written "490–27th," then corrected it to read "519–31st.") His thinking has led him to consider the possible resale of the property by Mother and "Charley" after it has come into their possession. Since, he states blandly, neither of them cares to make a profit out of him, it is only fair that if and when the property is resold by them, any increase in its value, which, he admits, he has surrendered by selling it to them, should come to him and not be retained by them as profit. He therefore asks them to give him a document to cover the years until Bess is twenty-one that will ensure his receipt of this profit.

It is odd that he first wrote "490–27th," the address of the house he had bought for Grandma London, and then, three times, corrected it to "519–31st," as if, despite his "agreement, promise and guarantee" of February 1, he was deeply unwilling to sell the bungalow.

More significant is the altered salutation and the signature. They had not spoken these affectionate names for a long time, although until he left on the *Snark*, Daddy had used them in the inscriptions he placed in the copies of his books he gave her. Now they appeared again, an incongruous frame to a letter with whose spirit and contents they had nothing in common.

Incongruous, yes. But I am sure they did not seem so to Daddy, for in thus boldly reasserting the enduring bond between them, was he not perhaps also reasserting his claim upon her, a claim older by all his life than their marriage, which it had encompassed. The point is too delicate to belabor. It is an ancient device of men, hungering for what was denied them in childhood, to find in the mother of their children a mother-surrogate for themselves. Having found it, a second rejection is unendurable to contemplate, and the once-bereft child in the man will stop at nothing to safeguard his possessions.

Hence, I suggest, Daddy's wrath the night they discussed the coming marriage, his incredible charges and thinly veiled accusations. In his desperate need for something that would conceal, especially from himself, not only his panic but its true nature, he had seized upon the issue of the bungalow, impugning Mother's and Charlie's motives, insinuating that they were attempting to take advantage of his love for his daughters to obtain the bungalow for themselves, and not hesitating to doubt their veracity when they indignantly denied his assertions. But beneath his vividly expressed outrage at the picture he had invented of their conspiracy to rob him of his property, he was frantically seeking a way to prevent the marriage and preserve the status quo which suited him so admirably. It was not in his power to forbid the marriage, no matter how much he may have wanted to do so, and even in the midst of his emotional turmoil, he recognized that Mother had the same right to remarry as he, who had already exercised it.

I am sure that his tantrum lasted longer than was needful, that Mother and Uncle Charlie, shocked and dismayed by his intemperate manner and language, were helpless to stem his rage until it had run its course. When, as soon as the opportunity came to end the scene, they quickly accepted his proposal to sell the house to Mother upon their marriage, I think Daddy felt he had won a victory. There is a little air of triumph in the follow-up letter from Papeete two weeks later in which he made the astounding demand that, "in all fairness," they should freely relinquish for many years their right to dispose of the house at a profit—triumph, and a little complacency, too, as if he was happily certain that his new scheme of harassment would demolish the already shaky marriage plans. But the agreement bound him to sell, not they to buy, and before his letter reached Oakland their plans were underway to build the house on Jean Street.

Daddy's anger on the night of the discussion, his excessive discourtesy and the certainty that this would undoubtedly continue and increase, had their effect, however, not upon Uncle Charlie, who urged immediate marriage, but upon Mother, who, for all their sakes, dreaded a repetition, actual or in letters, of the distressing scene. But I wonder if what really determined her to postpone the marriage was not Daddy's substitution of "Mother-Girl" for "Bessie" in the letter from Papeete. Long afterward she would occasionally say, "I wonder what made him call me 'Mother-Girl' at the beginning of such a letter?," and sometimes she was genuinely puzzled and sometimes pleased that he had invoked the old affectionate term at that critical time. "He never called me so again," she would add wistfully.

She did not understand then or ever, any more than he did, what that love-name out of a happier past had probably come to mean to him, but she must have felt its urgent, unspoken plea. "Dear Mother-Girl, such you will always be to me"—thus, more than once after their separation he had inscribed his books to her. Now he was begging her to keep the special bond between them intact, to change nothing, to remain his mother-girl. And because all her life she never ceased to love him and could not bear to hurt him, she yielded, putting off the marriage to that more propitious time which never came.

He never forgave her, however, for that one attempt to make her life whole again, and to the end of his days his dislike of Uncle Charlie equaled hers of the Beauty.

It seems to me sad that this marriage was prevented. It would have been a good marriage, I think, a happy one. And time was to come when, if it had been consummated, I believe it might have permitted the realization of one of Daddy's most cherished hopes. Knowledge of this episode in 1908 came to me long after it had occurred, but understanding of it came even later, as part of a larger understanding. It is with that understanding that I have set it down here, in justice to everyone.

The house on Jean Street was my first acquaintance with planning for a tangible future since Daddy's move to the ranch had compelled me to alter my perspective and accept the painful knowledge that my hopes and dreams would be neither quickly nor easily realized. So much depended upon Daddy himself, but because his actions, as I had learned early, were rarely predictable and because, in any case, I had to grow a good deal older before I could attain the least of my goals, what I thought of as my future stretched ahead like a straight, empty road, featureless, without landmarks, slowly vanishing in a hazy distance in which, I was confident, would some day loom the faint outlines of what I longed for so ardently. Besides, before I even saw Daddy again, space and time had to be traversed: immeasurable, unthinkable spans of oceans and islands and continents, and years that were inconceivable to me, who had so few of them.

Now, however, the house on Jean Street was in a near future. I could clearly see that house, the new garden, the new way of life; perhaps, I dared to think secretly, there might be a baby brother. For a long time work was going to be started on the new house "very soon," not "some-time" or, vaguest of all, "bye and bye," which in my limited experience usually meant never. We pored happily over the house plans, arranged and rearranged the garden, chose and rechose color schemes for the rooms, and, night after night, playing "Let's imagine," Bess and I dreamed aloud, turn and turn about, of living in the house on Jean Street.

At the same time, new knowledge and new ideas, along with new people and experiences, were widening my horizons. Slowly, impercep-tibly, the void created by Daddy's absence began to be filled. As he receded from me in time and distance, echoes of his voice and laughter grew ever fainter, memory-pictures faded and only at intervals would a sense of loss and a longing for him return to haunt and sadden me.

"_She trieth real hard, but does not succeed in breaking the Camera._**"**

This photo, and all subsequent photos, are from the album Joan, Her Book, _assembled by Jack London. Courtesy of Waring Jones._

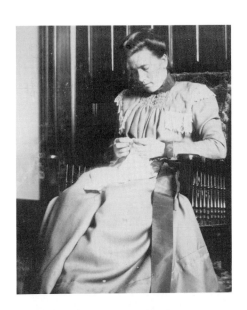

"The Mater, before she was the Mater.
What is it she worketh so busily upon?**"**

"The Pater, before he was the Pater. Behold
the cheerful Countenance!**"**

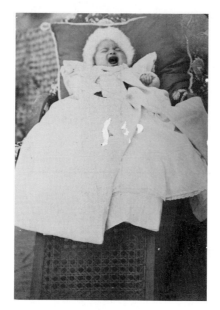

"She Smileth at Three Months . . ."

*"And Cryeth immediately after . . .
at Three Months and Five Minutes.
N.B.—And Weigheth Fifteen
Pounds."*

"_She prepareth to discard her Nipple,_
after four months' Wear and Tear,
wherefore the Mater looketh
exceeding Melancholic.**"**

▌She inclineth the Pater to scratch his Chin.▐

"At Six Months Joan sitteth on the Beach at Sunny Cove and looketh Sphinx-like."

"Her Grandfather Maddern, who
maketh her first bed, which
happened to be a Basket."

"Grandma London, who yearly
presenteth one marvelous Spoon."

❝The Tent in which she Sleepeth, at
Camp Reverie. Behold the Wash
upon the Line: Whose Wash?❞

❝The Pater remembereth that all
Good Things and Camp Reveries
come to an End, and that it is Time
to depart to the City Folk.❞

"At Nine Months she Biketh with the Pater, who is the Pater no longer, but Daddy. Behold Joan's House in the Distance."

"At Ten Months she Walketh, in the Walker, likewise by holding on to Things and preventing them from Tumbling Over."

"Her Favorite Nook by the Heliothrope."

"And at Twelve Months, which is her Second Birthday, she holdeth her First Birthday Party."

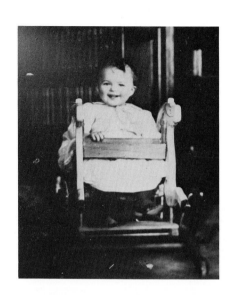

❝Thirteen Months—she rideth in Uncle Fred's Horseys.❞

❝Eighteen Months—Her Daddy Pulleth his Freight for South Africa, but Windeth Up, instead, in the 'Awful East.'❞

❚_Nineteen Months—While Daddy is away, Joan trieth to break the Commandments, her Neck, and the Mater's Heart._**❚**

❚_Twenty Months—She gathereth in Everything in Sight._**❚**

"She beginneth to Become Aware of Herself."

SEVEN

All this time as I have explored the past, remembering people, places and events, I have not deliberately denied Grandma London her place there, but unconsciously I must have pushed her into the background, mollifying her impatience for recognition by mentioning her once in a while but really counselling her to wait and promising that she would have her chance to parade across my small stage. Now, as I recall this second year that Daddy was away on the *Snark* voyage and note with surprise how frequent a visitor she was to the bungalow, I find that she has flung open the door and entered my story. She was always a willful woman, and she has not changed in my memory of her. I yield to her insistence.

There is a picture of her in *Joan, Her Book.* When I pored over the album seeking the lost memories of my babyhood, I used to glance at it only briefly; no child could read that inscrutable face. The caption under the photograph, however, was an attractive one:

> Grandma London, who yearly presenteth one marvellous
> spoon.

I knew about those spoons. There were four of them in the Korean chest—heavy, beautifully wrought, sterling silver teaspoons with gleaming golden bowls. "Joan" was engraved on the handles, and on the back, "From G.M.L." and a date. It was a long time before I realized that those baffling initials stood for "Grand Ma London." Her wish was to provide each of her granddaughters with a full dozen of these beautiful

113

teaspoons, but this soon proved too extravagant an ambition for her limited income. The latest of my four spoons bears the date January 15, 1904; of Bess's three, October 20, 1904.

Years later I came to understand the significance of those "marvellous" spoons: this was the way proper people had behaved in Grandma's youth, a way whose value she had realized too late perhaps to preserve for herself, but which she wanted for Bess and me. Even today, however, the face in the photograph is only a little less inscrutable, although now I can at least report what I see there.

She is dressed in black, and her small, black hat—I think it may be a bonnet—is topped by a cluster of flowers, the whole conveying a certain elegance and distinction which was not really typical, but which I like to associate with her. It is her face which commands attention. Spectacled, large-nosed, square-jawed, it could be the face of a man. Beneath well-defined brows her gaze is disconcerting, faintly hostile, even a little contemptuous; above the determined chin, her mouth is a firm straight line. Humorless, stubborn, opinionated, intelligent—it is an extraordinary face.

No other person influenced Daddy so greatly as his mother. It was their common tragedy, however, that her role was almost wholly negative, and, because of this, its effect upon him, especially during his earliest years when impressions are indelible, was damaging. I had no knowledge of this for many years and could not even have suspected it when I was younger, having been brought up in the old-fashioned belief that all mothers were good mothers merely because they were mothers. Even then, however, it was obvious to me that Daddy did not love his mother in the same way as Bess and I loved ours. He was invariably gentle with her, but never tender, not especially interested in her ideas or what she did, not really glad to see her or be with her. I used to hear them talk together seriously of many matters, but never laugh together.

Familiar as she was to me then, she was a figure of mystery; to this day she invites endless speculation. In a sombre, unnaturally quiet way, she was also a compelling figure, so compelling, in fact, that I believe that is really why I have not allowed her to come forward before this, doubting my ability to keep her within bounds.

There were several Grandma Londons. The one in the album I could accept as mine, although she had aged greatly in the several years since the picture was made, but the others whom I heard about from Mother and Aunt Jennie, and even from Grandma herself, bore little resemblance to the one I knew.

First, there was a little girl named Flora Wellman who lived in a big house in a town called Massillon in far-off Ohio, whose mother with the lovely name of Eleanor Garret Jones had died a few weeks before the little girl's third birthday. After that, there was a girl of twelve or thirteen lying desperately ill with a fever, and when at last she recovered, her eyesight was ruined forever, all her pretty hair had fallen out and very little of it ever came in again, and she herself scarcely grew afterward. That girl, although she would never tell me why, hated her stepmother so much, she said, that she ran away when she was a little older and never went home again. "Where did you go?" I asked her once. "My sisters, Mary and Susan, were older than I and had their own homes by then," she replied, and would say no more.

The Flora who ran away was a young woman, not pretty at all, she recalled, but with an attractive figure despite her short stature, and with beautiful small hands and feet. This was the one who had danced with the Union soldiers during the Civil War; and made lint for bandages out of old linen sheets and handkerchiefs. She was twenty-one years old when Abraham Lincoln was assassinated, and she remembered the great mourning throughout the land. (Did she say that once she had seen him? I cannot be sure.)

This Grandma London, who was still Flora Wellman then, interested me greatly because it was so difficult to believe that she had ever existed. She was young, always elegantly dressed and vain enough to leave her thick-lensed spectacles at home whenever she dared, although she could scarcely see without them. Until she ran away, she had lived in a large, luxurious house, a mansion, she called it, set in the midst of well-kept grounds that covered half a block. I have seen a photograph of that house, thanks to Sue Eleanor Jorgeson, whose father, Flora's half-brother, was also born there. Grandma London did not stretch the truth when she described her home to me. Simple, elegant, beautifully proportioned, it was typical of the homes built by the wealthy in the 1830s. Its two stories contained thirty-three rooms; a wide, pillared porch surrounded the lower floor; underneath was a huge basement. A tall, wrought-iron fence enclosed the garden with its trees and shrubs and sweeping lawns. When young Flora Wellman lived in this house, she was waited upon by servants and rode in fine carriages; she sat for her portrait (long since vanished, but I have seen the one of her half-brother which was done at the same time); she did not go to school but was educated by private tutors; she studied music and painting and elocution, but learned none of the household arts except breadmaking and, especially, needlework, at which, despite her wretched eyesight, she was extraordinarily proficient.

"Did you have a cruel stepmother?" I asked one day, settling myself comfortably to listen to a new and intimate version of the cruel stepmother story I had read in many fairy tales.

"Not at all," she replied surprisingly. "She was a kind and lovely woman."

"Then, why . . ." I began, but she went on, "As a matter of fact, I can't remember now why I quarreled with her. I suppose it was probably all my fault. Because I was so young when my own mother died, and then was sick for so long, I was spoiled by my father and sisters. I think I must have been very difficult to get along with."

"But didn't you love your Daddy?" I could not believe that any girl would run away from her father.

"Certainly, but I guess I disliked her more." Then, abruptly terminating the conversation, she said, "Oh well, it's all so long ago now that I can hardly remember it. Besides, it doesn't matter any more."

I would look at the tiny, stooped old lady who was my Grandma London and try in vain to see in her the rebellious young Flora Wellman. The faded blue eyes peered through thick glasses, the large, domineering nose commanded a slack-mouthed face that had fallen into wrinkles, the once-pretty hands were misshapen and liver-spotted. Only her feet were still young, and smaller than mine by the time I was seven; even in the high-laced old-lady shoes, it was not hard to imagine them dancing.

The darkest part of the mystery—and how long it was to be before I could unravel even a part of it—came between the rich and fashionable Flora Wellman and the next one. Ten years after the end of the Civil War, she was living in poverty in San Francisco, giving piano lessons and doing needlework and paying Aunt Jennie to take care of her baby.

"She was the littlest woman I ever saw," Aunt Jennie remembered, who was not very tall herself. "And I never knew anyone with a mind so set on getting ahead. She was on the go from morning till night, teaching and sewing and seeing people. She seemed to be sad and angry at the same time and all the time, but her angriness would not let her just be sad for a while and get over it, but kept driving her and driving her. I took care of her baby, but she was so busy that she couldn't even come to see him very often."

What had happened? I used to wonder. Why had she left Ohio and her wealthy family? All she would say when I asked her was that she had grown tired of Ohio and had welcomed the opportunity to go to California as the traveling companion of a rich woman. Once she told me that she had made this journey only a little while after the completion of the first railroad that went all the way to the Pacific Coast; if so, she could have arrived in San Francisco as early as 1869 or 1870.

I had no reason, of course, to suspect that she was not telling me what really happened; now I know that this was part of the story she had invented and stubbornly adhered to until she died, to account for the years between the end of the Civil War and 1876—surely the most interesting years of her life. But even then questions arose in my mind to which, when I voiced them, she would give no answer. Why didn't her family help her when she was so poor? Had she finally quarreled so bitterly with them that they would not, or had they lost their money and were poor, too?' What became of the rich lady? Did she go back to Ohio? Why did Grandma stay in California? And most interesting of all, what did she do before Aunt Jennie became acquainted with her? Grandma would never say, and no one else knew.

We shall never know how, or when or why Flora Wellman came West; actually, we shall never really know where she was and what she did after she left Massillon, or even when that was. But it is possible to pick up her trail with some certainty in Seattle in 1873, and definitely in San Francisco in 1874, and find there a little later the bizarre, tragic and least recognizable of all the Grandma Londons, who, as Flora Chaney, achieved a brief notoriety in 1875. My Grandma London would furiously protest Mrs. Chaney's entrance on the scene, would deny that there ever had been such a person. But she had existed; it was Flora Chaney who married John London. I was twelve years old when I first learned of her—from her son.

There were two more Grandma Londons, both difficult to reconcile with mine, before, at the age of fifty-eight, she became my grandmother. There was a picture of the first of these two, taken when she was in her early forties, and if I looked at it closely enough, I could recognize her—the spectacles, the big, ugly nose, the scanty hair, still pale brown at that time, Aunt Jennie said; a hard, determined face, with an aggressive jaw-line and an unsmiling mouth. Together with the small, square shoulders and neat bust, these features gave the impression of a woman who knew her mind, laid down the law and expected to be obeyed.

The other Grandma London was the one immediately preceding mine; it was her picture that was in my album. My only source of information about this Grandma was Mother, but I could make little sense of her anecdotes. The metamorphosis from enemy to friend which had taken place between mother-in-law and daughter-in-law in a relatively short time was clear to Mother, but not to me. As far back as I could remember they were friends, sharing a common interest in Daddy and us two little girls and a common fate in having been set aside and left behind by Daddy.

But it had not been that way in the beginning. Scarcely acquainted with each other, and unequipped either by experience or temperament to meet one of the oldest and most difficult situations involving two women, they found themselves sharing the same household. Mother, three days married, had unwittingly deposed Grandma as "the lady of the house." "Deposed" is too harsh a word for Mother's shy assumption of her position as Daddy's wife, but it was precisely how Grandma regarded it and she reacted accordingly. It is a common enough story, but this one had an uncommon ending in that friendship was finally achieved.

The ascent from the depths of poverty and despair into which Grandma had been flung by catastrophic events in the months preceding Daddy's birth had been long and arduous. For a quarter of a century she had labored stubbornly against heavy odds to regain a certain cultural and economic status, not the wealth and social position of her youth in Ohio, for she had turned her back on that, but an equivalent of what she had known later. A mere escape from poverty, desirable as that certainly might be, would not have satisfied her. Insofar as poverty meant merely a lack of creature comforts or even security, I do not believe she either feared or hated it. What she did hate was the part it played in denying her opportunity to achieve distinction in some way, to use whatever talents or abilities she may have possessed and especially to know people who were making rewarding use of their own.

Then she had unexpectedly found herself on the threshold of the kind of life she had longed for, and one, moreover, in which she felt she had earned a place because she had contributed to it. Was it not she who had first encouraged her son to write stories when he was seventeen years old, by urging him to enter the writing contest conducted by a San Francisco newspaper, in which he had won the twenty-five dollar first prize? Now his stories were appearing in magazines, and an eastern publisher had signed him up to do a novel. People, interesting people, were beginning to seek him out, to visit him and sometimes stay for supper. She was his hostess, cooking and serving their simple meals; afterwards she could listen to good talk once more; she could even express her own ideas to courteous listeners. And to cap it all, they had just moved into the finest house she had lived in since she left Ohio all those years ago.

It is not to be wondered that she bitterly resented the young stranger her son had married. The violent outbreaks of temper and the bitter moods which had characterized her behavior since childhood had begun to subside; now they again sprang free of control. An irreparable situation might have resulted, except that Mother was not only incapable of quarreling with anyone, but was eager to like this tiny, vital woman for her own sake as well as her son's.

By her own admission after she and Mother had become friends, Grandma behaved very sadly. Matters reached a climax within a few months in a tragi-comic scene at the supper table when, either by chance or design, Grandma sank without warning into one of the trances she had experienced throughout many years of spiritualistic beliefs and practices, and began to speak in the deep and terrible tones of her "control," who in life, as Grandma had long since established, had been an American Indian named Plume. Startled, and believing that the older woman was in the throes of some kind of seizure, Mother immediately picked up the glass of water beside her plate and dashed its contents in Grandma's face. Grandma was furious, Mother was unbearably embarrassed when the manifestation was finally explained and Daddy outraged both of them for different reasons by roaring with laughter. A few days later Grandma moved to a nearby cottage and the two women never again lived under the same roof. Nor was the truce they tacitly established ever broken. Instead, a curious, sympathetic friendship began to grow between them, culminating in Grandma's outspoken loyalty to Mother during the separation and divorce and continuing to the end of her life.

And, finally, there was *my* Grandma London.

For twenty-two years, from the time I was born until I was a young married woman with a baby of my own, she occupied a definite place in my life, and yet how little I really knew of her. And for all her insistence upon her place in this story, she seems reluctant now to appear as I remember her, but only as I came finally to understand her. Melissa, who passed away when I was barely four, is easy to recall: I can find her in every garden and well-kept house and fragrant kitchen. Aunt Jennie comes to mind as readily, with the instant rekindling in my heart of the unchanging love that bound us to each other. But it is not so with Grandma London.

There are people who feel a gulf between themselves and children and all their lives are unable to cross it. Grandma was one of these. Her inability to communicate even with her own child had compounded her tragic failure as a mother; she was little more successful in the easier role of grandmother.

If she was happy to see Bess and me when she came to visit us, we did not know it; if she loved us, we were not aware of it. This did not distress us, for we were amply provided with warmth and affection from other sources. We simply accepted it as Grandma's way. Besides, even if it lacked enthusiasm, her interest in us was sufficiently evident. When we really had something to show or tell her, she gave us her full attention, and although it was more fun to exhibit our accomplishments to Aunt Jennie, who was always gratifyingly amazed, we nevertheless valued Grandma's terse approval.

She did not talk *with* Bess and me, but *to* us, and that rarely. Most of the stories of her youth in Ohio and of San Francisco in the 1870s, where were her favorite reminiscences, were told in long monologues directed to Mother, although Bess and I made the better audience. When we interrupted to ask questions or to urge her to continue when she ceased talking as abruptly as she had begun, we were generally ignored. Watching her impassive face, I used to wonder where her thoughts were taking her in the profound silences that followed, broken at intervals by slow, deep sighs. When she and Mother discussed their special, private topics, their conversation was brisk and ambiguous and I could make neither head nor tail of it.

In some way, these private conversations were connected with yet another mystery surrounding Grandma: although she frequently spent the day and had supper with us at the bungalow, we were never allowed to visit her. When Mother eventually explained this prohibition, the mystery merely deepened; there is something incomprehensible about it to this day. But I regret that I have no childhood memories of Grandma London in her own home, of having supper at her table or—oh, unimaginable!— of spending the night with her.

Slowly, now, I begin to see her as she was in those days, small, old, moving with greater deliberation and stooping a little more each year, dressed always with scrupulous neatness in her grey or black old-lady clothes and never without a bonnet or gloves when she was on the street. I can see her shading her eyes with her hand, watching us noncommittally as we performed stunts for her on the swing and rings and acting bar in the backyard. And I can see her sitting in the small Morris chair, making buttonholes in the dresses and panties and petticoats Mother had sewed for us—and never were there buttonholes so exquisite, and always outlasting every garment—peering through her spectacles at her work, or at us or over our heads at Mother, with whom she shared a rich vocabulary of flashing glances that supplemented their cryptic remarks whenever they talked about the Beauty.

Solitary, self-contained, undemonstrative, she laughed seldom, smiled rarely, never complained. She had a poor opinion of most people, usually expressed with flat finality, although once in a while her voice would rise in brief indignation. That her life had not been what she had striven for, that it had, in fact, turned out badly in comparison with her grandiose ambitions, she had accepted at last without rancor, blaming no one, least of all herself. I do not believe that she ever admitted defeat, however; she merely stopped fighting.

That she had struggled long and fiercely for what she wanted and against what she hated I sensed even as a little girl. But what had she striven for? What did she desire, what did she hate?

I think that she had hated ordinariness and dullness and had striven in every way to escape them. Her youthful rebellion against the dullness of her comfortable life in Massillon had won for her a dozen exciting, intellectually and emotionally stimulating years, but when these had ended in disaster, the deadly dullness of poverty and of toil for which she was ill-prepared became the enemy she fought henceforth without respite. It was an unequal contest. She had an excellent mind and a better education than most, but she was not a gifted woman. No hunger to create drove her to seek expression in any of the arts; it is doubtful if she even enjoyed them. Year after year she had taught music, yet none of us ever heard her play the piano; through all my childhood I longed for piano lessons, but it was never suggested that she instruct me, nor did she volunteer. She was a superb needlewoman, but she took no pleasure in her skill, although a hand-turned hem, a row of delicate featherstitching or a buttonhole fashioned by her made other needle-women exclaim over their perfection. Unlike Melissa Maddern, she could not discern beauty in the commonplace or delight in the fine performance of humdrum tasks.

And I think that perhaps she did not really know what she sought, or, so profound and habitual was her dissatisfaction, would she have recognized it if she had chanced upon it. Spiritualism probably came closest to answering her need, and if she believed in anything, it was in a spirit-world and in her ability to communicate, meaningfully or other-wise, with those who inhabited it. It set her apart from others, made her different, out of the ordinary, and that was important to her. In the end, of course, it failed her. She could not overcome her son's disbelief and active dislike of her practices, and as her circle of interested friends and acquaintances diminished with the years, she finally abandoned her attempts to impress others with her gift.

Bess and I never witnessed any manifestation of her powers, and she did not speak to us of her beliefs, but they were obliquely referred to from time to time in her conversations with Mother. Thus I became familiar with the name "Plume," although I did not know who or what it meant. Sometimes Mother would tease her gently: "What does Plume tell you about that?" Grandma took no offense, replying with dignity, or more often courteously ignoring the question. Once only, during the few years she lived after Daddy's death, did she directly mention the subject to me, confiding matter-of-factly, "I see and talk with your father every day," and changing the subject while I was still searching for a proper response.

She read omnivorously and talked to Mother with zest about the books that especially interested her. At such times she grew animated, spoke quickly and moved her hands in small, emphatic gestures. What were the books she enjoyed? I do not know, but I have one clue to the kind of book she liked. Years later, when she could no longer leave her house but sat all day in her armchair, in summer by the sunny window, in winter by the stove in the dining room, there was always a stack of public library books beside her. "I read all day," she told me when I commented upon them, but when I bent over to see the titles, she stopped me. "They're only novels," she said scornfully. "I read them and forget them. They pass the time and don't make me think. There's enough of thinking and remembering at night when I can't sleep. At least the days go by quickly." So the books she enjoyed and discussed with Mother must have rarely been fiction.

I have wondered why my first viable memories of Grandma London date from this period and not earlier. Partly, of course, it was because, no longer blinded by the blazing light of Daddy's omnipresence in my life, I was able for the first time to see her clearly as a person in her own right; partly it was because I had reached an age when I could begin to know and wonder about this complex and difficult woman. But there is another reason, knowledge of which came to me only recently and has made me realize that I could scarcely have failed to be impressed by her at that time. At the age of sixty-five, Flora Wellman was making a final effort to be distinctive and outstanding, if only within a small circle, and for a little while was a more vivid and outgoing person than she had been for a long time, or would ever be again.

No hint of this venture that I can remember reached me then, nor did Mother ever refer to it in after years. Yet she must have known about it, if not from Grandma herself, then certainly from Aunt Jennie, who invariably recounted the incidents of their quiet lives. It is probable that Mother did not appreciate its significance and simply forgot about it.

Grandma must have conceived the idea when the emptiness of her life after Daddy's departure on the *Snark* could no longer be endured. She must have hesitated over it for months, then, committing herself to it, made careful plans before issuing invitations to several young journalists with whom she had become acquainted through Daddy to gather at her home on Sunday evenings for supper and conversation. And it was a success. They probably came the first time out of curiosity, hoping perhaps for a story or feature article, but replete with an excellent supper, they stayed afterwards enjoying the talk and discussion of their colleagues and the unique, well-informed little woman who was their hostess. And this was Grandma's triumph: they returned again and again at her invitation.

It was Franck Havenner, then a young Oakland newspaperman, later, after years of public service, to be sent to Congress from San Francisco, who described these gatherings to me. "I remember those evenings with great pleasure," he said. "Good company, good food, good talk—we young men appreciated and enjoyed all of it. . . . Your grandmother was an extremely interesting woman, you know."

On her behalf, I am grateful for this small tribute. The measure of praise she received in her lifetime was scant. She was not pretty, or attractive, or charming or even pleasing, although at one time or another she must have wanted very much to be all of these, but she *was* interesting. I regret that there were not more who found her so. Her detractors have been many. Some have dismissed her as eccentric or freakish, as cold-hearted, selfish and egotistical. Others, with intimate knowledge of her misfortunes, have smugly declared, "She brought it all on herself . . . she had only herself to blame," ignoring not only the colossal handicaps that burdened her, but also the valiant spirit with which she battled, rightly or wrongly, to achieve ends that were not ignoble.

I could wish that she might have been a loving mother to Daddy—more to the point, perhaps, that life had so shaped her that it was possible for her to have been such a mother. I could wish that I might recall her as a grandmother with warmth and affection. But if I did not love her, I liked her, as I know she liked me. If she did not praise me, she gave me her tacit approval when I had earned it, and I valued her good opinion. If she was critical of my shortcomings, she was either silent or tactful about them, for she never hurt my feelings or bruised my young ego. She did not complain, or blame anyone or pity herself in my hearing. She was interesting, and I liked and respected her. Out of that liking and respect, nourished by Mother's appreciation of her loyalty and friendship, grew slowly my compassionate understanding of this strange, lonely little woman who was my grandmother.

EIGHT

It was during these same years of Daddy's absence that I entered and wandered curiously for a long time in a wilderness of ideas and traditions whose gateway was Sunday school and church, but at whose heart lay the great concepts of life and death. Although I tried earnestly, I failed to understand most of what Sunday school and church offered me, but because I was under no compulsion to believe or have faith without understanding, I was free to explore at will this realm of beauty and mystery.

No emphasis was placed on religion in our home, and Bess and I received no formal religious instruction. Mother had not attended church since her marriage, but she taught us to recite "Now I lay me down to sleep" when we were very small, and later, the Lord's prayer. Thus we early had the fundamentals of a religious vocabulary, but no inkling of the meaning of the words.

Little by little, we learned more: Christ, whose other name was Jesus, was a great and good man who had lived a long time ago and who had happened to be born on Christmas day; he loved children and the poor and unfortunate—he loved all people. There was a storybook, the Bible, that told about Christ, and about other men and women who had lived even longer ago. The stories were interesting, more like fairy tales than real happenings, and we liked fairy tales.

It was God, whom Aunt Jennie always and other people sometimes called the Lord, who puzzled us. Dimly we sensed that he was not a person, as Christ had been, but the word "spirit," the only answer grown-ups gave us, conveyed nothing. We were very curious about God, yet every path we followed in our search for knowledge and understanding led us further from belief and nearer to a cheerful agnosticism. We even developed a sort of catechism in the hope of some day finding a clue.

"Who made the world?" one or the other of us would begin.

"God."

"Who made God?"

"Oh, a little bird."

"Who made the little bird?"

"A tiny shell."

"Who made the tiny shell?"

"A grain of sand."

"Who made the grain of sand?"

"Oh, well . . . a speck of dust."

"And who made the speck of dust?"

We could go no further; our progression toward a First Cause, always from the larger to the smaller, had come to an end. Besides, we knew that if we did manage to name a creator smaller than a speck of dust, the inexorable next question would immediately present itself. So we remained unbelievers, although we were ready and even eager to believe if someone could convince us.

My first knowledge of death came when I was very young, but it was imparted so simply and gently and the hereafter was so appropriately named that I felt neither shock nor grief.

One day I realized that I had not seen Grandma Maddern for a long time.

"She has gone away," Mother said when I questioned her.

"Isn't she coming back?"

Mother shook her head. "She was very tired and ill, you know, so she went where she would be well again and happy."

"But *where* is she?" I persisted.

Mother hesitated. "In God's garden," she said softly.

Of course! I thought, pleased. Where else but in a garden where she would be well and happy?

"Can I see God's garden?"

"Sometime," Mother promised, "when you are a little older."

And when we eventually did go to the cemetery, it was indeed a glorious garden, with great trees and stretches of lawn, and statues and charming, little stone houses and birds and flowers everywhere. Looking back, it seems to me that the concept of God the Gardener was the finest and most satisfying of the many suggested to me in my childhood.

Everyone at Miss Merriman's went to Sunday school. Dominated by my passionate desire to conform in all ways, I begged Mother to let me go, also.

On the corner of Twenty-ninth Street and Telegraph Avenue, shadowed by huge, old trees, still stands the little Trinity Episcopal Church, where, because it was conveniently near the bungalow, Bess and I first attended Sunday school. It is a quaint, storybook kind of church, austere, angular and old; it belongs in an old-fashioned town, not in a modern city. Ever since I can remember, the wooden exterior has seemed freshly painted dark red, and the shrubbery and lawn are meticulously tended.

Sunday school was a disappointment. Eagerly at first, and then conscientiously, I paid close attention to everything, joined enthusiastically in the hymn-singing and prayers, listened to the Bible stories related by the teacher and shared in the questions and answers that followed. It was no use. Always I felt that something was escaping me that the others seemed to find in the hymns and prayers and stories. I thought Uncle Charlie's music was more beautiful than the Sunday school songs, and only the magic-stories—the ones about miracles, and of the flood and the ark and the dove and of Jonah and the whale—held my interest; despite a growing skepticism, I still clung to my belief in magic. Then Mother's friend, Mrs. Morrow, who was our courtesy-Aunt Edith, briefly checked my growing boredom by persuading Mother to have us baptized.

When Mother discussed this ceremony with the rector of Trinity Church, a controversy arose. It appeared that we were not properly named. "Joan" was outlandish; in all his years of ministry, the rector said, he had never baptized anyone with this name. (Joan of Arc had not yet been canonized; actually, I was the only Joan I knew until I met a single contemporary when I was eighteen.) As for "Bess," it was no name at all but a nickname; she would certainly have to be baptized Elizabeth. Finally, neither of us had a middle name. This omission must be rectified; everyone should have a middle name.

Mother was adamant: we would be baptized Joan and Bess, without any middle names, or we would not be baptized at all. The rector yielded unhappily, and in return, Mother volunteered her own, never-used middle name for the record. The parish register shows that Joan London and Bess London were baptized in the Trinity Episcopal Church on May 17, 1908; the names of the parents are listed as Jack London and Bessie May London, the godparents as Edith Eliza Allen Morrow and Charles Harold Milner.

Of the ceremony itself I recall only that I had a new dress, that the baptismal water was shudderingly cold and that I protested indignantly when it ran off the top of my head and spotted my new tan shoes. But I do remember the church that day, empty save for ourselves, the chill and gloom unrelieved by the pallid daylight that came through the high north window near the font—so different from the warmly beautiful church I later came to know so well.

Just when my interest in Sunday school had receded to the vanishing point, I was invited to join the girls' Friday afternoon sewing circle, and there began for me the only satisfying association I was to have with the Trinity Church. We gathered after school in one of the parlors, a dozen or so little girls. What we sewed I do not know, but I remember the friendly grey-haired lady who taught us to take tiny, even running-stitches and to turn almost invisible hems. It was very pleasant, sitting there with the other girls in a circle near the windows where the light was best, all of us chattering at intervals but mostly intent on what we were doing, relaxed and comfortable because school was over for the week and the next day would be Saturday. But for me, it was merely a prelude to the best part of the afternoon. At five minutes to four, we put our sewing away and quietly, quietly, went along a narrow passage and through a door into the church to attend the four o'clock Litany service.

And now the little church glowed with color, and from red-carpeted floor to high-peaked roof was vibrant with organ music. Late afternoon sunlight streamed through the tall stained-glass window behind the altar, transfiguring everything it touched: the pages of an open prayer book, the rector's cheek, my own hand would be violet or green or ruby-red. And the music itself, so unlike the Sunday school hymn-music, took on the same rich hues as it swelled out from the organ pipes and filled the church.

A handful of elderly women and a few men, silent, withdrawn, sat apart from each other in the pews or knelt on the fat, red cushions in brief prayer before the service began. Observing their actions, I solemnly imitated them, feeling self-important as I performed the ritual, but understanding no more of it than of the service itself. Its fascination lay, I believe, as much in its incomprehensibility as in its beauty of color and sound. The rector intoned the words so that their shape was blurred and their import lost; the congregation murmured the responses. Unfettered by meaning, the rising and falling of the single voice, the uninflected drone of the replies, the soft sibilances and curiously drawn-out -ings of the participles were another kind of music that merged in beauty and mystery with the jewel-toned prisms of light and the muted thunder of the organ.

It did not occur to me that this was a religious rite, for it did not seem to involve either God or Christ in any way. They belonged with the Sunday school singing and Bible stories, while the Litany service was like a play, with music and color taking the place of words—a very ancient play in which I was both participant and spectator.

The lilies and massed blossoms of Easter, the tall candles, fragrant pine boughs and joyful songs of Christmas delighted me, but the four o'clock Litany on Friday afternoons was the best. For three years I rarely failed to attend. And yet it was during that same period that I became, once and for all, an unbeliever.

Bess and I had a tiny flock of tiny chickens. We were very proud of these bantams, took care of them ourselves and loved them dearly. Mrs. Kendall gave us the nucleus, three miniature hens, speckled brown, speckled white and snowy white. When they began to lay, we were astonished by the tiny, perfect eggs and needed no coaxing to eat our breakfasts on the mornings they were served to us. Not long afterwards, Glen's friend, the milkman, presented us with a gorgeous bantam rooster, all scarlet and black and gold and vivid blue. He accepted his status as chief of the barnyard seriously and with intense pride, and the little hens were obviously delighted with him.

We could not find a perfect name for so perfect a bird for a long time. Then one of Daddy's numerous hobo friends, who for years used to appear at our back door, greet us by name and, in exchange for a meal, chop kindling for Mother or spade a garden bed, proposed that we give our rooster two names, and recommended "John Henry." Its significance was lost on us, of course, but after considering it gravely, we reached the mysterious conclusion that John was not a fitting name for a rooster and that we would therefore call him Jim Henry.

The snowy white hen, Whitey, I remember we called her, was the first to set, and as an experiment, we slipped one black Minorca egg under her. How huge it was among the bantam eggs! We counted the days until they were ready to hatch, running out to the pen each morning during the last week to peer excitedly through the looped wire. But it was in the middle of the afternoon that the first chick made its way out of its shell—the black Minorca. We brought it into the house, found a shoebox and a piece of old flannel to keep it warm, and from time to time let it run around on the newspaper-covered kitchen table and fed it bits of hard-boiled egg, just as Mrs. Kendall always did with her baby chicks.

I was overwhelmed by the miracle of birth. Just a few hours earlier this chick had been curled inside its shell, beginning to be aware that the time had come for it to peck its way out to life and movement. And here it was, complete and perfect, a fluff of smoky black down, with sharp beak, bright, inquisitive eyes, and strong golden legs and feet! It ran tirelessly about the table, pecked at the food, peeped in a small, shrill monotone, and I watched it with awe and wonder and love.

At nightfall, no other chicks having hatched, we returned the little black one to Whitey so that it would be warm during the night. Early the next morning Bess and I raced out to the pen. The three small eggs had hatched, but I had no eyes for the exquisite bantie babies; the first-born was lying, lifeless, among the discarded shells on the edge of the nest, inadvertently trampled by the distracted mother-hen during the night. Heartbroken, I carried it to Mother. "Bury it in the garden," she said.

I knew where I would put the little chick—in the flower bed below the front porch, bright and sweet now with purple and white violets that had come from Melissa Maddern's garden—but nothing else was clear. This was my anguished first actual encounter with death. In my hand, I thought confusedly, is death . . . no, this is what death has done to the baby chicken who was so wonderfully alive only yesterday. Death denied life . . . death was un-life. It brought stillness where there had been quickness, ugliness where there had been grace and beauty. Worthless now were the baby chick's tools for living, the eyes to see, the beak to peck, the legs to run, all shaped miraculously inside the egg, used so briefly and never to be used again.

Shaken with sorrow, angered by the senseless injustice, fighting blindly against the irrevocableness of the catastrophe that had befallen the little black chicken, I rounded the corner of the bungalo and stood, transfixed. Through an open window on the top floor of Mrs. Kendall's big house was pouring wild, sweet strains of music; the young lady violinist who was living there just then was saluting the spring morning.

The throbbing notes of the violin, the sunlight, golden and dazzling, the fragrance of opening, dew-fresh blossoms came together in a magic interval, vibrant with life, and suddenly I *knew* with absolute certainty that this was a moment of miracle, that I had only to ask. Stretching forth the hand that held the tiny, crumpled body, I raised my tear-filled eyes to the morning sky and asked God to let the baby chick live again. Confidently, I waited. Nothing happened. The magic moment passed. In the violet bed, together with the little black chick, I sadly buried my belief in magic and miracles and the God they talked about in Sunday school and church.

The Litany service still drew me to the Trinity Church on Friday afternoons, and before long, as if to balance my loss, I was to make a tremendous discovery, far more beautiful to me than the Litany and more deeply satisfying because I could understand a good deal of it: the Bible, not the storybook Bible, but the Bible of the Psalms and Ecclesiastes and the Song of Solomon.

One Friday afternoon the rector visited our sewing circle, complimented us on our handiwork, and expressed gratification for our regular attendance at the Litany service. Then, after stressing the importance of preparing ourselves for confirmation, he gave each of us a little book containing the catechism he said we must memorize. I had not the faintest notion of what "confirmation" or "catechism" meant, but memorizing I knew very well and enjoyed. As soon as the service ended I opened the little book. "Catechism" proved to be a collection of questions and answers. It did not matter in the least that most of them were neither interesting nor comprehensible. Before I reached home I had mastered the first two pages and had started on the third. Whatever "confirmation" was, I would be ready for it.

Cousin Minnie was staying with us just then, as had been her custom for several years. Her visits, which lasted a week or two and sometimes longer, were always happy ones for all of us, but especially for Mother, for they were great friends as well as cousins. A pleasant air of excitement pervaded the bungalow while she was there. Everything was different. Aunt Jennie came to stay, because Mother often went out in the evenings with Cousin Minnie, who slept late. It seemed I had known Cousin Minnie forever, although I could not remember what came before the long-ago day in Ben Lomond when she had bade me find a four-leaf clover. It was during this visit, however, that she emerged for me for the first time as a real person, a mentor, and a kindler of hopes, ambitions and dreams.

Supper was ready when I reached home that Friday afternoon, and I had no opportunity to ask Mother about "confirmation." Afterwards I went back to the catechism, keeping my eye on the clock, as it was my turn to awaken Cousin Minnie at half-past six. This was a great privilege, shared by Bess and me on alternate evenings. She was rarely asleep when I tiptoed into the darkened room, but if she was, she awakened easily and at once, and then I was permitted to stay and talk with her while she dressed to go out.

Bess and I adored Cousin Minnie. She was very beautiful, with eyes like violets and glorious red-gold hair, but her allure was far greater than her beauty, extraordinary as that was. Just to be in the same room with her and, more than anything, to listen while she talked was electrifying. At such times I felt a-tiptoe with excitement, as if something wonderful was going to happen at any moment. Her gestures, her movements, but especially her speech, were marked by a sort of staccato grace, uniquely and inimitably her own. I did not yet know the words to describe the way she spoke—cadence, inflection, modulation, pace—but I was keenly aware of these qualities and of the delicate, almost unnoticeable precision with which she shaped her words.

"I've been learning the catechism," I announced that evening when I was settled in my place at the foot of her bed.

"Mm?" She was putting up her hair and her mouth was full of hairpins. "Is it hard?"

"Oh no, it's very easy. Do you want to hear me?"

"All right," she agreed.

"Here, you take the book and ask me the questions. It's only the answers we have to know."

She propped the booklet in front of the mirror and began, but we had covered less than a page when she stopped me. "Do you understand what you are saying, Joan?"

"Understand?" I echoed blankly.

"Yes. Does it mean anything to you?"

"Well . . . I guess not," I confessed. "I know what most of the words mean, but I don't really understand it."

"I thought not." She glanced at her little traveling clock, then said rapidly, "Listen carefully because I haven't much time. I want to tell you something that I hope you will always remember. Never, *never* memorize something you do not understand. Think about it, work at it, ask questions about it, until it has meaning. Perhaps you will not understand it in the same way other people do, but that doesn't matter. Some things have different meanings to different people. Anyway, it will be *your* understanding, and then when you say the words aloud, what they mean to you will be clear to anyone who listens to you. Of course," she went on comfortingly, "this catechism is pretty hard for a little girl to understand. Have you learned anything else from the Bible? Do you know the Twenty-third Psalm?"

"Oh yes!" I answered eagerly, and immediately began to rattle it off as we did in Sunday school.

"No, no, no!" she interrupted sharply. "Not like that! Never like that!"

Again she looked at the clock, and then went on, "Let me show you how to begin to understand. In the first place, you should know that a psalm is really a special kind of song, a religious song, not a hymn or a prayer, but a little like each of them. The psalms in the Bible were composed so very long ago that we don't know how they were sung, so we speak them, but the music is still there in the thoughts and the words. Now, do you know anything about the people who made up these songs?"

She did not wait for me to answer, but began to tell me about the tribesmen who had lived many centuries ago in a land called Judea. They were herdsmen, depending almost entirely on their flocks of sheep and goats for food and clothing, and because these animals had to have grass to eat, the shepherds and their wives and children moved constantly with their flocks in search of grass. Judea was an arid land, with long, hot summers and little rain even in the winter, so they wandered endlessly from lowland to highland and back again, following the springing of the grass from the parched soil after the rains. But the flocks, as well as the people, also had to have water to drink, so every lake and river, every spring, even every trickle, was precious to them. By day, the sun blazed in the vast expanse of sky; by night, myriads of stars hung in the overarching darkness. It was a hard land, a lonely land, filled with peril. And it came to them, who were so often in danger and afraid, that just as they protected and cared for their flocks, so, surely, someone mighty beyond their understanding watched over them in much the same way.

Then, in her unforgettable voice, she slowly spoke the ageless, beautiful lines, and I heard the music in the words, luminous now with meaning:

> The Lord is my shepherd; I shall not want.
> He maketh me to lie down in green pastures;
> He leadeth me beside the still waters. . . .

I see her again, standing small and still in the cramped, little room, the light from the chandelier burnishing her hair, chin lifted to complete the long, lovely line from throat to brow; standing so near I could have reached out my hand and touched her, but so far and remote in time and space that she was speaking to and for those shepherds of long ago.

I shall not, I cannot forget those moments of wonder and beauty, even if the countless others she gave me later through many years were to fade from memory, for Cousin Minnie was Minnie Maddern Fiske, and this private performance by the great actress will ever remain, for me, her finest.

Did I ever memorize the catechism? I don't remember, but I doubt it. Was I ever confirmed? No; of this I am sure. In my memory, catechism and confirmation vanished together that evening beneath the still waters of the Twenty-third Psalm, never to reappear. But the very next day, drawn irresistibly to the source of the enchantment Cousin Minnie had laid upon me, I began the solitary, unguided explorations of the Bible that I was to pursue at intervals for many years.

Eagerly, I sought other verses that, by following Cousin Minnie's instructions, I might bring to glowing beauty as she had the Twenty-third Psalm. The model she had given me was impossibly fine for a little girl to emulate, but I was not easily discouraged. Besides, the forays I made into the Bible—up mountain peaks where the view was breathtakingly clear, across sandy wastes, into impenetrable thickets where I lost my way and sometimes along wide, sunny valleys where the going was easy—were among the greatest adventures of my youth.

Neither the archaic language, so reminiscent of the captions Daddy had written for *Joan, Her Book,* nor the unfamiliar, frequently mystifying concepts diminished my ardor. I had fallen in love with language, and forever after would be in thrall to the evocative power of words spoken with understanding. Heightening the pleasure of my quest was the Bible I used, a small, stubby volume bound in thin, worn leather, printed in London in 1855; on the flyleaf, in faded ink, was written: *Melissa Jones, Feast of S. Barnabas, June 11th, 1858.*

My memory, so excellent in details of my early years, tells me that I discovered many remarkable passages in Melissa's Bible during my explorations. I learned them, whether I understood them or not, because I could not resist the beauty of their words and cadences, and because, in indefinable ways, they brought me close to the people of long ago whom Cousin Minnie had brought so vividly to life. Many of these passages I remember still for the same reasons; some, which a little later were to be quoted by Daddy with portentous meaning, I can never forget.

One of the earliest to be embraced with my whole heart I found among the Psalms in the poignant story of the Israelites on their long march into bondage, who were ordered by their captors to amuse them with singing and laughter. Torn between anger and sorrow, I made the lovely lines my own: "By the rivers of Babylon, there we sat down, yea, we wept when we remembered Zion. We hanged our harps on the willows in the midst thereof . . ." And walking home from school on spring afternoons when buttercups and wild mustard were beginning to bloom in empty lots and the air was sweet with lilacs, I would chant ecstatically:

> For lo, the winter is past, the rain is over and gone,
> The flowers appear on the earth.
> The time of the singing of birds is come . . .

Then there was Ur of the Chaldees. Placing those magic words on paper now, I experience again the excitement I felt at the moment of discovery. That I did not know what they meant, whether Ur was a person, place or something to eat, like honey or manna, did not matter. For me, they made a single, prolonged sound that was sometimes a great, echoing shout, sometimes a trumpet call and sometimes a wordless whisper about something almost remembered.

Little in the New Testament caught at my imagination, although "In my Father's house are many mansions" never failed to raise goose bumps on my arms. Always it was the Old Testament that drew me. Even when meaning was elusive, I was not lost, for on every hand were references to what was dear and familiar, flowers, fields, birds, animals, wind and rain and sun and stars, and out of these I contrived meanings of my own.

In another of the Psalms, I found, for instance:

As for man, his days are as grass;
As a flower of the field, so he flourisheth.
For the wind passeth over it, and it is gone,
And the place thereof shall know it no more.

The flower, the field, the grass, the wind passing over . . . for a long time this meant the unforgotten, the longed-for, the forever lost poppy field, and only much later did I grasp the thought of the psalmist when I found it stated uncompromisingly in that sombre book, Ecclesiastes:

For to him that is joined to all the living there is hope; for
a living dog is better than a dead lion.
For the living know that they shall die; but the dead know
not anything, neither have they any more a reward; for the
memory of them is forgotten.
Also their love, and their hatred, and their envy, is now
perished; neither have they any more a portion forever in
anything that is done under the sun.

When I first came upon this I recognized in it what I had felt as I buried the little black chicken, but without the anguish and resentment and tears. I was to remember it later in a time of great desolation, but as the years passed I came to question its finality; my own dead was not forgotten, either by me or the world, and his portion in what was done by many remained vital.

Having thus taken in stride some of the harshest lines in Ecclesiastes, how gladly I carried away with me from the same book, only to hear them spoken later at a tragic time, fragments of the serene verses that begin:

To everything there is a season, and a time to every
purpose under the heaven:
A time to be born, and a time to die; a time to plant, and
a time to pluck up that which is planted . . .
A time to get, and a time to lose; a time to keep, and a
time to cast away . . .

And, finally, accepting the challenge of their sequence, I learned the "whatsoevers" of St. Paul, concentrating on the precise order of "true . . . honest . . . just . . . pure . . . lovely," relaxing when I reached "of good report" and finishing triumphantly with "if there be any virtue, if there be any praise, think on these things."

Sunday school and the four o'clock Litany, Cousin Minnie, the thoughts and songs of the ancient people in the Bible, language understood to the best of one's ability and spoken beautifully out of that understanding—how fine and innocent and good they were! Yet in their midst lay the seeds of dissension and grief that would one day bear bitter fruit.

Slowly, imperceptibly, the months of Daddy's absence grew into a year, then another. Often in the beginning and then at longer and longer intervals, I tried to picture, to make realizable in some way, the eventual termination of his voyage and our longed-for reunion, but seven years, or six years, or even five years were still inconceivable. Arithmetic, which I was finding a potent though somewhat mysterious tool, failed to help. Simple addition gave me the incredible date of Daddy's planned return: April, 1914. Sometimes I would say it aloud to myself; it had no meaning at all. As soon as I learned the six-table I converted the years that remained into months, but the result was so appalling that I hastily abandoned any attempt to discover the number of weeks and days that must elapse before I would see him again. As time passed and my life was filled with people whom Daddy did not know, experiences and interests in which he had no part, I missed him with diminishing intensity, until it no longer hurt very much either to think about him or to be momentarily aware that I had not remembered him for some time.

Now it was winter again, the second since Daddy had left. Christmas had come and gone; there was a dreary wait before school would recommence. Since morning the day had been cold and grey, with a savage wind and a constant threat of rain. Bored from a long day of indoor amusements, Bess and I had welcomed the diversion of an early supper and were bickering halfheartedly to pass the time until Mother had washed the dishes and was ready to read to us.

"Look at the sunset, girls!" Mother called from the pantry.

We dragged a chair to the back door, the top third of which was the only window in the kitchen, and gazed in wonder at the western sky. Jagged fissures were opening in a towering black cloud-wall and through them we could see the blaze of the December sunset. After a bit Bess tired of watching, but I lingered, voyaging far and swiftly through the flaming gorges and out at last into a calm sky-sea of purest gold. It was long since I had sailed thus, but as always the same wish companioned me: somewhere in that glowing cloudscape I might find Daddy, perhaps on one of the gleaming beaches that edged the golden sea, or high in the shifting rose-and-bronze mountains. Then, with sudden pain, I realized that I could not see his face or hear his voice. Have I forgotten Daddy? I wondered frantically, striving in vain to recall his features and hear him speak my name in the old, loving way.

The rifts in the cloud-wall were closing, shutting me out from the light and the color and warmth of the far places where Daddy sailed on without me, and I was standing on a chair in the kitchen, peering into the gathering darkness.

Softly at first, by ones and twos, then in a swelling chorus, factory whistles began to blow somewhere in downtown Oakland, just as they did on weekdays, but more of them now and longer sustained.

"What is it?" I cried to Mother. "Why are the whistles blowing?"

"It's the last day of the year," she answered. "They're saying goodbye to the old year and getting ready to welcome the new one."

I remembered then that last year and other years before that, there had been one day when everyone hailed each other with the gay greeting, "Happy New Year!" As soon as we understood, Bess and I always tried to be the first to say it. Once—and I remember it because I wished I had thought of it—Bess was so exuberant that, standing on a chair in front of the telephone, she had lifted the receiver and shouted, "Happy New Year, Central!"

But on that New Year's Eve I felt no elation. The whistles, rising and falling mournfully, the storm clouds that barred me from the golden seas where Daddy moved forever farther away from me, the thought of Daddy himself, whose face and voice had been lost to me somewhere in this year that was coming to an end, combined to overwhelm me with a grief so poignant that I have never forgotten it.

"Happy New Year!" Bess said experimentally.

"Oh yes!" Mother echoed. "A happy new year, for a change!"

And suddenly I was no longer sad. Jumping down from the chair, I danced around the kitchen, shouting "Happy New Year!" until I was breathless.

"What number year will it be?" Bess asked, and Mother said, "1909."

NINE

In June, 1909, we received a letter from Daddy that took us totally by surprise.

Quito,
Ecuador
June 3/09

Dearest Joan:—

 Get mamma to tell you about this country, which is one of the highest in the world. This city is nearly 10,000 feet high.

 We are leaving here soon and going to see the Canal at Panama. Then we go to Mexico, and after that to California.

 There are no dolls in this country, but I am sending you in this letter a handkerchief.

 It is a long time since I received a letter from you.

 I am still sick, but I shall get well in California.

With hugs and kisses from
Daddy.

I read this letter in stunned disbelief. If, unannounced, he had walked into the bungalow at that moment, I could not have been more shocked. Daddy was coming home? But he had said over and over again that he would be gone for seven years! My acceptance of that monstrous length of time had been so difficult and painful that it was impossible for me to adjust myself to the prospect of his imminent return. In a brief note from Australia many weeks before, he had said he was ill, but there had been no hint that this was serious enough to make him abandon the voyage. Hearing nothing further, I imagine we assumed he had recovered and had long since sailed west from Australia.

Where, I finally began to wonder, were Quito and Ecuador? After a long search I managed to locate them on the map, and received my second shock: he had indeed recrossed the ocean and was now on our side of the Pacific! But, as could be seen on the map, he was far, far to the south of California, and although Panama was very small, Mexico was huge and would take a long time to visit. Clearly, there was no telling when he would return.

For a few days after the arrival of his letter I was torn by conflicting emotions, from which I escaped, despite the letter and the corroboration of the map, into a calm skepticism. It was much more comfortable to doubt that I would see him soon than to remember guiltily how his image and the sound of his voice and laughter had faded from my mind. The old excitement rose unbearably whenever I dared to think of him actually coming up the walk as he used to, sitting in the big Morris chair, romping with Bess and me, but the excitement gave way almost always to uneasiness. Would he be pleased and proud of me or disappointed? I was eight and a half years old now and had just been promoted to the high fourth. I could read and write quite well, I could speak a little French, I knew all my tables and could even do long division. Would it be enough? In comparison with the multitude of wonders he had seen on his travels, could I hope to impress him favorably?

Yes, it was better not to think about his return. Besides, Cousin Minnie had recently been staying with us again, and this visit had been extraordinary. I must have seen her perform prior to this year, but I have no sure memory of any of her roles before *Salvation Nell*, which she played in Oakland in the early summer of 1909. There were excellent reasons for me to remember this play. I saw it three times, first at a matinee, then at an evening performance, the first time I had been permitted to go to the theater at night, and finally, crowning all, at Cousin Minnie's invitation I sat on a chair in the wings throughout another evening performance, alternately bemused and entranced by the backstage activity and the sights and sounds and smells I would forever associate with the theater, and afterwards I went home with her on my first and only ride in a hansom cab.

But this was not all. Cousin Minnie was not the only Maddern in the cast of this play. There was also Cousin Minnie's Aunt Mary Maddern, a very old lady who had been an actress for more than sixty years. I remember her from a long Sunday afternoon of "keeping her company"—a stern, straight-backed, formidable little person, and the first woman I ever saw smoking cigarettes. Noting my astonishment, she explained curtly that they were a special kind of cigarette, a cubeb, which relieved her asthma.

And even this was not all. Also playing a role in the same play was my very own, instantly beloved first cousin, Merle Maddern. Tall and slender and very beautiful, with a thrilling low voice and captivating manner, she delighted me by evoking pictures of my forgotten babyhood when, as a girl of fourteen, she had amused me and taken me for airings in my baby carriage. Finally, although she was not in *Salvation Nell*, photographs were brought out by Cousin Minnie and there were inquiries and reminiscences about yet another actress-cousin, lovely Emily Stevens, whom I still remembered from Ben Lomond the summer after the earthquake.

It was a fortnight of dream and ecstasy for Bess and me. Our days, and especially our evenings when we talked together in bed before going to sleep, were dominated by the theater, the play, and the amazed realization that these actresses with their beautiful speech and manners were actually members of our own family. Adored and adoring, how could we escape feeling that we belonged to them as much as they belonged to us? And how could the bungalow be the same when such a casual remark as "What a lovely day it is!" by one of the cousins was like a flight of bright birds across the sombre living room?

Of paramount importance, however, was the moment when the opportunity came for me to tell Cousin Minnie of my discoveries in Melissa's Bible, and, in response to her immediate interest, to recite for her some of the verses I had learned. Her praise and warmly expressed gratification that I had not forgotten the brief lesson she had given me the year before filled me with pride and a determination to learn more and perform even better. Of the discussions between Mother and Cousin Minnie that must have followed I have no knowledge, nor do I remember any special announcement of the agreement that was reached, but from this time on it was understood that when I was older, if it was my wish to go on the stage, I would be sent to Cousin Minnie for training and experience.

To go on the stage, to learn to speak and move like these beautiful cousins, to enchant audiences as they did—what a prospect to be placed before an eight-year-old, already enamored of the spoken word and long since in love with the theater itself as a play-goer!

I gave myself joyously to this dream that, if I wished, would one day become a reality. It did not supplant the plan I had already made for myself, whose sole aim was to recapture Daddy, but enlarged and extended it and, I never doubted, guaranteed its success. I could not think of a surer way to please Daddy and make him proud of me.

This cherished dream was a golden thread woven distinctly through the next half-dozen years. Obscurely, I sensed in myself a dedication to the dream, an awareness of destiny. As the time for decision approached, a passionate affirmation was slowly shaping. Never again would I want to be and do anything as much as this.

And then, sooner than seemed possible, Daddy returned, almost on the heels of his letter from Quito.

"It's Daddy!" Mother called to us a moment after she had answered the telephone. We crowded around her, pulling at her skirt and whispering urgently, "Let me talk to him! Let me talk to him!" I waited in agonized impatience while Bess, her round face alternately smiling and serious, listened to him (what *was* he saying to her?), answering at intervals, "Yes . . . Yes, Daddy . . . I'm fine . . . Oh yes, Daddy!" And at last it was my turn.

The voice, the beloved voice, was unchanged! How could I have forgotten it! There was so much I wanted to say, to ask him, but my thoughts flew past too quickly to snare with words. Worse, my agitation was such that I could understand nothing of what he was telling me, so that I, too, repeated at intervals, "Yes . . . Yes, Daddy . . . Yes . . ." until he suggested gently, "You'd better let me speak to your mother again."

An hour later, dressed in our prettiest, Bess and I were walking down Telegraph Avenue, trying to remember Mother's admonitions: "Walk slowly so you won't trip over something and take a tumble. . . . Be sure to look up and down the avenue before you cross Twenty-second Street. . . . When you reach the Key Route Inn, go in the main entrance . . . Daddy will be waiting for you just inside. . . . He is visiting some old friends there. . . . Remember your manners. . . ."

Past the little Trinity Church at Twenty-ninth, past the flat on the other side of the avenue near Twenty-eighth where we had gone long, long ago to visit Daddy and I had seen the strange, silent woman who stared at us, past Twenty-seventh where Grandma London and Aunt Jennie lived, past Twenty-fourth, only a block from Melissa Maddern's one-time house and garden and finally to Twenty-second; then we were safely across the avenue and down the long block to Broadway and the Key Route Inn. The distance seemed interminable, but never had we covered ten blocks so quickly. An iron-hard ball was lodged in my chest so that it was difficult to breathe. Impatience to reach Daddy and, simultaneously, a perverse desire to delay the meeting as long as possible were equally unendurable.

Just inside the entrance we halted, standing close together, excited, apprehensive, searching the dark lobby. There he was, not ten feet away.

For a moment he looked full at us without recognition, then, smiling with his whole face and calling our names delightedly, he swept us into his arms. Past time flowed into present time and merged; the gap was closed. For Bess and me, the long voyage had ended at last.

Laughing, chattering, breathless, we made our way to the little suite where Daddy's friends were waiting for us. Smiling a welcome from the doorway was a tall, quickly recognized figure, George Sterling, whom I had not seen since the surprising encounter on the beach at Carmel, and with him his wife, Carrie, whom I did not remember because she had vanished with many others when we left the Bungalow.

It was a bewildering afternoon. We had been instantly at ease with Daddy when we had met downstairs, but in the presence of the Sterlings we were overcome with shyness that slowly lessened but never completely wore off. Perhaps the Sterlings only intensified the constraint we would have felt in any case; perhaps this first meeting after long separation would have been even more uncomfortable without their friendly presence. I think that Daddy was as ill at ease as we were. He had not foreseen that our relationship could not be resumed unchanged from what it had been two and a half years before. He had said goodbye to babies, Bess only four and I six; he had returned to find girls. I am sure he had not the least idea of what to say or what to do with us now that we were together again.

So the long summer afternoon lives in my memory as a kind of montage of conversation:

> . . . Martini, Jack? . . . You bet, but make mine very dry. . . .
> How you little girls have grown! But I would have recog-
> nized you anywhere, I think. . . . Dry Martinis, waiter . . .
> Carrie? . . . Make it two, waiter, and be sure they're dry. . . .
> Oh, what about the girls? . . . Would you girls like lemonade?
> . . . Two lemonades, waiter. . . . How old are you now,
> Joan? . . . And Bess? . . . Do you go to school? . . . And how
> is your mother? . . . You wrote me about cannibals and
> head hunters, Jack. . . . Did you really . . . ? . . . Well, it was
> in the Solomons, and we. . . . How long do you plan to be in
> town? . . . Only a day . . . we'll probably leave tomorrow. . . .
> I must go up to the ranch and get to work and make some
> money. . . . But not so soon, Jack! Everyone here wants to
> see you. . . . Two more Martinis, waiter . . . dry . . . and two
> lemonades. . . . That fellow you wrote me about, George, he
> hunted me up in Sydney . . . very interesting man. . . . And
> say, Carrie, you and George simply must see Hawaii . . .

*no place like it in the world. . . . Carl and Laura Bierce for
sure. . . . Dinner tonight? . . . Let me call them. . . . Stories?
Hundreds of them . . . enough to keep me busy for years. . . .
Did I tell you about the leper? . . . Two Martinis, waiter, and
two lemonades. . . .*

One voice, solo, then two and sometimes three questions, answers,
sudden bursts of hearty laughter, the frequent jangle of the telephone
and over all a deepening blue haze of cigarette smoke.

Bess and I sat utterly still on straight-backed chairs, all ears and eyes,
but unable to follow much of the conversation. A good deal of it was
like the "Martinis" Daddy and George were drinking, "dry," when it
was obvious they were wet. But the real problem was the lemonade. It
was served in the tallest glasses I had ever seen, and the first round
taxed our capacity. After that, however, we were not asked if we wanted
another; fresh glassfuls arrived with each round of Martinis. We tried
our best to drink them, fearing it would not be polite otherwise, but we
could not manage it. Finally noting our plight, Carrie rescued us. "You
don't have to drink them," she whispered. "Just leave them there on
the table. It's all right."

The discomfort of sitting still so long, the lemonade-nightmare, the
near-certainty, from what he had said, that this would be our only visit
for quite a while, the plans being made over the telephone for that very
evening and Bess and I, of course, not included—none of these mattered.
My surrender to the happiness of actually seeing and being with Daddy
again was complete; nothing could mar or diminish this long-awaited joy.

Then came the remembered moment. In the sudden silence that fell
when both George and Carrie were occupied with the telephone in the
adjoining room, Daddy opened his arms wide to us, and in a trice we
were out of our chairs and in his embrace.

"Isn't this fine!" he exclaimed, adding quickly, "though I guess this
sort of thing isn't very much fun for little girls."

"Oh yes, Daddy, yes, it is!" we protested.

"I've just had a dandy idea!" He lowered his voice. "Have you girls
anything on for tomorrow?" We shook our heads vigorously. "Well
then, when I take you home later, we'll ask your mother if it's all right
with her, and if it is, I'll come by for you tomorrow morning, and we'll
go to San Francisco and spend the whole day together—just the three
of us! What do you say?"

We were speechless, but he understood. "Not a word now," he cautioned. "This is just for us."

It was nearly dusk when we started for home; I remember seeing the evening star low in the west as we walked, two by two, toward Telegraph Avenue to take the streetcar, Bess and Daddy ahead and George and I just behind. The men were in high spirits, and I thought it must be because of the gay dinner party that had been hastily arranged over the telephone for that evening. Although I was more tired than I had ever been in my life, I wished with all my heart that I might go with them. It seemed to me that I had lived forever, and yet I was still a little girl who had to go home at nightfall. But I was not sad; Daddy had come back! Besides there was tomorrow—a whole day with Daddy!

George squeezed my arm. "Isn't it great to have him back! I've missed him, too, you know." After a bit he began to chant, "Joan, Joan, what a beautiful name. . . . Green-eyed Joan . . ." He broke off, looked down at me and added solemnly, "When I become a really good poet, I shall write a poem about your beautiful green eyes."

It was my first compliment, and all the more stunning because I had not known that my hazel eyes were green. I felt I should say something, but before I could find words Daddy was calling, "Hurry, here comes the streetcar!"

And there, as I ran with George the last few feet to the corner, my memory of that afternoon, which marked an end and a beginning, ceases.

The years of my life with Mother were many, thousands of days lived, one after the other, under the same roof, and as I grew older our relationship adapted itself to my changing status so gradually and painlessly that it is not possible to say: on such and such a day everything began to be different from what it was before. But my association with Daddy was discontinuous over a relatively brief span of years, and many changes, often abrupt and sometimes violent, can be marked with dismal accuracy, usually by year, month and sometimes even by day. His return from the *Snark* voyage in July, 1909, was the beginning of a new period that promised, at the start, to be a happy one. Certainly, the day in San Francisco augured well for the future.

Some days are familiar; you know you have been in them before even if you cannot remember when. But that long, lovely day was brand-new, like no other before or since. We were new to each other; we did new things together; even the city, still rebuilding after the earthquake and fire, was new. I remember, because Daddy pointed them out to us, the freshly laid cobbles along the Embarcadero and how the white and brown and silvery grey buildings gleamed in the July sunshine.

We talked incessantly on the train and ferryboat and all through lunch, rediscovering each other, confiding our ideas and interests, exchanging experiences, sharing our disappointments and triumphs, daring even to hint at some of our hopes and dreams. Swiftly, because we were all so eager and needed it so, the loom of our relationship was rethreaded, new patterns shaped, and the weaving begun.

One item in our conversation I was to recall a few years later when its significance suddenly became apparent; at the time it was only one of many exciting exchanges. This was my account of Cousin Minnie's recent visit and how I had watched the play from the wings backstage.

Daddy listened intently. "You like the theater?"

"Oh yes, I love it!"

"So do I," he agreed. "As a matter of fact, I plan to write some plays before long. But I find it much more interesting and pleasant to write plays for other people to act than I would, I'm sure, to play a part that someone else had written."

I was dazzled by the possibilities his announcement presented. "Do you think Cousin Minnie will act in your plays?"

"No, I think not. I don't write her kind of play."

"But maybe you will sometime?" I persisted.

He smiled then. "Maybe I will—sometime."

Lunch over, he proposed, "Now let's decide what we shall do the rest of the day. Shall we go out to the Cliff House and the beach? Or to the park? Or maybe there's a matinee somewhere. . . . I've got it! Let's go shopping! What do you say?"

We looked at him dubiously. Shopping, as we knew it, was not very much fun—a great deal of walking, a great deal of waiting while Mother decided on her purchases and then a long walk home. But as he described what he meant by "shopping," our doubts vanished.

"I haven't bought anything for you girls for a long time. There must be lots of things you've been wanting. Books? Games? Think!"

The titles of half a dozen books and the "Pirate and Traveler" game we had long coveted were instantly on our lips.

"You see?" he laughed. "What else? Isn't there something special you have wanted without expecting to get it? . . . Joan, I can see by your face that there is. Tell me."

He was irresistible. In a shaking voice, I described the small, silver coin cases for holding nickels and dimes that girls were wearing about their necks on long, silver chains, and told him how Bess and I had yearned over them in jewelers' windows.

"That will be first on the list," he decided. "We'll think of the rest as we go along." Beckoning the waiter, he consulted him as to the best stores to visit.

And the fabulous afternoon began.

The recommended jeweler was only three blocks distant, but to our astonishment, Daddy insisted on taking the streetcar. We never rode on streetcars except when it was raining or our destination was unusually far away. That afternoon we rode everywhere, once for only a single block.

The coin purses were carefully selected and left to be engraved with our names and delivered in two days. Assuring us that a five-dollar goldpiece was the same size as a nickel, Daddy slipped one into the larger of the two receptacles in each case, because, he said, "I don't like empty purses." Then the expedition was resumed.

I cannot remember the numerous stores we visited or even much of what he bought for us. Reality vanished with the purchase of the coin purses. From then on I moved in a dream in which a wish had only to be uttered to be granted. Books we bought, and games, and a punching bag and small silk parasols. . . . Once, I remember, I tried to think up something practical and came up triumphantly with hair ribbons. I can still see the dazed saleslady measuring and cutting length after length of different shades and patterns of ribbons chosen with abandon by Daddy after Bess and I had exhausted our own small preferences.

At some time in the midst of our orgy Daddy proposed, "Let's get something for your mother, something really nice! What would she like?"

Anything was possible that day. "A fireless cooker!" I said wildly. "I know she'd like that." They were new then and Mother greatly admired one that a friend had recently acquired.

"Splendid! That's what we'll get."

But housewares were on an upper floor, and somehow we did not think of the fireless cooker again until it was too late. "Next time," Daddy promised.

As we cruised through a large department store we came face to face with a man who hailed Daddy with, "Well, Jack London, this is the last place I'd expect to find you!"

Daddy introduced us to his friend with such pride in us that I thought my heart would burst, and told him about our shopping spree and the fun we were having. Not listening so much as watching Daddy while the two men spoke briefly, I think I saw him for the first and very nearly the only time as a person, not solely and completely Daddy. There was a difference. His holiday air did not alter, his gaiety was undiminished, but his voice and manner underwent an impressive change. I had loved him all my life; now, with almost equal intensity, I also admired him. I forgot his friend's name immediately, but years later, in the *San Francisco News*, I was to read John D. Barry's tender account of how he had once chanced to meet Jack London and his little girls in a San Francisco department store.

In the late afternoon, the sun dropping toward the hills behind the slowly receding city and fog just beginning to flow through the Golden Gate, we sat together on the upper deck of the ferry, going home. After the clangor of the city streets, the quietness of the bay was a benediction. The gulls, dipping and turning watchfully above our wake, were silent; the water whispered against the gently vibrating boat; at intervals, muffled and far away, the first of the fog horns were blowing.

"Tired?" Daddy asked.

"Oh no!" I answered quickly, knowing that was for later, not now. "I guess I'm just happy."

He pressed us close to him for a moment. "That's what I am—just happy. I haven't had so much fun in a long time. Let's do it again soon, shall we?"

"Oh yes, Daddy!"

But we never did.

TEN

There was no cloud in the sky, the sun shone every day, birds sang, flowers bloomed . . . so it seemed to me for a long time after Daddy's return. The joy his relative nearness brought me was a measure of the despair I had known when he departed on the planned seven-year voyage and of my unacknowledged fear that I would never see him again. Now he was only seventy miles away, and what was seventy miles after the thousands that had separated us?

We saw him infrequently and briefly at first. Long afterwards I learned that not only had his recovery from the tropical illnesses that had brought the voyage to an end been slow and painful, but that, despite ill health, he had written almost incessantly for months to reduce the mountain of debt that faced him on his return. There was little exchange of correspondence between us for some time, and that did not matter, either. The three or four lines scrawled on a penny postcard, saying he would be in Oakland on a certain day and would telephone on his arrival, had traveled such a little distance compared to the letters that had come by ship from the far-off South Seas. Unfailingly, he would telephone as promised, and even if it was a school day, Bess and I would be ready and waiting for him at the appointed time.

Although we still engaged in them when he visited us, the romps were no longer our principal amusement. If it was rainy or cold, or if Daddy had only an hour or so to spend with us, we played games—lotto, Pirate and Traveler, jackstraws and tiddley-winks. Sometimes we worked on a jigsaw puzzle he had brought us, a portion of which, a barn roof bearing a huge painted advertisement for something called Hood's Sarsaparilla, I have never forgotten. Nor can I forget the way he played the games that required a certain skill, such as jackstraws, scrupulously honest but giving no quarter, playing to win, and gloating over his victory when he succeeded.

The times we played games together I remember with especial tenderness, realizing now that his bleak boyhood had lacked even these small diversions, but at the time they were far less exciting than the afternoons we went out for our pleasures. Usually, this meant taking the streetcar downtown to attend a matinee, most often at the Orpheum but sometimes at the Bell, followed ritually by a stop at Lehnhardt's for ice cream before Daddy took us home.

How large a part the theater played in the lives of almost everyone in those days! Motion pictures were already available (a tiny theater named the Bijou showed nothing else), but they were still a novelty and could not compete with the road shows at the McDonough, the stock company plays at the Ye Liberty or the endless marvels of vaudeville.

Like everyone else, Bess and I had our favorite vaudeville acts and personalities, and welcomed their return year after year with zest and affection. There were Alice Lloyd and Sophie Tucker and Melrose the clown, the beloved skit *School Days*, and the intriguing act involving a dozen or more colorfully costumed characters, male and female, two or three of them apparently on the stage at the same time, which was immediately repeated with transparent scenery to show that a single actor played all the roles. The richness and variety of the bills are hard to believe in these vaudeville-less days—toe dancers and tap dancers, famous actors and actresses in scenes from their Broadway hits, cyclists, jugglers and acrobats, singers and comedy teams . . .

We used to come out through the glass doors that bisected the Orpheum's long lobby and turn, blinking in the late afternoon sunlight, toward Broadway, replete and content, yet already anticipating the final scene in the drama of those afternoons with Daddy.

I remember Lehnhardt's as fragrant and spacious and beautiful, with a softly carpeted floor and crimson-draped mirrors on the walls of the "parlor" that was filled with small, round tables, each with four small chairs. Never was there such candy, never was there such ice cream and never anywhere in the world were there such macaroons and ladyfingers as at Lehnhardt's! We would sit down at the little table and in a moment a black-clad waitress with a frilled white apron and cap would place a paper napkin, a menu and a tiny glass of ice water in front of each of us, and wait, cool and detached, for our orders.

One warm afternoon Daddy was scarcely settled in the too-small chair when the waitress came to our table.

"Oh, fine!" he exclaimed, reaching for the glass of water and emptying it in one gulp. "I'm really thirsty!" he confided to the waitress. "What I'd like before anything else is a *big* glass of water!"

To swallow ice water so quickly and then immediately ask for more was impressive, and I waited with great interest to see him drink the "big" glassful. The second glass was brought, a duplicate of the first. The contrast between what we had expected and the absurd little glass that arrived was so great that for a moment we simply stared. Then our eyes met and we laughed and laughed and laughed. I remember that even the impassive waitress was startled by our merriment, while the other customers regarded us with lively curiosity.

Another afternoon at Lehnhardt's is also memorable for its laughter. I felt very daring and adventurous that day and scanned the menu for something I had never tasted before. The widespread dark green oak tree on the cover was magnificent, but in those pre-fancy sundae days the "suggestions" inside were neither numerous nor imaginative. Disdaining the familiar vanilla, strawberry and chocolate ice cream, I considered and rejected pineapple, banana, cherry and maple-nut, and came at last to an exotic unknown.

"Pistackee-oh," I announced. "That's what I'm going to have."

"Pistackee-oh?" Daddy echoed. "What's that?"

"I don't know," I answered happily. "But it's what I want."

He turned to the waitress. "What's this pistackee-oh? What's it like?"

"Pistachio," she corrected and added, "It's green."

That decided it. *Green* ice cream!

Daddy eyed the pale green mound when it was placed before me and watched while I put a cautious half-spoonful in my mouth. "Well? Is it good?"

"It's . . . funny," I said dubiously. It certainly was different, but was it good? I tasted it again, and this time I knew that I didn't like it very much; in fact, I didn't like it at all.

Reaching across the table, Daddy dipped his spoon into the ice cream, and now it was I who watched as he tasted it gingerly. After a moment he grimaced, drained my glass of water, his own being empty as usual, and gasped, "It's awful! It tastes like . . . like . . ." He burst into laughter. "It tastes just like hair-oil!"

Neither Bess nor I knew what hair-oil was, but Daddy's mirth was infectious and we joined him enthusiastically. The waitress took away the despised pistachio, replacing it with one of the reliables. Daddy teased me about "pistackee-oh" for a long time afterwards but I was never embarrassed. It was a happy memory and evoked only renewed laughter.

The best, though least frequent, of our expeditions with Daddy were to Idora Park. For a few years after his return he took us there two or three times each season, but in my memory those many visits merge and I recall incidents of only the first and last times we were there together.

Idora Park was the East Bay's one amusement center, so filled with wonders that no child of that time and place could ever be impressed by travelers' tales of an allegedly more remarkable Coney Island. We would listen, but we simply would not believe. Idora seemed enormous to me, not only because I was small, and not only because of its many large installations—theater, skating rink, roller coaster and ferris wheel, merry-go-round, cages of monkeys and bears, a picnic place; even, for a while after the 1906 earthquake and fire, a baseball diamond complete with grandstands and bleachers—and not even because of the wide spaces around and between the buildings and the tall, old trees, but because it actually was large. Today, no trace, no tree, nor stick, nor stone remains. Long since, its forty splendid acres were carved into city blocks with neatly squared corners, and neat houses behind neat lawns face each other across quiet streets.

When we went there with Daddy we rarely rode on the merry-go-round and never went to the theater, even when Ferris Hartman was playing in *The Toy Maker*, for, thanks to Uncle Charlie, these were delights that were already familiar and we knew we could enjoy them at other times. With Daddy, the whole park was ours, and we could try anything and everything that, until his return, had been labeled "wait until you're older."

And so, having paid the entrance fee at the front gate and fortified us for the afternoon's adventures with ice cream cones and bags of candy and popcorn, Daddy would set forth, hat pushed to the back of his head, coat unbuttoned, Windsor tie fluttering and with a wide-eyed, excited, skipping-and-jumping little girl on each arm.

Sometimes the trees, green-budded, stood a-tiptoe in glittering spring sunlight; sometimes they leaned into heavy, late-summer air, their dusty leaves drooping wearily; once, on the very last day before the park closed for the winter, a chill wind tore tattered leaves from the branches and flung them helter-skelter along the walks. First and last in our ears, and always audible no matter how far we wandered, was the mechanical, unmusical, hurdy-gurdy beat of the merry-go-round, against and over and under and through which all the other carnival sounds emerged, faded and re-emerged: the crack of rifles at the shooting galleries, the high, thin screams of passengers on the roller coaster, the chanting of barkers, the wails of tired children, the roar of roller skates through the rink's open doorway and, always and everywhere, laughter.

We went through the "Crazy House," alternately amused and mystified, and Daddy explained how the mirrors were made that reflected us as tall and thin or short and wide, and why some of the walls leaned crookedly but were not crooked at all. We rode on the toy train that we could easily see Daddy enjoyed more than we did. We watched admiringly while he shot at moving tin rabbits and ducks, and we lingered long outside the monkey cage, listening but only half-believing, while Daddy told us of the long, long ago, before early man lived in caves, even before he had lived in trees, when he, our ancestor, had looked very much like the monkeys there in the cage, only larger and heavier and more intelligent. There was a dreamy interlude when, in a little boat, we traversed quiet waterways in total darkness except, at intervals, for dimly lit grottoes in which scenes had been contrived, some of them eerie but many of them strangely lovely, like pictures in a book of fairy tales. With some trepidation, we rode on the ferris wheel, which looked formidable but was not even very exciting, though the view of the hills and the bay from the top of the great wheel was magnificent.

At the end of the first day's adventures we came to the roller coaster, known then or perhaps a little later as the scenic railway, and still later, rebuilt and enlarged, as "The Race Through the Clouds." Unsuspectingly, for the ferris wheel had proved only mildly interesting, we clambered into the front seat of the first car and sat down, Daddy in the middle.

"Hold on tightly," he cautioned as the car began to move. "And don't forget to scream . . . that's part of the fun!"

We screamed, of course. Daddy screamed, too, but he was having fun. As the flimsy open car swung around sharp curves, dropped sickeningly through emptiness, then climbed straight up to drop again and again and again, unendurably, we were utterly terrified.

The moment the car came to a stop we scrambled out as fast as we could and, not waiting for Daddy, started down the platform toward the exit. He was still laughing when he caught up with us.

"Wasn't that fun!" he exclaimed. "Let's . . ." He saw our faces and his laughter died. "Didn't you like it?"

"Not very much," we answered carefully.

"Were you afraid?" he asked, so severely that we knew we must admit the shameful truth.

"Wait here," he ordered.

We watched him stride to the ticket office and return with what seemed to be yards of tickets. Back we went and into the front seat of the first car.

"This is fun," he said firmly. "If it were not fun, it wouldn't be in an amusement park. There's nothing to be afraid of. You can't fall out. You'll see, you'll have as much fun as I do."

Twenty-five trips in succession later, he had proved his point, and we tumbled out onto the platform, breathless from screaming and laughing, fear lost forever. Afterwards, whenever we went to Idora Park with Daddy, the scenic railway was the best of all.

How fine that year and a half was! My confidence in the outcome of my hopes and plans, badly shaken for so long, began again to grow. Daddy loved us, I could tell, was proud and happy to be with us. Always he said goodbye with a promise to see us again soon, and we never doubted that that was his wish, even when many weeks elapsed between his visits. Perhaps, he would suggest, if the weather was good the next time he came down to the city, we would go to the beach and he would teach us to swim; perhaps we would go to Lake Merritt and he would take us rowing or sailing; somehow we never did either.

Even the first Christmas after his return was special: for the first time, and I do not remember whether it was on his initiative or ours, he provided Bess and me with a small sum apiece so that we might buy gifts to exchange with our young friends. And that Christmas, although I have no clear memory of the event, he came to see our Christmas tree.

It was all shining peaks with lovely sunlit valleys in between; all fun and happiness and anticipation. That was the tragedy, of course. It was as if, each time we were together, we sat down to a banquet composed only of fabulous desserts, while what we desperately needed was meat and potatoes and bread and butter. Always we were brushed and combed and dressed for "company"; always we awaited his arrival with impatience; always, like "kept" girls, we sought in every way to please and divert and entertain him.

While we basked in the sunlight of that joyous first year after his return, we were sometimes faintly aware that those who were nearest to us, Mother and Grandma London and Aunt Jennie, did not entirely share our happiness. More and more frequently as the months passed, their conversations in our presence were cryptic and unintelligible, accompanied by sighs and head-shakings. But if they saw deepening shadow where we saw only brightness, if they sensed peril while we rejoiced in a dazzling present-without-end, we were not taken into their confidence. Not until the danger had passed and the shadow seemed to them to have lifted did we know what they, as well as Daddy, had kept from us.

This knowledge was so incredible, so bitter, that I instantly dismissed it as something that did not concern me in any way. It was only later when, hurt and bewildered, I was striving to understand the defeat of all my hopes, that I remembered the little half-sister who had been born the first summer after Daddy's return, and suffered, in a moment of unendurable anguish, the greater rejection I might have felt had she lived.

That summer of 1910, when I was nine years old, and later, at thirteen, my attitude toward this baby was exclusively personal: I fiercely resented her birth and was grateful that her existence had been brief. Now with pity and compassion for all of us who were joined together in love and conflict and pain, I can comprehend what the loss of this longed-for child must have meant to Daddy and to her mother, and can wish that she had lived.

Perhaps the memory of Joy London abides only with me today, this half-sister I never saw and of whom Daddy never spoke to us. Her whole life-span was just thirty-eight hours, but she was inextricably woven thereafter into the cruel pattern from which we could not escape.

Guarded by silence from knowledge of Daddy's joyful anticipation of the birth of his child and his subsequent grief, Bess and I were caught up in an astonishing series of events during the year and a half following his return from the *Snark* voyage. Whether he initiated all of the innovations that marked that exciting period, I do not know, but there is no doubt that he made most of them possible. Even when we did not see him for weeks, we felt his active presence in our daily lives as we followed through on changes he had proposed, saw our scarcely hoped-for plans miraculously come into existence and were overwhelmed from time to time by unexpected largess. Forgotten were the many months when our only contact with him had been the letters that reached us at intervals from remote distances—letters written to little girls he no longer knew and who scarcely remembered him. From the moment of our reunion at the Key Route Inn we had ceased to be abstractions to one another, but reacquaintance was slow. We were shy with him at first, over-careful, and perhaps, even if he had been aware of our uncertainties and our unacknowledged fear of somehow losing him again, he would not have known how to help us overcome them. Nevertheless, we were making progress during those remarkable months.

The year 1910 began with a change of tremendous importance to me. Just as I was about to celebrate my ninth birthday, rejoicing that this was the last of my single-digit years, Bess and I left Miss Merriman's forever and entered public school. I had urged this for nearly two years, pointing out to Mother how long it had been since I was seriously ill, and concealing my undiminished distress from her, as I always had, under the plea that I wanted to go to a "real" school. There was, certainly, nothing spurious scholastically about Miss Merriman's, which was amply demonstrated by the excellent grades Bess and I continued to receive in public school, but I could not bring myself to confide to Mother my wish to escape my tormentors.

Rarely are a child's extravagant hopes fully realized, but, for me, public school was an exception. At the Grant School, no one cared that I was Jack London's daughter or that my parents were divorced; I was a whole person again, free to meet challenges and competition on my own. It did not last, of course; before I graduated from the grammar grades the shadow of the famous name had again fallen upon me, but by then I was older, a little surer of myself and able to assert my own individuality and accomplishments with greater confidence.

My enthusiasm for public school as I found it was boundless. I admired Miss Gallagher, the teacher under whose instruction I passed through the fifth and sixth grades; I especially liked fractions; and I liked, even though I did very badly at it, the manual training the fifth-grade girls were then required to take. (Hoping to surprise Daddy, I wrote him with admirable restraint: "I have manual training at school, we make such things as key tags, fish line winders, etc. I have finished my fish line winder and I am at work on a key tag.) And I found my first chums, Helen Dickie and pretty, red-haired Hallie Poole.

The single, distinct memory I have of those pleasant years, however, is one of acute embarrassment. Miss Gallagher placed great stress on reading aloud at sight, and introduced this technique into as many of our studies as possible. Pupils were called upon in turn and permitted to read without interruption until a word was mispronounced. I excelled in this, as I certainly should have, and could go on and on triumphantly until Miss Gallagher would gently suggest that someone else should have a turn. Thus, reading aloud from our history book one day, I fell ingloriously into a classic trap: "Step-hen Douglas," I read distinctly, and the next moment, horrified, heard a half dozen of my fellow pupils and Miss Gallagher correcting me.

Reading aloud . . . when did we not read aloud at home? As far back as I can remember, Mother had read stories to us at bedtime or to fill the long hours of inactivity when we were ill. Later, as one after the other we mastered the art, Bess and I became the readers while Mother ironed or sewed or mended. Rainy days, summer afternoons, winter evenings, how excitingly they passed while we journeyed through the jungle treetops with Mowgli and the Bander-Log, nibbled the opposite sides of the magical mushroom and grew taller or shorter with Alice and shared the adventures of the Scarecrow, the Tin Woodman and the boy who was really the enchanted Ozma of Oz.

For a long time we had few children's books in our home. There was

The Golden Heart, of course, and *The Marvelous Land of Oz*, both of the stories about Alice and several collections of fairy tales. Unique among these fantasies were two slim volumes by Katherine Elizabeth Dopp, *The Tree-Dwellers* and *The Early Cavemen*, gifts from Daddy, who had read them prior to writing *Before Adam*. We read and reread these books, acted them out in imaginative games and for a long time planned to be anthropologists when we grew up.

It was during the *Snark* voyage that Mother made us acquainted with Daddy's stories. The prophecy he had inscribed in her copy of *The Cruise of the Dazzler*, "Some day you can read this to the two youngsters," came true a half dozen years later. *The Call of the Wild* had been the first, followed by *White Fang* and the short story *Brown Wolf*, about Brown, the father of our lost Glen. Then had come *The Cruise of the Dazzler* and *Tales of the Fish Patrol*, and the boy Daddy had been became more vivid to us than the Daddy who was sailing on far, strange seas. Had he not written in Mother's copy: "Find here, sometimes hinted, sometimes told, and sometimes made different, the days of my boyhood when I, too, was on the Fish Patrol."

Daddy's books, so different from the fairy stories and even from those about the tree-dwellers and cavemen, whetted our appetites for more, and at the rainy beginning of the second winter of Daddy's absence Mother had searched her own library for works we might be able to enjoy. Was *David Copperfield* the first, or *Great Expectations?* And did *Kidnapped* and *David Balfour* come before or after *Sentimental Tommy?* I no longer remember. At some time during the years of what might have been our premature entry into the world of adult books, but fortunately was not, we found *Vanity Fair* and excitedly recognized in its heroine Cousin Minnie's Becky Sharpe, about whom we had heard from Mother but were yet to see on the stage. Sir Walter Scott was not precisely to our taste, but we read at least two of the Waverly novels from beginning to end. Balzac, the dark green bindings filling an entire shelf, was forbidden until we were "older" (I was twelve when I defied this prohibition and was permanently ensnared by *La Comédie Humaine* and its author), but it mattered little then, for we could and did rove at will among the elegant, wine-red volumes of Dickens—so many still to read for the first time and the others to reread with increasing pleasure.

And once during this time Mother read aloud to someone—was it Uncle Charlie? I don't remember but I listened—a story by the man who had written *The Jungle Book*. It did not resemble the tale of Mowgli in any way, and I did not understand the title, *Without Benefit of Clergy*, or parts of the story, but its sadness reached deeply into me. When she read the closing lines about the destruction of the house where the man and the woman and the baby had known such happiness—"It shall be pulled down, and the municipality shall make a road across . . . so that no man may say where this house stood."—I wept. "Jack loved that story," Mother said softly.

Mother did not deceive herself that our reading, no matter how much we enjoyed it, was a satisfactory answer to our book-hunger. Our leap from fairy tales to novels had inevitably left untouched a rich store of children's books, and she was concerned lest we miss them entirely. From her own girlhood she remembered and brought to us two old-time classics, *The Wide, Wide World* and *The Lamp Lighter,* and from the public library, *Little Lord Fauntleroy*, which did not greatly impress us, and *Sara Crewe*, which we read with delight. Unfortunately, however, the library was too distant for us in those days for frequent borrowing. Mother's determination to provide us with the reading we had missed was inflexible; she made lists of wanted titles, adding to them as others came to her attention; some day we would read those books.

And so it was that, returning from school one afternoon in the spring of 1910, we found Mother on her knees beside a huge packing case, prying off the top boards with hammer and chisel.

We ran to her, touching the box with curious fingers. "What is it? What's in it?"

Under the boards were sheets of brown wrapping paper, and under the paper were books, hundreds of them, large and small, some jacketed, others in bright bindings that sparkled with newness.

"Where did they come from?" we cried, scarcely believing what we saw, but already sure of the answer.

And, of course, they had been ordered for us by Daddy, not book by book, and probably with not even one title chosen by him, but selected at his request from Mother's lists by someone in the East, forever nameless to me, who knew children's books, for there were more titles in the packing case than there had been on Mother's lists.

Those titles! *Don Quixote, Gulliver's Travels, The Dog of Flanders, Black Beauty* and *Beautiful Joe, Rebecca of Sunnybrook Farm, Mrs. Wiggs of the Cabbage Patch, The Arabian Nights* come instantly to mind, and dozens of others could be as readily listed.

For hours that afternoon we sat on the floor beside the packing case, reverently examining the volumes as Mother lifted them out and placed them in small piles, abashed by their crisp newness as much as by their number and variety, scanning the titles, recognizing some and even some of the authors, a little giddy from the heady fragrance of new paper, new ink, new bindings, not trying yet to decide which to read first. After supper we helped Mother stack them on the long window seat in the living room to await the building of their special bookcase, and before we went to bed we wrote ecstatic thank-you letters to Daddy.

From that afternoon, I remember especially Mother's smiling face, at once triumphant and content, and from that evening, my exasperation that I could not find adequate words to convey to Daddy the wonder of his gift and my immense joy.

There was no end to the marvels of that year. Soon after the arrival of the books there began to come, as another surprise, *The Youth's Companion*, addressed to me, and *St. Nicholas Magazine*, addressed to Bess, the subscriptions to which were faithfully renewed by Daddy for several years thereafter. And as summer neared, even the heavens participated, for, as predicted, Halley's comet returned after seventy-six years to stream in blazing magnificence across the sky for many nights.

Cousin Minnie stayed with us for a month that summer, playing in *Pillars of Society* and a revival of *Becky Sharpe*, which the Bay Area had not seen since January of 1901. Bess and I do not remember *Pillars of Society*, perhaps we did not see it, but *Becky Sharpe* we have never forgotten.

And sometime that summer, the incredible, the improbable, the un-dreamed-of occurred: we went, overnight on a Pullman train, to Shasta Springs on a two-week vacation. Which of these triple wonders, Shasta Springs, going away for a vacation, or the overnight trip on the train, was the greatest to me then, I have not the slightest doubt: to sleep on a train was incomparably the best.

In a letter describing a second journey several months later, I wrote: "This time it was not a 'soap bubble' as I called it before. It was a really truly journey." Alas, I do not recall what I had tried to convey to him by "soap bubble," perhaps in a letter that no longer exists, perhaps in conversation. That I should have referred to it months afterwards surely indicates that the impression was lasting and that I had not found in retrospect a better term for the experience. But, remembering the soap bubbles Bess and I used to blow out of slender, white clay pipes, bubbles irridescent, crystalline, so fragile they would burst at a breath, I think I can feel again the sense of unreality and awe that overwhelmed me as I climbed up the steps of a Pullman car for the first time. Walk softly, do not breathe, I might have counseled myself, else all will vanish.

So self-absorbed was I, as unforeseen events succeeded each other in that amazing year, that my memory holds no clue to Daddy's state of mind and heart during that time. Was he amused or touched by my extravagant reaction to the trip to Shasta Springs? I do not know. It had been one of several generous impulses that he acted upon in that happy spring that preceded the birth of Joy. Telling Mother one afternoon of an unusual arrangement he had made with a western magazine to accept railroad passes as part payment for material it was publishing, he had suggested, probably on the spur of the moment, that we might use such passes for a vacation.

Did he, I wonder, fear that the actual presence of the coming child in his home might cause him unknowingly to slight Bess and me, or was it the overflowing of that springtime's euphoria that prompted further proposals? When school began again, he suggested, we should go to dancing school and join a class in gymnastics, if such could be arranged. Most wonderful of all, he promised that, later in the year, I might begin to take piano lessons. One obligation he required from us in return: each month we were to send him the receipted bills for the dancing and gymnasium lessons and he would then send us his check for these amounts. This duty devolved upon me, as the chief letter-writer for the three of us, but I did not find it onerous: on the contrary, my memory brings back distinctly my pride and self-importance in performing this responsible and business-like task. Mercifully, I had no intimation then of how painful my dual role of family letter-writer and financial trans-actor would become in time.

Everything he promised came true.

Soon after school resumed in August, we joined a dancing class also attended by Aylen, Hesper and Hope Lewis. We met every Saturday afternoon from two to four in a large, shabby hall belonging to a fraternal organization in East Oakland, wearing pretty dresses and hair ribbons and shining patent leather Mary Janes, and the cost was a dollar a month apiece. In November I reported to Daddy: "I am learning how to dance now nicely. I know how to dance the Fairy Dance and my teacher is going to give me a new dance today." In the same letter I explained apologetically, but importantly nonetheless: "I have misplaced the receipt to last months dancing school bill. I will get the receipt for this month today . . . so will you please send three dollars, because I was the only one that took last month." Then, perhaps to assure him further of my reliability in business matters, I added at the end of the letter: "P.S. I will send the receipt as soon as I get it."

Organization of the gymnasium class began that fall, but when eight or ten little girls had signed up for weekly Saturday morning sessions in our big back yard, the early winter rains forced a postponement until the following spring.

And one October afternoon the long awaited letter from Daddy arrived at last, giving me permission to start taking piano lessons. I remember that after supper Mother and I hurried through the early dusk to the home of her friends, the Tuttles, on Thirty-second Street, to tell Miss Jennie Tuttle the extraordinary news. And I remember Miss Tuttle saying briskly, "I am going to give Joan her first lesson right now."

How long ago that evening was, but how well I remember it: the warm, fire-lit room, the lamp on the table at which Miss Tuttle and I sat, the sharp pencil in her thin, strong fingers, the sheet of paper crossed by group after group of five parallel lines, staves, she called them, the clear, matter-of-fact instruction she gave me. Miss Tuttle was an excellent teacher; I was all eagerness to learn; in less than half an hour she had taught me to read music. Afterward, we went into the front parlor where, at the awesome grand piano, she introduced me to middle C and showed me the relation between the music I had just learned how to read and the gleaming black and white keys.

In a long letter to Daddy early in December, I was able to tell him: "I have a pretty duet that Mother and I can play together and some very pretty pieces." Christmas plans and secrets, my just-recorded chest expansion of three and a half inches—"the measurement of a thirteen year old child," the receipt for the dancing school bill, the possibility of a trip to Los Angeles—"but Mother says it is a great big maybe," a request for Christmas money—"so can you spare some this year?," a hint of the present we were going to give him—"You can't guess what you are going to get. No sir. But it is something you will like," are jumbled happily together in this excited, confident letter. Not even the poignant closing sentence is cautious: "Are you going to be down Christmas to see our tree like you did last year, I hope you will because we have such a nice time when you come down."

The trip to Los Angeles did take place, a second journey overnight in a Pullman, but this time my wits were about me, and in a letter to Daddy on the very morning of our arrival, I made my first effort to describe to him in written words an experience that I had clearly found hilarious: "I had an upper berth. . . . Every time the train would lurch, over I would go on one side and then before I had a chance to breathe another lurch would send me into the corner. So I went from one side to another, sometimes half falling out and again bumping my head so violently that it made me see stars. . . . I finally managed to get hold of the hammock with one hand and some of the bed clothes in the other and to lie flat on my back. In that way I went to sleep but I woke up soon finding myself in the corner again and with a very sore head. . . . I send lots of love and hopes that you will not have such a time in an upper berth."

Perhaps the Christmas of 1910 really was an exceptionally fine one in

Oakland; perhaps it was myself, so buoyant and exhilarated at the end of this year of unprecedented happiness, so confident and sure of an unclouded future that I was bedazzled by everything. Two days before Christmas, when we arrived back from Los Angeles, I found the downtown streets and stores blazing with lights, ringing with bells, garlanded with pine boughs and scarlet ribbons, thronged with joyful people.

Hastily we bought our Christmas tree and Bess and I trimmed it ourselves. We had not heard yet, but we still hoped that Daddy might come to see it. In the kitchen, Aunt Jennie was making mince pies and cranberry sauce and readying the turkey for the next day's roasting, for she and Grandma London were to be with us on Christmas day as always. Then Uncle Charlie telephoned to tell us that Tetrazinni was going to sing at Lotta's Fountain in San Francisco that very evening and offering to escort us. I had never heard of Tetrazinni, but the idea of listening to a famous opera singer in the midst of thousands on Christmas Eve, out-of-doors in San Francisco, was enchanting and I begged Mother to agree. She almost yielded to our combined entreaties, but the thought that Daddy might come after all—he had arrived at the last minute the year before—sobered us and we decided to stay home.

Daddy did not come, but chains of rosy coral from the South Seas were under the tree for us the next morning. And in my day-after-Christmas letter to him, telling of our Christmas and the gifts I had received and thanking him for the coral, there was no hint of reproach. All was well.

ELEVEN

Thoreau used to say "You cannot see anything till you are clear of it." Although I shall never be entirely clear of the effects of the tragedy that was shaping during my childhood, it became possible, after a long time, to see it and to understand, with grief and compassion, why it had happened. Throughout those crucial years there was so much that Bess and I did not know. Lacking knowledge or even the faintest hint of the growing bitter conflict between Mother and Daddy, we gave to both, spontaneously and without reservation, our love and implicit trust. Because, unlike Mother, Daddy was not always with us, there was inevitably a special ardor in our love for him, but when the four of us were together in a fleeting illusion of a family, our happiness in loving and being loved merged into pure contentment.

As I look back at the fateful year of 1911, now that I am at last clear of it, most of its mystery has vanished, but then and for long afterwards it was for me a year of inexplicable, unhappy events, perplexing questions and an uneasy awareness that Daddy, whom we saw rarely, was somehow different. It was the year of my greatest personal triumph to date; Daddy was pleased, but I remember still my disappointment that he was not as enthusiastic as I had expected him to be. It was also a year when it sometimes seemed that Bess and I were punished by Daddy without knowing why. Outwardly, however, there was little change. We wrote to each other as always, and at least on my part, more frequently than ever before; in Daddy's files were fourteen of the slightly smudged, punctiliously dated letters I sent him during 1911.

The serene confidence I carried over from the preceding year, heightened by reaching my tenth birthday, starting the sixth grade and undertaking to write my first story, came to an abrupt end one afternoon early in February.

I was miserable that day with the onset of a heavy cold, but when Daddy telephoned that he would come to see us that afternoon, I persuaded Mother to let me move from my bed to the couch in the sitting room, once our bedroom, at the front of the house. Daddy was glad to see us, but almost at once he turned his attention to Mother. They had scarcely sat down when what I recognized as an argument began. I have no memory of what they said to each other. Drowsy with fever and baffled by their evident intention to talk over our heads, I remember only my surprise that they were quarreling, for this had never happened before.

Nine-year-old Bess, eyes sparkling and round face wreathed in smiles, was too excited by seeing Daddy for the first time in many weeks to notice the set faces and anger-roughened voices. Daddy's visits always meant romps and she was eager to start, especially that day when, because I was ill, she could monopolize him. For what must have seemed to her a very long time she restrained her impatience, then, unable to endure it longer, she touched his hand: "Please, Daddy, romp with me?" Ignoring her, he brushed her hand away and continued the argument. Again, a little later, she sought to gain his attention, bending over and looking up into his face beguilingly, and again he ignored her.

The third time she touched his hand he stopped in mid-sentence. "If you put your hand on mine again, Baby B," he told her, "I'll put you through that window!"

This was a new game, the most thrilling yet! I sat up, the better to watch. I shall never forget Bess's face as, tense with anticipation, she slowly put her hand on his: for the first, and probably for the last time in her life, it mirrored the ultimate in trust.

The next moment, springing to his feet and grasping both her hands, he swung her up and thrust her, feet first as far as her knees, through the big front window, then quickly pulled her back.

Blocked off forever is any coherent memory of what happened next. The crash of breaking glass, Bess's scream of pain and terror, Mother leaping from her chair to take Bess from Daddy, the glimpse of bright blood spurting from Bess's leg—these I remember. And I also remember a special shock in the midst of the larger one—Daddy's incredible violation of three basic laws of childhood: Bess had not done anything to merit such terrible punishment; Daddy was bigger than she; he did not say he was sorry.

Then and for long afterwards it was the latter that troubled me the most. I used to ask myself: did I really remember that he had not said he was sorry? And if that was true, then what *did* he say or do when he saw that Bess had been hurt?

Many years later I reread a letter I had written him on February 10, 1911. It awoke no memory of the sequel to the shattered window, the screams and the blood, but because of that letter, I know now what Daddy must have been saying while Mother comforted Bess and bandaged her leg and only I listened and understood his great need. "Dear Daddy Tiger," I began, and ended, "I send lots of love, from your little tiger cub, Joan."

A few days later there arrived in the mail for Mother an inscribed copy of Daddy's just published volume of short stories, *When God Laughs*. She read the inscription, then, her face inscrutable, firmly closed the book and placed it on the shelf with the others. "Dear Bessie," he had written, "God often laughs—especially at glass windows."

In a letter dated March 4, telling him that the gymnasium class was at last under way, I apparently could not forbear to reprove him, albeit gently: "Bess is only able to take the arm and wand exercises on account of her leg. Her leg was worse than you thought. An abscess formed on it and it is not well yet." Thereafter, neither the grievous incident nor "Daddy Tiger" reappears in my letters or my memories of when the three of us were together.

We ignored it, we did not speak of it, we "forgot" it; Daddy had not meant to hurt Bess, Mother said, and we could be sure he would never again play so roughly. We believed her, not only because we wanted to so badly, but because nothing really could have persuaded us that Daddy would ever want to hurt either of us. He was always physically gentle with us after that; even the romps came to an end. But—and how reluctant I am even now to speak of that tragic time—the scars left by a traumatic experience are permanent, even if recognition of their existence is steadfastly refused by those who bear them. Of these, I will not speak.

My reticence does not extend, however, to my efforts to understand Daddy's action. I had responded instinctively and with a compassion beyond my years to the anguish behind his desperate attempt to save face ("I'm a tiger, I play rough tiger games with my cubs!"), but the inscription he had placed in Mother's copy of his book baffled me. Prefacing that collection of short stories is a small anonymous verse:

> "As any one is
>   So is his God,
> And thus is God
>   Oft strangely odd."

Even today I am not sure that I really understand the relevance of these lines to God's laughter at glass windows. At first, I think I was shocked, as Mother surely was, by the apparent flippancy of the inscription. Mother and I were intimately aware that laughter could not have attended a little girl's agony and fear when an abscess was lanced. But a Daddy who could be flippant about fear and pain was so utterly unlike the Daddy we knew and loved that my shock gave way to a hope that, strange as his words seemed, he was really trying to say he was sorry. Long afterwards I recognized the bitterness implicit in the inscription and, taken with the verse, what might have been a tacit expression of remorse. Perhaps so; I shall never be sure. But if he regretted it, I wish we might have known it then.

From my subsequent letters to him, from a startling opinion of me he expressed in a letter a few years later, from memories of our conversations, I can perceive now the immediate effect of the incident I had witnessed on that February afternoon. I became careful; careful of what and how I wrote him, careful of my opinions and comments when we were together. It was a child's reaction, a longing to accomplish what she did not know was impossible—to return somehow to "the way things used to be." A new lightness began to appear in my letters, and my efforts to interest him and make him proud of me were redoubled. Deeply buried was the more drastic effect: my blind confidence in his unquestioned wisdom and goodness had been irreparably damaged; thenceforth, unhappily, always unwillingly, I could be critical of Daddy and dare to question his judgment and even doubt his kindness.

Thus, hidden from Bess and me for another two years, the bitter conflict between Mother and Daddy had begun. It was to be a conflict in which all of us would suffer wounds that did not heal, that no one won, and that would end in disaster. It was not, of course, a conflict uniquely our own, arising out of special circumstances. Long before Bess and I were caught in its toils and during all the decades since, countless divorced parents have fought over the same terrain, with their children the chief casualties. Details, personalities, the intensity of the struggle differ; the cause and the almost invariable results are heartbreakingly similar.

The final decree in the divorce that ended Daddy and Mother's marriage was issued on November 18, 1905. Agreement on community property and support had been reached out of court. Custody of Bess and me was awarded to Mother, with visiting rights only to Daddy. The following day he and Charmian were married.

The terms of the divorce had been accepted by both, by Mother numbly, by Daddy, I imagine, eagerly, in order that he might consummate his second marriage as quickly as possible. The dispute over the property settlement that arose two years later when Mother was considering remarriage revealed that certain verbal understandings would not be honored. Mother had not insisted. But when, in 1910, Daddy challenged a provision to which, apparently without reservation, he had earlier agreed, she did insist.

I do not know exactly when or under what circumstances he first appealed to Mother to ease the restrictions the custody provisions had placed on his access to his daughters. A letter written to her on January 8, 1911, indicates that his overtures were probably made toward the end of 1910 and had already been rejected. I think that he had approached her straightforwardly, telling of his great need and confessing frankly that when he had agreed to the custody provisions at the time of the divorce he had not known how much his children would one day mean to him. (In a letter to me two years later, he would be equally frank, reporting that he had told his Japanese houseboy, "When I knew these daughters they were little babies and did not count.") I am sure that he had expected resistance from Mother, but was confident that in the end she would yield to his pleading. When she did not, he was outraged.

His tardily recognized desire for full fatherhood, which must have become overwhelming after the loss of baby Joy, anger against Mother for frustrating his hope to know his daughters and be more to them than a mere visiting relative—all these went into the headlong, emotion-packed letter of January 8. He insulted Mother with calculated cruelty, taunted her with invidious comparisons to Charmian, complained piteously of how hard he worked and what little happiness he won from his labors; he blustered and threatened, and in the midst of his imprecations was the poignant appeal: "Let me have the children part of the time."

And Mother? Although there were many reasons for her refusal to share her daughters with their father, only one was compelling. Lacking this, I believe that anxiety over our health (how often we had been ill), the appalling prospect of the empty bungalow while we would be away, even the possibility that we might prefer the richer, more exciting life with Daddy and return to her unhappy and dissatisfied, might have been overcome by his moving entreaties. But one reason, and possibly the only one she gave him, outweighed all others. She believed, and this was based on bitter personal experience, that Charmian, whom she despised and mistrusted, was not a fit person to care for her little girls. Whether this opinion was justified or not, Daddy could not have doubted her sincerity, but he was in no mood to appreciate this. In the January 8 letter, which surely reflected their stormy interview, he charged her furiously with being a dog-in-the-manger, vindictive, a "sexually-offended, jealous, peasant-minded female creature."

I do not know how, or even if, she attempted to defend herself; she had no talent for arguments or quarrels. She held firmly to her position, undoubtedly aware that, apart from her condemnation of Charmian, she was powerfully backed by public opinion, the churches and the courts, which traditionally supported the dictum that children belonged with their mothers. She was never to regret her decision, only the reason for it, since her opinion of Charmian did not change; and because she knew the anguish her refusal had brought to Daddy, she winced under his punishing attacks but accepted them in the end without rancor. But from my vantage point of today, I sometimes dare to wonder if, all unaware, she did not act as woman first and mother second in denying his plea, and punished *him*—for the divorce and remarriage, for the loss of the man she loved to another, for the loneliness of her life, and for what, as a mother, she may have regarded in her darker moments as his blithe abandonment of Bess and me to her when, as babies, we would have been a nuisance in his new life.

No, I cannot question my mother's sincerity, nor will I assail as false the strongly held principles that Charmian had violated years before. That Mother consistently chose, at no matter what cost, what she honestly believed to be best for her daughters is impossible to doubt. She was a good mother, gentle, loyal and devoted; a generous, open-hearted woman whose special gifts and skills I admired and respected. But, deeply and painfully, I feel that her decision, like those of many other mothers in similar situations, to deny to Daddy and Bess and me the one way we might have achieved a genuine father-daughter relationship, was a tragic error. And, in my opinion, she was mistaken in her judgment of Charmian as a potential danger to Bess and me. Years later I came to know Charmian. She was not a particularly admirable person, to be sure; she was egocentric, pretentious, had an inordinate love of material possessions; she was superficial, even a little silly; nevertheless, I am certain that she would have been a conscientious and not unfriendly stepmother, who would have welcomed us properly on arrival and watched us depart without regret.

And Daddy? His longing for his daughters was deep and true, his need for them was desperate. But did anyone ever bungle more badly in striving to realize his desire? Surely, patience, gentleness and understanding might, in time, have won some concessions, made a beginning. Instead, he lost his temper. He was not prepared, apparently, to negotiate. If his first proposal—for Bess and me to live with him on the ranch during part of each year, preferably not just during vacations—were rejected, he would, and did, bring forth an alternate plan that I am sure he believed would answer Mother's objections. This plan—to build a permanent home for the three of us on the ranch—far from meeting Mother's objections, profoundly shocked her. She had been nurtured, after all, on Victorian proprieties; even Charmian, for different reasons, perhaps, would have strenuously objected. Unwilling or unable to see any point of view but his own, Daddy met the rejection of both of his cherished plans by declaring war on Mother, a fatal, self-defeating course that would later involve me and lead irrevocably to failure and alienation.

Thus matters stood, and Bess and I did not know, on that February afternoon when Bess placed her hand on Daddy's and I sat up to watch.

TWELVE

We saw little of Daddy in the following months, although we kept in touch by letter. In the fall, after one wonderful year of studying piano with Miss Tuttle, he abruptly announced, without explanation, that I was to have no more lessons. Concealing my disappointment, I promised him, unasked, that I would continue to practice every day; oddly enough, I did, but he never again proposed that I resume the lessons.

That year also, Daddy inexplicably brought an end to the beauty and wonder of the Friday afternoon Litany services. "What do you know of the Immaculate Conception?" he demanded angrily of me when he learned that we sometimes went to Sunday school at the Trinity Church. I stared at him blankly, but he did not wait. "If you must go to Sunday school, then you are to go to the Unitarian!" I have never regretted the change of denomination, but then I was sad because the magic was gone.

And that year I finally saw the Beauty, learned her real name and discovered who she was. The dim memory of the picture in Daddy's watch, the even dimmer memory of the lady who sat in the dark corner and did not speak, merged in a painful reality: this was Charmian, this was the usurper, my ancient enemy.

The year 1912 began with Daddy going East and thence on a five-month voyage around the Horn in a sailing ship. We did not see him again until August. Letters were few and brief, but I do not remember being sad about his absence (this was no *Snark* voyage) or the diminished communication between us, for during this time undreamed-of progress was being made in the grand design I had planned long before to win him back.

When Bess and I had changed schools the previous year, and I found myself with a remarkable teacher, a tiny, energetic woman who, at the start of

171

the new term in January, 1912, announced to her low seventh grade class that if we were willing to work hard, she would do her part to cover the seventh and eighth grades in one year, so that we would graduate in December. This, I thought dazedly, would put me a whole year ahead of my schedule! Although, at eleven, I was much younger than my classmates, Mrs. Greenman managed to persuade Mother to let me try her plan.

Mother was not well that spring and in the summer underwent surgery followed by a slow convalescence. School began again, and now it was I who was not well. With my sights fixed on the December graduation, I made heroic efforts to ignore my illness, but daily I felt worse. Then Daddy took us to Idora Park—the first time we had ever gone in the evening, the last time we would ever go there with him. The next morning I gave up. The diagnosis was typhoid.

I remember little of the next many weeks. There was Mother, always, and the doctor and the nurse, and, unbelievably, there was Daddy. Thyphoid fever in pre-serum days was a long drawn-out, cruel experience for the victims and those who loved them. Days and weeks, nights and days vanished from my awareness in an endless, icy nightmare. But it seemed very often that, coming briefly to consciousness, I found Daddy beside my bed, anxious-eyed but warming me with his quick, encouraging smile as I sought his face. I had not seen him so frequently nor felt so near and dear to him since the long-ago days of the Bungalow and the poppy field.

Out of the long illness came something wonderful: Daddy would build us a new house. The spring of 1913 began with finding the building site high in the Piedmont hills, a stone's throw from the long-vanished Bungalow. My letters to Daddy and his replies were exuberant; our new house was underway, his own Wolf House on his ranch would soon be completed.

In May I faced a crisis: the new house was ready for occupancy, but Mother's slender income could not provide the moving expenses and she firmly refused to ask Daddy's aid. The luster of my new closeness to Daddy dazzled me. Without telling Mother, at once confident and a little frightened at my temerity, I wrote him of our predicament, mercifully unaware of the grievous chain of events my letter would set in motion.

I was so elated by the check that arrived by return mail that my uneasiness about the letter that accompanied it was only momentary. Daddy had not failed me, and now we could move! The letter worried Mother, who recognized its implicit threat: failing to persuade her to share their daughters, he would appeal directly to me.

And then the year that had started so happily began to change, not all at once, but step by irrevocable step. We moved into the new house, I graduated from the eighth grade, Daddy came to Oakland for an appendectomy, recovered swiftly and returned to the ranch; in August I excitedly entered high school, a few days later the Wolf House was totally destroyed by fire; and through it all were the ever more insistent letters from Daddy and my agonized replies. Concern for my education, now that I would soon be entering high school, had initiated his campaign. In August he proposed that I ask Mother's permission to go to his ranch for "a few hours talk with me about your education"; at the end of September the next stage of his battle was signalled: "The time has come," he wrote, "for your mother, you, and me, to have a talk."

The letters that were exchanged between us that summer, and the last of the series written the following February, are the record of Daddy's heartbreaking attempt to be more than a visiting father and the bitterness of his failure. They are extraordinary letters, written with all his skill with words, but ever present, implied in the beginning but openly and brutally expressed more and more frequently as the correspondence developed, was his anger against Mother. He addressed his twelve-year-old daughter as a person free to make her own decisions, and I think I really was, and at the same time, by betraying his fear that Mother would continue to thwart his wishes, he inevitably strengthened her influence over the decision I was to make. In those coldly furious passages, he lashed her with such cruelty and contempt that I was shocked into realizing for the first time how much I loved her, and a fierce loyalty to her kindled a resentment of his injustice and unkindness that distressed me.

Truly, I was torn apart. Unexpectedly—so many years before had I dared to hope for it—the opportunity I had sought for so long had arrived. Daddy's yearning for me matched mine for him. But, oh, my mother!

Our talk on a Sunday afternoon in October was long and painful. Daddy was deadly serious, unsmiling, visibly controlling his anger each time it was roused; Mother was tense and mostly silent, although outrage compelled her to bitter protest from time to time; and I—I remember that I was actually hopeful at the start that somehow Mother and Daddy would forget their differences and be friends again, that Daddy would say he was sorry for his unkind words about Mother, that Mother would finally see that no harm would come of my visit to his ranch.

Daddy had carefully prepared for this talk. He had never spoken in this way to me before. Incredibly, he referred at length to Christ and quoted many passages from the Bible, one of which I knew well and would recall with anguish when I read the February letter: "To everything there is a season, and a time to every purpose under the heaven

. . . a time to get, and a time to lose; a time to keep, and a time to cast away. . . ."

In the ensuing discussion I did my best, I remember, to make my situation clear whenever I could, trying desperately to wound neither as I reiterated my love for both. I defended Mother, I pleaded for time to grow up a little more; more than once tears threatened but I would not shed them. I am sure I was not very effective, and I accomplished nothing. There was another who assisted in that interview, invisible but evoked over and over again—Charmian—and Mother and Daddy were adversaries, not parents seeking only the happiness of the daughter they both loved.

Once, striving anew to express a father's love and need for his children, Daddy exclaimed, "You cannot realize what it means not to have known a father at all, never to have seen him, never to have heard anything good of him!" He broke off, and turning to Mother, asked, "Will you tell the girls about Chaney? I can't."

Our talk ended inconclusively. I was to think over carefully all that had been said and write him of my decision. That evening, because we could not yet bear to speak of the long afternoon's talk, Mother told us what she had learned from Daddy about Chaney. It was not a pretty story. Many years were to pass before I was able to discover a great deal more about Chaney himself and his tragic union with Flora Wellman, from which had come Jack London. I wish Daddy had known these facts and placed the events in their context. I like to think that he might have forgiven his mother, that he might even have come to feel the respect and affection that I have for the strange, perverse crusader for a better world who fathered him.

My letter to Daddy, surely the most difficult I have ever had to write, is missing from the file he kept, but I remember its essence and the despair in my heart as I slowly put into the least hurtful words I knew the only decision I could reach: I would not visit him at his ranch until I was older. My wordless plea for him to appreciate my dilemma and to be patient just a little longer was to be ignored. I know now that nothing in his own childhood had prepared Daddy to understand the plight of a sad, confused little girl, torn intolerably by conflicting loves and loyalties, but then I did not know this. During the following weeks, although Daddy's letters were few and a little remote, I began to believe that the crisis had passed, that my letter had reassured him, that his harshness to Mother and his threatened loss of interest in Bess and me if he could not share us with Mother had been spoken in anger and that he had really not meant what he said.

For four months he brooded over the defeat of his cherished plans for his daughters before reaching his own decision. I had no knowledge then of the extent of the reverses he suffered that year. The Wolf House was gone, his first-born had failed him, he was in the forefront of the fight being waged by writers to protect their works from the depredations of the expanding motion picture industry, financially he was in poor shape and he was far from well. But everything he had accomplished thus far had been won by fighting for it, and he was not yet ready to yield, to acquiesce, to wait patiently. Grief over what he surely persuaded himself was my rejection of him gave way to wounded pride—for I think he had been confident of victory—and then to anger.

Even today, rereading his letter of February 24, 1914, I am appalled by the relentless, calculating cruelty with which he wrote to me, his daughter, just turned thirteen. These brief excerpts from four closely typed pages must suffice here:

> Let me tell you a little something about myself. . . . When I grow tired or disinterested in anything, I experience a disgust which settles for me that thing forever. I turn the page down there and then. . . .

> Years ago I warned your mother that if I were denied the opportunity of forming you, sooner or later I would grow disinterested in you, I would develop a disgust and that I would turn down the page. . . .

> I shall take care of the three of you. You shall have food and shelter always. But, unfortunately, I have turned the page down, and I shall be no longer interested in the three of you. . . .

> When you were small, I fought for years the idea of your going on the stage. I now withdraw my opposition. . . .

> Please, please remember that in whatever you do from now on, I am uninterested. I desire to know neither your failures nor your successes; wherefore please no more tell me of your markings in High School, and no longer send me your compositions. . . .

> Unless I should accidentally meet you on the street, I doubt if I shall ever see you again. If you should be dying, and should ask for me at your bedside, I should surely come; on the other hand, if I were dying, I should not care to have you at my bedside. . . .

A final sentence halted the door he was closing, leaving a crack through which a sort of communication could be maintained:

> *Whenever you want money, within reason, for clothes,*
> *books, spending, etc., write me for it, and if I have it at the*
> *time, I shall send it to you.*

The signature was *"Jack London."* *

The tiny line of communication he had left open, and the incredulity that dominated my emotional turmoil after my tears had ceased (don't cry when you are hurt, he had taught us long ago, but this time my conditioning did not hold) brought us at length through the crisis. I rejected his rejection simply because I could not possibly accept it. Little by little, with the initiative on my side for each cautious easing of the tension, but with its immediate tacit acceptance by Daddy, an affectionate correspondence was resumed. When once again he began to express his hope that I would decide not to become an actress, the shadow of the shattering letter seemed to have lifted at last. Overcome with gratitude, I wrote him reassuringly, renouncing my dearest ambition forever. It was long, however, before we met again. On November 19, 1915, we saw each other for the first time in more than two years. Now one year and three days remained.

Only now can I see that, in indefinable ways, our relationship was no longer the same. Neither in our letters nor in my memory can I find the slightest evidence that he had accepted the gradual return to the *status quo ante* with any reservations; no reference to the near-disastrous letter of February, 1914, was ever made by any of us. He did not renew his request for me to visit him at the ranch, but often he expressed the hope that some day we would come to know certain of his friends of whom he was especially fond.

And yet, Daddy was different. I did not know then, of course, how rapidly his health was deteriorating, and perhaps that would explain his new, easy-going, uncritical attitude toward us. Except on rare occasions, his old exuberance was gone. Fewer letters were exchanged than before, but they were loving letters, and when we were together, he expressed his love for us and his interest in what interested us in ways I shall never forget. He spent much time in Hawaii during those last two years, and, missing him, I wished that he would telephone me when he sailed to the islands or returned, but he never did.

No, all was not well for us, although I had no suspicion that it was

---

* See the Appendix for a complete version of this letter.

not. The future seemed very bright. I was fifteen now, a senior in high school; slowly my decision was forming to spend the summer after my graduation with him.

The last crisis, in August of 1916, was, in all innocence, precipitated by me. Ironically, its origin was the life-line, the crack left open in the closing door: "Whenever you want money, within reason, for clothes, books, spending, etc., write me for it." Mother's monthly "allowance" from him sufficed only for necessities, and so when we were small my letters had contained awkward requests for skates and sweaters and tickets for plays we especially wanted to see; later, I had to ask for monthly carfare and lunch money for high school, books, summer coats, a school pin. Most adolescent yearnings I suppressed, a few greatly daring hints went unnoticed. As time passed I grew embarrassed and then humiliated by the need to make these endless petty requests. The solution seemed eminently reasonable to me: Bess and I were older now, Daddy must increase Mother's allowance.

Courageously, and at the same time pretty sure of his approval, I broached the subject when we were lunching together in Oakland soon after his return from a seven months' stay in Hawaii. How very ill he must have been, I think, for how else explain the totally unexpected violence of his reaction. He was furiously angry, and although I immediately withdrew my proposal, he insisted upon discussing it further. "Discussing" is scarcely the right word for what followed: accusations, upbraidings, erection of straw dummies that were instantly demolished, self-justification that sank finally into self-pity. Whatever I tried to say was cruelly twisted into its opposite intention. Frustrated in every attempt to get through to him, stung by the injustice of his accusations, I felt the beginnings of anger and then, to my horror, tears. I struggled desperately to hold them back, but he saw them.

His tirade ended at last. He asked me to send him some figures to help him make up his mind, and said he would let me know. Bess and I walked down Twelfth Street with him to the Orpheum where he was to meet Charmian and some friends. None of us had much to say. In front of the theater he kissed us perfunctorily and moved toward the glass doors that led into the lobby. With one hand on the door, he looked back for a long moment at us, still standing disconsolately on the sidewalk. My impulse to run to him, to fling my arms about him, died at sight of his set, unsmiling face. He turned then, pushed open the door and went inside. We were never to see him again.

I sent him the figures he requested, but weeks went by—and again we had no knowledge of how dreadfully ill he was—before he approved my proposal and agreed to double our income. The document providing for this bore Mother's signature, but he delayed adding his own. His business-like letters gave no inkling of his attitude toward me; he wrote without anger, but also without the love he usually expressed. He was planning to go to Europe at the end of November, but he did not say he would see us before he left.

He died on November 22; mercifully, we did not know for some time that he had taken his own life. But on the morning after his death, his last letter to me was delivered. Dated November 21, it invited us to have lunch with him in Oakland at the end of the week, and afterwards, if the weather was good, to go for a sail on Lake Merritt—the excursion we had looked forward to for so long. In the days of grief over a loss so great that disbelief constantly challenged inexorable fact, that last letter, a legacy of love, comforted and sustained me.

A final blow awaited us, however, and it fell with the filing of his last will and testament nine days after his death. The solace of his last letter endured the impact of the small bequest to Bess and me; nothing withstood the diabolically conceived provisions that followed: If Bess and I should need any additional aid, it was not to come from his estate; we were to be "beholden" to Charmian, and whatever she allowed us would be "a benefaction and a kindness" arising out of her "goodness and desire." Near the end of eleven scrawled pages, he stabbed directly at Mother, and in advocating the disposal of Bess and me almost as if we were chattels, he robbed us of the little pride and dignity the earlier provisions had left us:

> I recommend that my daughters, Joan London and Bess
> London, be personally housed, cared for, and managed, by
> my beloved wife, Charmian K. London, of whose fitness and
> goodness for this duty I am amply confident.

The will had been written on May 24, 1911; a codicil in regard to an executor was dated April 17, 1914.

A thousand times I have asked myself: could this possibly have been his last will and testament? The significant dates—May, 1911, while he was losing his first battle with Mother, and April, 1914, less than two months after his letter thrusting us out of his life forever—indicate the state of mind in which he had composed the will, and three years later, having "turned down the page," reaffirmed it by adding a codicil. But afterwards, when we had come together again and he had shown in countless ways his love and pride in us, was he content to let this harsh document, inseparable from the past years of strife, stand as his final judgment upon us?

I shall never know the answers. But I find it as hard to believe that in 1911 he intended to inflict lasting punishment upon two little girls who did not even know their parents were quarreling over them as it is, remembering the later years when we felt encompassed by his love and when he seemed even to have forgiven Mother, to accept that malevolent ghost of a past war as the testament he desired to leave.

APPENDIX

The following is the complete version of the letter from Jack London to Joan London, February 24, 1914, excerpted on pages 175–76.

February 24, 1914.

Dear Joan:—

In reply to yours of February 10, 1914. I have just got back from the East, and am taking hold of my business. Please find herewith check for $4.50, according to account presented by you. When I tell you that this leaves me a balance in the bank of $3.46, you will understand how thin the ice is upon which I am skating.

I note by your letter that you have been charging schoolbooks in my account at Smith's. Never again do a thing like this. Never be guilty of charging to anybody's account when you have not received permission from that person to charge to their account. I shall make a point of sending you the money for your schoolbooks when you write to me for same, or, if I have not the money, of giving you permission to charge to my account. If I am away, and if Mrs. Eliza Shepard has not the money, she may also give you permission to charge to my account. Under no other circumstances except those of permission, may you in the future charge anything to any account of mine anywhere. This is only clean, straight, simple business, Joan.

Now I have what most persons would deem a difficult letter to write; but I have always found that by being frank and true, no thing is difficult to say. All one has to say is all that he feels or thinks.

Let me tell you a little something about myself: All my life has been marked by what, in lack of any other term, I must call "disgust." When I grow tired or disinterested in anything, I experience a disgust which settles for me that thing forever. I turn the page down there and then. When a colt on the ranch, early in its training, shows that it is a kicker or a bucker or a bolter or a balker, I try patiently and for a long time to remove, by my training, such deleterious traits; and then at the end of a long time if I find that these vicious traits continue, suddenly there comes to me a disgust, and I say Let the colt go. Kill it, sell it, give it away. So far as I am concerned I am finished with the colt. So it has been with all things in my whole life from the very first time that I can remember anything of myself. I have been infatuated with many things, I have worked through many things, have become disgusted with those many things, and have turned down the pages forever and irrevocably on those many things. Please believe me—I am not stating to you my strength, but my weakness. These colossal disgusts that compel me to turn down pages are weaknesses of mine, and I know them; but they are there. They are part of me. I am so made.

Years ago I warned your mother that if I were denied the opportunity of forming you, sooner or later I would grow disinterested in you, I would develop a disgust, and that I would turn down the page. Of course, your mother, who is deaf to all things spiritual, and appreciative, and understanding, smiled to herself and discounted what I told her. Your mother today understands me no more than has she ever understood me—which is no understanding at all.

Now, do not make the mistake of thinking that I am now running away from all filial duties and responsibilities. I am not. I shall take care of you; I shall take care of Baby B., I shall take care of your mother. I shall take care of the three of you. You shall have food and shelter always. But, unfortunately, I have turned the page down, and I shall be no longer interested in the three of you.

I do not imagine that I shall ever care to send you to the University of California, unless you should develop some tremendous desire to do specific things in the world that only a course in the University of California will fit you for. I certainly shall never send you to the University of California merely in recognition of the bourgeois valuation put upon the University pigskin.

I should like to see you marry for love when you grow up. That way lies the best and sweetest of human happiness. On the other hand, if you want career instead, I'll help you to pursue whatever career you elect. When you were small, I fought for years the idea of your going on the stage. I now withdraw my opposition. If you desire the stage with its consequent (from my point of view) falseness, artificiality, sterility and unhappiness, why go ahead, and I will do what I can to help you to it.

But please, please remember that in whatever you do from now on, I am uninterested. I desire to know neither your failures nor your successes; wherefore please no more tell me of your markings in High School, and no longer send me your compositions.

When you want money, within reason, I shall send it to you if I have it. Under any and all circumstances, so long as I live, you shall receive from me food in your stomach, a roof that does not leak, warm blankets, and clothing to cover you.

A year from now I expect to have a little money. At the present moment, if I died, I should die One hundred thousand dollars in debt. Therefore, a year from now I may be more easy with you in money matters than I am capable of being now.

I should like to say a few words further about the pages I turn down because of the disgusts that come upon me. I was ever a lover of fatherhood. I loved fatherhood over love of woman. I have been jealous of my seed, and I have never wantonly scattered my seed. I gave you, well (we'll say my share at least) a good body and a good brain. I had a father's fondest love and hope for you. But you know, in bringing up colts, colts may be brought up good and bad, all according to the horseman who brings up the colts. You were a colt. Time and fate and mischance, and a stupid mother, prevented me from having a guiding hand in your upbringing. I waited until you, who can dramatize "Sohrab and Rustum," could say for yourself what you wanted. Alas, as the colt, you were already ruined by your trainer. You were lied to, you were cheated. I am sorry; it was not your fault. But when the time came for you to decide (not absolutely between your mother and me)—to decide whether or not I might have a little hand in showing and training you to your paces in the big world, you were already so ruined by your trainer, that you declined. It is not your fault. You were trained. It is not your mother's fault—she was born stupid, stupid she will live, and stupid she will die. It was nobody's fault—except God's fault, if you believe in God. It is a sad mischance, that is all. In connection therewith I can only quote to you Kipling's "Toolungala Stockyard Chorus":

"And some are sulky, while some will plunge.
    (So ho! Steady! Stand still, you!)
Some you must gentle, and some you must lunge.
    (There! There! Who wants to kill you?)

Some—there are losses in every trade—
Will break their hearts ere bitted and made,
Will fight like fiends as the rope cuts hard,
And die dumb-mad in the breaking-yard. "

Whether or not you may die dumb-mad, I know not. I do know that you have shown, up to the present time, only docility to your trainer. You may cheat and fool your trainer, and be ruined by your trainer. I only think that I know that you are too much of a diplomat to die over anything—result of your reaction over your training, plus your inherent impulse to avoid trouble, kick-up, and smashing of carts and harnesses.

You cannot realize all this letter. You may when you are older. Save it for that time. But I have lost too many colts not to be philosophical in losing you. It might be thought that I am unfair to your youthfulness— yet you dramatized "Sohrab and Rustum," and calmly state to me narrow-minded, bourgeois prejudices (instilled into your mind by your mother), such as: My present wife, my Love Woman, is all that is awful and horrible in that I do truly love her, and in that she does truly love me.

All my life I have been overcome by disgust, which has led me to turn pages down, and those pages have been turned down forever. It is my weakness, as I said before. Unless I should accidentally meet you on the street, I doubt if I shall ever see you again. If you should be dying, and should ask for me at your bedside, I should surely come; on the other hand, if I were dying I should not care to have you at my bedside. A ruined colt is a ruined colt, and I do not like ruined colts.

Please let me know that you have read this letter in its entirety. You will not undertand it entirely. Not for years, and perhaps never, will you understand. But, being a colt breaker, I realize that a colt is ruined by poor training, even though the colt never so realizes.

Whenever you want money, within reason, for clothes, books, spending, etc., write me for it, and if I have it at the time, I shall send it to you.

Jack London